Hospitality Services

Student's Book

TVET FIRST

NQF Level 4
M Postma

TROUPANT · PUBLISHERS

TROUPANT

IN PARTNERSHIP WITH
macmillan
education

TVET FIRST Hospitality Services NQF Level 4 Student's Book
TVET FIRST

© M. Postma 2008
© Illustrations & design Guidelines – a division of Macmillan South Africa (Pty) Ltd,
2006

First published
2008

20 22 21
15 17 16 14

Published by
Macmillan South Africa (Pty) Ltd
Private Bag X19, Northlands, 2116,
Gauteng, South Africa

Typeset in Zapf Calligraph 11 pt by The Purple Turtle Publishing
Services Cover design by Deevine Design
Illustrations by Jean Black

ISBN 978 177017 315 6
WIP 0383G000
e-ISBN 9781431020898

Note: Any reference to Further Education and Training (FET) in this book should be taken to mean Technical
and Vocational Education and Training (TVET).

To order any of these books, contact Macmillan Customer Services at:
Tel: (011) 731 3300
Fax: (011) 731 3535
E-mail: customerservices@macmillan.co.za

Printed by: Atlas Printers

Contents

Topic 1:
Serve bottled wine

Module 1

Assist customers in the selection of wine and serve wine in the appropriate manner

In this module you will…

- identify and explain the uses of appropriate service equipment and glassware.
- understand the wine making process and its impact on the end product.
- identify different wine varieties, know their basic characteristics and the appropriate food items with which to serve with.
- provide customers with accurate information on wines, promote certain wines and offer alternative options.
- take drinks orders accurately.
- explain the importance of serving wine at the correct temperature.
- serve and clear bottled wines.
- deal with customers in a polite and friendly manner.
- understand the impact on customer service of working within prescribed time limits
- explain how customer service could be improved.
- understand the license requirements and the consequences of serving alcohol to customers under the legal age.
- deal with unexpected operational situations as they occur.

Unit 1:

Service equipment and glassware

This unit will enable you to identify and use appropriate service equipment and glassware.

Glassware

A wine glass is generally composed of three parts: the bowl, the stem, and the foot. The shape of a glass can influence the overall flavour of a particular wine and how people perceive the wine. Wine glasses can be shaped with particular inclines and angles so as to enhance the type of wine that is in them. There are certain wine glasses that are designed specifically for each of the different types of wine.

It is important to note the most obvious, but often most neglected, part of the wine glass – the stem.

The proper way to drink from a wine glass is to grasp it by the stem. The reason for this is that the temperature of the wine is not affected when you are holding the glass because the stem is not in direct contact with the wine. It is more difficult to control the temperature of the wine if you hold the glass by the bowl because the bowl is in direct contact with the wine. Holding it like this also prevents your fingerprints from smearing the glass, and it makes it easier to swirl the contents of the glass.

Wine glasses with large, broad bowls are used for bold red wines with bigger bouquets while narrower wine glasses are used for lighter white wines. If champagne is your beverage of choice then use a tall, slender glass.

A well designed (and perfectly clean) glass should enable you to see the wine clearly, help to concentrate the flavours and aromas, and thus enhance your enjoyment of the wine.

Wine should never be served in cardboard cups, plastic containers or water glasses. Remember that "a good wine deserves a good glass!"

Think about it

What is soup without a spoon? What is a pen without paper? What is wine without the appropriate service equipment? If you said "incomplete" then you are correct!

What are wine glasses made of?

The most common material from which wine glasses are made is glass – cut or fused glass, blown glass or so-called lead crystal glass.
* Wine glasses made of fused or cut glass will often interfere with the flavor of the wine, as well as having a rough, thick lip from which it is not as pleasurable to drink.
* Blown glass results in a better glass, with a thinner lip, and is usually acceptable for casual wine drinkers.
* High quality wine glasses are often made of lead crystal, which is not technically crystal, but is conventionally called crystal.

- Wine glasses are generally not coloured or frosted since this would obstruct your appreciation of the wine's colour. Coloured glasses, although from time to time they pop back into fashion, have no part in the serious wine drinker's appreciation, tasting and drinking of wine.
- The wine connoisseur believes that wine glasses should be made from clear glass, so that the wine can be assessed for colour and clarity.

Washing and storing wineglasses

When you are washing wine glasses, make sure that you hold the glass up to the light to check that it is truly clean. (Remember that wine often leaves a fine coat of scum in glasses.)

Wine glasses should stored rims up, in a cupboard that is free of furniture polish and other possible contaminative odours.

Learning Activity 1.1

Do this activity with a partner.
1. Visit an up-market hotel, restaurant, bar or shop and ask them to show you wine glasses made from the following materials: cut glass, blown glass and lead crystal.
2. Take descriptive notes on all these glasses.
Keep these notes in your portfolio.

In the workplace

The age-old method of hand picking is mostly replaced nowadays by mechanical harvesting because mechanical harvesting is faster and more economical than hand picking. Grapes are hand picked when quality fruit, which is going to be used to make expensive wine, is growing in a boutique vineyard, and the grapes require the gentlest treatment possible and also when there is not enough space between the rows for a mechanical harvester to be used.

How are wine glasses shaped?

A general rule is that the opening of the glass should not be wider than the widest part of the bowl.
- The shape of the glass is very important since it concentrates the flavor and aroma (bouquet) to emphasise the characteristics of the wine.
- The shape of the glass also directs the wine itself into the best area of the mouth where the wine will taste best.

Did you know?

Rose bushes are sometimes planted at the end of a row of grape vines because rose bushes are readily attacked by aphids (plant lice). If the roses are under stress, it's time to look for lice in the grape vines.

Red wine glasses

Glasses for red wine are characterised by their rounder, wider bowl which gives the wine a chance to breathe. Since most reds are meant to be consumed at room temperature, the wider bowl also allows the wine to cool more quickly after hand contact has warmed it. Red wine glasses can have particular styles of their own, such as:
- Bordeaux: this type of glass is tall with a wide bowl, and is designed for full bodied red wines like Cabernet and Merlot because it directs the wine to the back of the mouth.
- Burgundy: This type of glass is larger than the Bordeaux glass. It has a larger bowl to accumulate the aromas of more delicate red wines such as Pinot Noir. This style of glass directs wine to the tip of the tongue.

A red wine glass

White wine glasses

White wine glasses are generally narrower, although not as narrow as champagne flutes, with somewhat straight or tulip-shaped sides. The narrowness of the white wine glass allows the chilled wine to retain its temperature for two reasons:
- The reduced surface area of the glass (in comparison with red wine glasses) means that there is less air circulating around the glass and warming the wine.
- The smaller bowl of the glass means that there is less contact between the hand and the glass, and so body heat does not transfer as easily to the wine.

A white wine glass

Champagne flutes

Champagne flutes are characterised by a long stem ending in a tall, narrow bowl. The shape is designed to keep champagne and sparkling wine desirable during its consumption by keeping the gas bubbles inside the glass.

The glass is designed to be held by the stem to help prevent the heat from the hand from warming the champagne. The bowl itself is designed so as to help retain the carbonation (gas bubbles) in the drink. This is achieved by reducing the surface area at the opening of the bowl.

Champagne flutes are often used at formal engagements, such as award ceremonies and weddings.

A champagne flute

Port glasses

The traditional port glass holds 190 ml liquid and is 15 cm high. It is shaped like a small version of a red wine glass. Port glasses should be completely clear to reveal the colour of the port.

A port glass

Champagne saucer

Champagne saucers are not used much these days because the champagne loses its sparkle quickly in these glasses because they are shallow and have a large surface.

Sherry glass

A sherry glass is generally used for serving aromatic alcoholic beverages, such as sherry, port, aperitifs and liqueurs, as well as layered shooters.

A standard sized sherry glass is 120 ml.

A champagne saucer

Types of sherry glasses

- The copita has an aroma-enhancing narrow taper
- The elgin has a curve in the middle of the glass.

Wine tasting glass

Wine tasting glasses should have a narrow mouth piece (rim). The narrower the mouth piece the further the nose has to go into the glass. The bouquet (the smell of the wine) is very important when you are enjoying wine and if you use a wine tasting glass, it is easier to enjoy the bouquet.

The narrow mouth piece also forces the wine tasters to tilt their heads back a lot to get the wine into their mouths: this ensures that the wine falls on the correct taste buds at the back of the tongue.

Wine tasting glasses are stemmed with elongated, tapered bowls. They have capacities of 120 ml (for sherry), 210ml, 300ml or 410ml.

A sherry copita

Measures

Wine comes in two main measures:
- 175ml (small glass of wine)
- 250ml (large glass of wine).

Service equipment

Service equipment consists of trays and salvers.

Trays are larger than salvers and are usually square in shape.

An Elgin shaped sherry glass

Salvers

A service salver consists of a round silver tray with a serviette on it.

It is used to:
- carry clean glasses and removing dirty glasses from a table
- remove from, or take clean crockery and cutlery to, a set table
- clear dirty side plates and knives after the main course has been consumed
- take coffee services to a table for the silver service of coffee
- serve as an under plate when you are serving vegetables.

Ice bucket

It is important to keep ice clean and cold to avoid rapid melting.

Most ice buckets are metal but acrylic ones are also made.

It is useful to have a removable container to hold the ice so that excess water can be drained easily into the lower compartment.

Wine cooler

Wine coolers are used to keep white or sparkling wines chilled.

Decanter

When wine ages it accumulates sediment. The sediment is not only ugly, but it tastes bad, too. This occurs most often with red wine. When you decant the wine, you pour it into a decanter. In this way you aerate the wine thus improving the taste. The decanter is shaped in such a way that the sediment will stay in the decanter when the wine is poured into a glass. A decanter is usually is a very stylish vessel to hold the wine and can be an attractive piece for a table setting.

Depending on organisational requirements, offer to decant the wine if your customers are drinking older wine. Decanting wine is an excellent way to improve the taste.

Wine cradle

Red wine bottles are placed on the table in a basket or cradle.
- The cork should be removed from a bottle of red wine as early as possible, after it has been ordered, so that it can 'breathe' and attain room temperature naturally.
- If the red wine to be served is young – up to 7 years old – it need not be served from a wine basket since there will be little or no sediment. If it is over 7 years old then more care must be taken and a wine basket should be used to serve it from. This will prevent disturbing, as far as possible, the sediment.

A wine cradle is an attractive way to hold a wine bottle

- If an old bottle of red wine is opened from a basket or cradle the wine waiter must place a side plate, inverted, underneath the neck-end of the wine basket. This tilts the bottle slightly and keeps the neck-end of the wine bottle raised. The reasons for this are:
  - The sediment is kept in the base of the bottle
  - It prevents any wine spillage on the table cloth.

Carafe

Carafes usually come in multiples of 250ml and should drain every drop at an angle of 120 degrees.
- If a restaurant or bar serves wine that is not bottled, they must sell it in a measured glass or carafe.
- If a carafe of wine is incorporated in the wine list it should state the specific quantities offered and the price.

Corkscrew

Opening a wine bottle can be difficult without the proper corkscrew. The corkscrew is twisted into the centre of the cork, and turned (not the bottle) until half a turn of the corkscrew remains visible. Depending on the type of corkscrew, the cork is then pulled out of the bottle.

Invest in a good wine opener. There are several styles to choose from. These range from very elaborate ones to simple pocket openers and include:
- lever-style
- twist-style
- waiter-style
- pump-style
- rogar uncorking machines
- wing corkscrews.

Each style of wine opener has its benefits.

There are a variety of types of corkskrew

Waiter's friend

A "waiter's friend" is an essential piece of service equipment for every drinks waiter. It consists of a corkscrew for opening wine, a bottle opener for opening bottles and a knife to cut and remove the lead seal at the top ridge on the neck of the wine bottle.

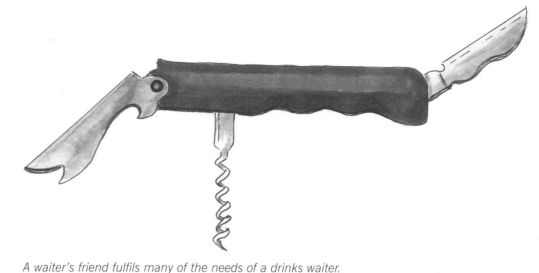

A waiter's friend fulfils many of the needs of a drinks waiter.

Wine humidity gauge

A popular wine accessory is a wine humidity gauge. This item helps test the overall humidity of the wine and can ensure that the wine is being held at the right temperature.

Most gauges are tested specifically for certain types of wine, so they are usable in wine cellars and wine fridges. Some can determine proper readings regardless of the type of wine. Many people use a humidity gauge in their wine cellars to ensure that the wine they serve to guests is always up to par.

Serving cloths

These are used to wipe the inside of the bottleneck to remove any residue after you have removed the cork. They should always be spotlessly clean and well ironed.

Words & terms

Mise en place duties These duties are carried out before the service starts. The term 'mise en place' is the traditional term used for all the duties that have to be carried out in order to have the room ready for serving guests. These will vary according to the particular food and beverage service area concerned.

Learning Activity 1.2

Do this activity with a partner.
1. Visit a restaurant with a large bar or visit a shop that sells bar equipment.
2. Make notes on what each of these corkscrews looks like.
3. Write down how each of the following corkscrews is used to remove the cork from a wine bottle:
   • lever-style
   • twist-style
   • waiter-style
   • pump-style
   • rogar uncorking machine
   • wing corkscrew.
Keep these notes in your portfolio.

The sommelier (wine butler or waiter) is responsible for the service of all alcoholic drinks during the service of meals. The sommelier must have a thorough knowledge of all drinks to be served, know about the best wines to drink with certain foods and know the licensing laws in respect of the particular establishment and area. The wine butler or waiter must be a salesperson who sells as much liquor as possible since this is one of the main sources of income in a catering establishment.

Mise en place duties before wine service starts

Confirm that there are sufficient stocks of the following service equipment before service starts:
- glassware
- trays or trolleys
- service silverware
- service cloths
- table linen
- knives
- candles
- corkscrews
- ice buckets
- coolers.

Also ensure that there is sufficient stock of wine and beverages according to the par stock levels of the organisation.

Ensure that all service areas are all clean and neatly arranged according to the hygienic standards of the organisation.
- bar center
- display
- cashiers
- fridges and coolers
- table areas
- seating areas.

Unit 2:

The wine making process

How is wine made?

The different stages of wine making are outlined in the table below.

Stage	Process
Harvesting of the grapes	Fruit is picked when it is ready to produce the particular type of wine.
Initial processing of the grape juice	A machine crushes the grapes and removes the stems. Maceration (the time spent while skins and seeds are left with the juice) will go on for a few days or weeks. Pressing, which may be done using a "bladder press" – a large cylinder containing bags that are inflated and deflated several times, each time gently squeezing the grapes until all the juice has run free, leaving behind the rest of the grapes.
Ferment-ation	Fermentation is the process through which grape juice is turned into alcohol. Grapes on the vine are covered with yeast, mould and bacteria. By putting grape juice into a container at the right temperature, yeast will turn the sugar in the juice into alcohol and carbon dioxide – this is fermentation. Malolactic Fermentation – the wine maker may choose to allow a wine to undergo a second fermentation process. When malic acid is allowed to break down into carbon dioxide and lactic acid (because of bacteria in the wine), it is known as "malolactic fermentation. It is much more prevalent in red wines than in whites.
Filtering and Fining	After fermentation, there still may be a lot of residue floating around in the wine. This can be removed by filtering or "straining" the wine. Alternatively, a "fining" process is used. This involves adding to the wine a substance that will attach itself to the residue enabling it to be effectively filtered out.
Aging	Barrel Aging: The winery may then keep the wine so that there can be additional clarification and, in some wines, to give it a more complex flavour. When wood aging is used, wines are stored most commonly in oak barrels. Some wines may be aged in stainless steel barrels. Wine may be barrel aged for several months to several years. Bottle Aging: Wine is bottled and is then laid down to mature in the bottle.
Blending Wine	During the barrel aging process, the individual containers of wine may develop differences. So the winemaker may choose to "blend" (mix) wine from different barrels to achieve a uniform result. Also, the winemaker may blend together different grape varieties to achieve the desired characteristics.
Bottling	Producers often use different shaped bottles to indicate different types of wine. Coloured bottles help to reduce damage by light.

Did you know?

The first stage in the wine making process is the crushing of the grapes. In days gone by the grapes would be loaded into a large vat and the wine maker(s) would gently tread on them to break the grapes' skins to release the juice. Nowadays this procedure is almost invariably carried out using a machine called, unsurprisingly, a crusher.

In the workplace

When the inside of an oak barrel has been charred (burnt) a 'toasty' flavour will be imparted to the wine as it matures in the barrel. Some red wines styles are not matured in oak but in stainless steel containers. These red wines will be lighter, have less tannin and can be quite refreshing. They are excellent wines to enjoy on a hot summer's day.

Wine varieties and the foods they go with

This unit will identify and describe the characteristics of wine varieties and help you to recognise which foods they go with.

The components of red wine

The different components of red wine include sugar, alcohol, tannin, acid, fruit and oak. Each plays a role in creating a harmonious wine.

Sugar

Sweeter wines have more sugar than dry wines. During the fermentation process a lot of the natural fruit sugar is fermented. However, in some wines the residual (remaining) sugar may be higher and therefore a sweeter wine will result.

Alcohol

One of the key components of wine is, of course, alcohol. Alcohol is fundamental to the taste of wine. The alcohol volume of most wines ranges between nine and fifteen per cent. The alcohol volume of fortified wine can be as high as twenty per cent.

Tannin

Tannin comes from the skin of the grapes. Therefore, tannin is much more fundamental as a taste component in red wine than it is in white. Too much tannin in a wine can result in the wine tasting spoiled. However, tannin helps to preserve a wine, which means that some wines can be kept for years. These wines improve with age. A small amount of tannin is also a positive taste characteristic for regular wine drinkers, though it can be a little overwhelming for inexperienced wine drinkers.

Tannin makes young wines taste harsh, but is a vital ingredient in any wine that will mature into a great wine.

Water

All wines contain water that has been extracted naturally from the grapes from which they were produced. Very rarely, if ever, would extra water be added to a wine. In fact, some wines may be criticised for being excessively watery if the other flavors are not sufficiently powerful.

Acid

The acid found in wine balances out the residual sugar that is left after the fermentation process has been completed. There are three key types of acid in wine: tartaric, malic and citric. All these acids are found in varying quantities in the skins of grapes. Alcohol may react with bacteria within the wine to create acetic acid. This is not generally a good thing since too much acetic acid will make a wine taste more like vinegar than anything else!

Acid gives the wine its crisp freshness. Too little acid makes the wine dull and lifeless while too much makes the wine unpleasantly sharp.

Fruit

This is what tends to differentiate one wine from the other. Fruity tastes are what we look for in a wine and different grapes will produce different fruit flavors. It is the combination of tastes that makes each wine unique and special.

Carbon Dioxide

During every fermentation process, carbon dioxide is produced. Most of this is normally released. However, in some wines a degree of fizz can be left in a wine to add a little extra to an otherwise very ordinary wine. Of course, in sparkling wines, the carbon dioxide is retained and is fundamental to the taste.

Oak

No longer an essential component of everyday wines drunk in large quantities, oak barrels are still used on occasion to add a vanilla, oaky flavor to special wines. Oak barrels can add an extra dimension to plain wines that will make them much more saleable and more enjoyable.

Important terms

You must know and understand these terms and be able to use them correctly.

Alcohol
This is measured in volume. Most South African unfortified table wines have between 9% (white wines) and 14% (red wines) alcohol by volume. Alcohol keeps wines in good condition, which is why red wines last better than white wines.

Blend
A wine made from two or more grape varieties or vintages or vineyards is called a blended wine.

Bouquet
This refers to the smell of the wine.

Cultivar
This refers to a grape variety. It is a contraction, or shortened form, of the words 'cultivated variety'.

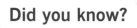

Did you know?

Rain falling just before the grapes are harvested is not good because it can cause the grapes to produce too much juice, thus diluting the flavours, sugars and acids.

Maturation

This refers to the aging of the wine, which gives it its complexity, subtlety and mellowness. It is the process by which a young harsh red wine is transformed into a smoother, more pleasant drink. The higher the tannin content of the wine, the more important it is that it is allowed time to mature. Because white wines are very low in tannins, they need less time to mature and they never reach the level of complexity typical of red wines.

Tartrates

These are harmless crystals that are formed by tartaric acid which forms in the bottle. In South Africa this is the result of the high potassium content in the soil.

Veritas

This is the name of a South African wine award. The highest award is the Veritas double Gold. There are also gold, silver and bronze awards. Wines winning double and gold awards are entitled to display Veritas stickers on their bottles.

Vintage

This indicates the year when the grapes were harvested.

Wood-fermented or matured

Wines that are aged in oak barrels are said to be wood-fermented or matured. The wood gives a wide range of flavours to the wine, and makes it mellower in flavour.

Methode Cap Classique

The classic method of making champagne as practised in the Champagne region of France, is by inducing secondary fermentation in the bottle, as opposed to adding carbon dioxide which is done in the making of sparkling wines.

Champagne

Champagne should never be confused with sparkling wine. Champagne is a lot more expensive than sparkling wine. Champagne is made only in the Champagne region in France. The Cap Classique wines (produced in South Africa) are made using the classic method of champagne making as practised in the Champagne region of France, by inducing secondary fermentation in the bottle.

Sparkling wine

This is a bubbly wine which is given its sparkle by the addition of carbon dioxide.

Rosé

This is a pinkish wine made either from a blend of red and white grapes, or from red grapes. The skins are removed quickly before the wine is macerated.

Did you know?

The syrah grape variety from France is a red grape, and it is known in various parts of the world as Shiraz or Hermitage. The Northern Rhone and Hermitage regions in France are known for their famous Shiraz wines. The 'spicey' quality often found in Shiraz can be described as 'peppery'.

Fortified wines

These are wines which have more alcohol – up to 16% – or more alcohol by volume. This is increased by adding spirits, for example, in the making of sherry or port.

Different wine varieties

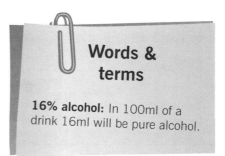

Words & terms

16% alcohol: In 100ml of a drink 16ml will be pure alcohol.

There are two types of grapes that are used to produce wines: red wine grapes and white wine grapes.

In this table the red grape varieties that are used to make red wine are listed and described.

Cabernet Sauvignon	This is one of the great classic red wine grapes. It is full-bodied. In a young wine it is a bit harsh, but it has the taste of blackcurrants and other berries. It also has herby, grassy, nutty qualities. Quality cabernets are usually matured in oak barrels. It usually needs some years of aging before it reaches its best.
Cinsaut	This varietal does not produce top quality wines on its own so it is usually blended with harder wines to speed up their drinkability. Unblended, it produces light, ordinary reds.
Gamay	In France this is used to make the light, fragrant reds in the Beaujolais style. In the South African Cape, it produces more full-bodied wines with a deep ruby colour, and a young fruity taste.
Merlot	This is currently a very fashionable grape variety. Its wines are drinkable earlier than cabernet. They are softer wines than cabernets, and are generally quite fruity.
Tinta Barocca	This is a Portugese grape used for making port. As a wine it is earthy and full-bodied.
Zinfandel	This is not yet currently very popular, but it produces a good full-bodied wine.
Shiraz	This produces wines that are quite heavy, savoury and full-bodied. It matures more quickly than cabernet, and it ages to a smoky, softish character.
Pinotage	This produces a full-bodied, flavourful wine, especially when it has been aged in oak. It is a hybrid of the pinot noir and cinsaut grape varieties. It tends to have a sweetish, acetone flavour, and is generally full-bodied and robust. Its coarseness disappears with longer aging.

In the workplace

In France Pinot Noir grapes are used to make Burgundy, which is a well known red wine.
These grapes are also used, along with the other traditional grapes, to produce a white Champagne, Chardonnay and Pinot Meunier.
In South Africa Chardonnay and Pinot Noir are the grapes most used for producing wine.

In this table the white grape varieties that are used to make white wine are listed and described.

Bukettraube	This is used for soft, off-dry and dessert style wines. It has a muscat style aroma, and is often used in blends.
Chardonnay	This is the most important of white wine grapes, producing the finest full-bodied white wines with fruity, lemon-lime freshness and elegance.
Chenin Blanc or Steen	This is the most commonly grown South African Cape white wine grape, making wines across the entire range of sweetness, dryness, fruitiness, still and sparkling.
Colombard	This can produce pleasant crisp wine with flavours of guava and granadillas. It is also used in producing brandy.
Gewurztztraminer	This makes spicy, boldly scented wines of great character.
Muscadel or Hanepoort	This is used mainly for dessert fortified wines, which have a distinct raisin bouquet and honey flavour.
Pinot Gris	This produces full-bodied balanced wines.
Rhine or Weisser Riesling	This is more aromatic, spicier, more complex, more subtle and more scented than Cape Riesling.
Riesling or Cape Riesling	This has a more 'steely', less complex character than the Rhine Riesling. It is not a particularly good variety.
Sauvignon Blanc	This produces complex and elegant wines.
Semillon	This is a soft grape with body and staying power that produces some very high quality wines.

What types of wine are available in the market place?

The different types of wines are:
- red
- white
- rosé
- champagne
- sparkling
- fortified – port, Muscat, sherry.

In this table the different types of wine are listed and described.

Blanc de Blanc	a white wine or sparkling wine made only from white grapes
Blanc Fumé or Fumé Blanc	dry white wine made from sauvignon blanc grapes, and not necessarily matured or finished in wood
Blanc de Noir	a light wine from red grapes
Champagne	sparkling wines made in the Champagne region in France
Dessert wine	a sweet wine that usually accompanies the last courses of a meal
Doux	sweet wines

Fortified wines	wines which are made stronger in alcohol, to 16% or more in volume by adding spirits, for example. sherry or port
Grand Cru	literally meaning "great growth", it is not an official rating, but is the producer's own subjective opinion of the wine
Jerepigo	a sweet, fortified red or white wine
Late Harvest	sweet wine made from grapes that are harvested later, and are therefore sweeter
Light wines	wines low in alcohol, light in body and usually dry and short on taste
Noble Late Harvest	a very sweet dessert wine made from grapes with "noble rot"
Nouveau	a fruity, young and light red wine usually made from Gamay grapes – a young red wine in the Beaujolais tradition
Perlé wine	slightly sparkling, carbonated wine
Rosé	pinkish wine made either from a blend of red and white grapes, or made only from red grapes, with the skins removed quickly before the wine takes up too much of the red colouring
Sparkling wine	a bubbly wine given its bubbles by the addition of carbon dioxide gas
Special Late Harvest	a South African dessert wine which is slightly less sweet than a Noble Late Harvest
Pinotage	a hybrid of the pinot noir and cinsaut grape varieties; a full-bodied, flavourful wine, especially when it has been aged in oak; tends to have a sweetish, acetone flavour; is generally full-bodied and robust; coarseness disappears with longer aging

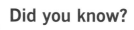

Did you know?

If you serve a vintage port after a meal, but only half the bottle is drunk the rest will keep for only a few days. Vintage port – unlike tawny port – is like a bottle of red wine. Open it, and drink it!

Tawny port does not age in the bottle, but it won't go off quickly either. There's no rush to drink it, and the small amount of air in a re-stoppered bottle will hardly affect a tawny port.

Making wine

In the making of white wines, after the crushing of the grapes, the juice is separated immediately from the pulp of the skins and stalks and fermentation commences.

In the making of red and rosé wines, the juice is allowed to remain in contact with the crushed pulp for a while to add color, body and flavor to the 'must' (the juice to be fermented).

Most modern wines are fermented at a relatively low temperature (around 20° C), which results in wine with a fruity character. White wines are commonly made in large, cooled, stainless steel containers but some better quality wines are fermented in oak casks or, alternatively, oak chippings may be added to the must.

Sherry, Port and Vermouth, and how to serve them

As a wine waiter you must know about these drinks and how and when to serve them.

Sherry

Sherry is offered as an aperitif before a meal.

In this table the different types of sherry are listed and described.

Fino	This is a very pale, light dry sherry.
Amontillado	This is an aged fino with an amber colour and dry nutty flavour. However, many wines carrying this label are sweet blends and "amontillado" is often used to describe a 'medium' sherry.
Oloroso	This is a dark gold, full-bodied sherry with plenty of body and a nutty flavour.
Cream, Brown and Amorosso	These are Oloroso sherries with sweet wine added to them.

Port

Port is offered after a meal. Port is usually served with the cheese and biscuits course. A port glass has the same shape as a sherry glass, except that it is a bit larger.

In this table the different types of port are listed and described.

Vintage Port	In a very good year, a winemaker will make a vintage port. This is a blend but only of wines of the same year. To preserve the fruit the wine must be bottled before all impurities have had time to settle out in the oak cask, so sediment will form in a bottle of vintage port. A white splash on the glass indicates the topside of the bottle during its early maturation so the crust will have formed on the opposite side. This crust will form again after the wine has been moved if it is left to rest for a few weeks. The port must be decanted off the crust before being served.
Late Bottled Vintage	This is port of a single year that has been matured in wood from four to six years before bottling. It is ready for immediate consumption. The label must bear the vintage date and the year of bottling.
Crusted Port	This is a blended port that has been bottled after five or six years in an oak cask. It is then cellared for at least seven years until it develops a crust.
Tawny Port	As port ages in oak, its colour changes from purple through to ruby to a light tawny. A fine tawny port has usually been aged in wood for about ten years and has a velvety consistency. Tawny Port can also be a blend of red and white ports.

Ruby Port	This is a blend of old and young wine. The old wine contributes softness and character, the young wine adds a fresh fruitiness. It is chilled before bottling to settle out any sediment and so lengthen its shelf life.
White Port	White grapes are fermented to make a dry wine which is then fortified. It is drunk as an aperitif, and is usually served chilled in summer.
Vintage Character	This is a quality blended port ready for immediate consumption. These ports must not carry a date on the label.

Date of Harvest	This is port that has been in wood for at least seven years before being bottled. It must bear the vintage date, year of bottling and an indication that the wine has been aged in oak. A "Reserve" port is an example of this style.
Indication of Age	These are Tawnies that have matured for ten, twenty, thirty or over forty years before being bottled. The label must carry an indication of age, the year of bottling and state that the port has been aged in oak.

Vermouth

Vermouth is an aromatised and fortified wine. It is also served as an aperitif before a meal.

Dry vermouths

The main types of dry vermouths are Martini Dry, Cinzano Dry, Chambery and Noilly Prat.

Dry vermouth is served on ice, using a 25ml measure, and garnished with a twist of lemon peel, or an olive.

Sweet vermouths

The main sweet vermouths are Cinzano Bianco, Noilly Prat Red and Punt e Mes.

Sweet vermouth is served on ice, using a 25ml measure, and garnished with a cocktail cherry on a stick.

Pairing food and wine

Instead of talking about rules for pairing food and wine, let's look at guidelines.

Match flavor intensity

Match delicate wines with delicate foods, and, conversely, match powerful wines with powerful foods. Light white wine goes with the poached fish, and the Bordeaux with the roast beef, and not vice versa.

Think about it

A few years ago the rule was this: Drink red wine with red meat and white wine with poultry or fish. Subsequently, that rule was replaced to read: Drink what you like. To drink what you like created more problems than it solved. Of course you can still drink what you like. But appropriate rules, or more precisely guidelines can increase your enjoyment of both the food and the wine. Isn't that what it's all about?

Not everything goes with everything. Would you wear Doc Marten boots with an Armani suit? Do you put Dijon Mustard on a Banana Split? If you drink a light white wine with Roast Beef, you won't notice the wine's fruity nuances, so you may just as well be drinking water and if you accompany a delicate Poached White Fish in Herbs with a massive, tannic red Bordeaux, the wine will overwhelm the fish. Don't even try to taste the herbs!

Take into consideration the spicing, the accompaniments, and sauce, if any, if you choose wine to go with a dish. Pair powerful wines with powerful sauces. It's often wise to use the same wine in the sauce as you serve in the wine glasses. If a wine isn't good enough to drink, it isn't good enough for your sauce.

Opposites sometimes attract

On occasion you may enjoy spicy foods such as curries with sweet dessert wines. But take into consideration the spicing, the accompaniments, and the sauce.

Balance sweetness

Avoid combinations in which the food is sweeter than the accompanying wine. Otherwise the wine may come off tasting 'thin'.

Avoid highly alcoholic wines on hot humid days. Either go with a beer or a low alcohol wine such as a Riesling.

Balance acidity

The food should never be more acidic than the accompanying wines.

Temperature counts

If you really want to do it right, use an ice bucket to chill most reds for five minutes before serving them and up to 15-25 minutes for most whites. A relatively small difference in temperature can make a big difference in taste.

When in doubt, open a bottle of Champagne or Sparkling Wine

If you can't afford champagne with most meals, choose a good sparkling wine and don't forget to balance the sweetness.

Drink your wines in the right sequence

Drink dry wine before sweet, white before red, young before old, simple before complex, and light before heavy.

Between wines cleanse your palate with water or a small piece of bread.

Did you know?

In a wine judging competition a wine wins a gold medal by scoring at least 18.5 points out of a possible 20. Unlike the Olympics, in which only one person can get a medal – gold, silver or bronze – more than one wine can score a gold medal, or it can happen that no medals are awarded at all: this is rare, but possible. Wine competitions are not about 'first past the post', but are about total and overall quality.

Unit 4:

Accurate information, promotions and alternatives

This unit will enable you to provide customers with accurate information on wines, promote certain wines and offer alternative options.

Giving guests information

Here are some guidelines for helping guests appropriately with their queries about wine.

- Answer their questions immediately if you can.
- If you do not have the answers to any questions, inform the guests that you will obtain the information and that you will get back to them. Then contact your manager or a colleague who is able to assist you with the required information.
- Ensure that you listen attentively to the guests, in order to address their actual queries appropriately.
- Give the guest your undivided attention. Do not display signs of impatience.
- Do not be amused at any query of the guests, no matter how misinformed it may be.
- Do not patronise the guests.

A glass of wine is often the first thing that customers will ask you for when they come to an establishment. It is therefore important that you have the knowledge to correctly provide customers with the correct information about what types of wine are available. This first contact with the customers will set the precedent for the rest of their stay.

It is extremely important to have a very good understanding of all the different types of wines that your establishment or outlet offers.

You will need to be aware of:
- what country or region the wine is from
- the vintage of the wine
- what it tastes like
- what food the wine is best served with
- what temperature the wine should be served at
- which glasses should be used
- which wines are new on the market and in demand at the moment.

When you are serving bottled wines, you must be aware of a number of issues including:
- customer requirements
- compliance with licensing legislation
- the correct service of wines
- adherence to organisational requirements.

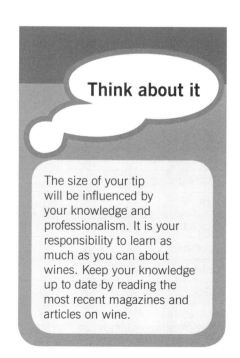

Think about it

The size of your tip will be influenced by your knowledge and professionalism. It is your responsibility to learn as much as you can about wines. Keep your knowledge up to date by reading the most recent magazines and articles on wine.

Do this activity on your own.
1. Get a copy of the wine list of the restaurant where you are doing in-service training.
2. Write down the names of all the wines on offer.
3. Now ask the head waiter or the manager to help you match items from your food menu with an appropriate wine from the wine list.
Keep this list in your portfolio.

Promoting certain wines

At all times it is extremely important to 'read' your customers. This means trying to work out what they are likely to require. This is most useful when you are promoting or suggesting particular wines.

*   The first opportunity to promote wine is when your customers arrive. This gives you the chance to tell them about the house specials, or, possibly, the wine of the month.
*   Presenting the customers with the wine list is also a form of promotion.
*   When your customers have finished a drink other than wine, suggest bringing them the wine list.
*   When they have finished one bottle of wine, suggest they have another. You may also like to suggest a different wine for them to try.
*   If given the opportunity, suggest wines to the customers that complement the meals that they have ordered. For example, if a customer says that she has ordered fish and therefore must drink white wine, but that she feels like red, reassure her that she should drink what she wants and that she does not need to stick to the old traditions.

Think about it

Selling wine allows you to make more money – it's like putting another guest at the table.

(Brown, Bob: The Little Brown Book of Restaurant Success.)

Pairing food and wine

This table lists some suggested pairings of food and wine.

Cold starters (Hors-d'oeuvres)	light, dry or fruity white wine
Seafood	Riesling, white burgundy
Soup	generally no wine is served with soup
Fish soup	dry white wine
Warm starters (Hors-d'oeuvres)	heavy white wines
Pastry dishes	light red wine
Fish	dry or fruity white wine
Vegetables	light white wine
Mushrooms	heavy red wine
Chicken	white wine
Duck	light red wine
Wild duck	light dry red wine
Offal	light to medium red wine
Veal	white wine

Beef	heavy full-bodied red wine
Pork	light to medium-bodied red wines
Lamb	medium-bodied red wine
Venison	heavy red wine
Dessert	dessert wine
Chocolate dessert	medium dry champagne
Cheese	light red wine/port
Fruit	medium sweet dessert wine

- If customers have started with a white wine to accompany their starter, you may suggest a red wine to accompany their main course.
- Don't forget to recommend a dessert wine for the dessert.
- Recommend a port or sherry during the coffee. You will generally not sell bottles of these, just glasses.
- If customers have not been drinking alcohol during the meal, it is not recommended that you suggest they have a dessert wine with their dessert.
- If customers appear to have had enough alcohol to drink, do not suggest more wine.
- If you know that a customer has to drive, this gives you the opportunity to promote low alcohol wine, if your establishment offers this type of wine.

Offering alternative options

Each customer has different requirements and different tastes. It is therefore important to identify these tastes, since what one person likes, another may not.

When you are asked for an opinion or recommendation about wine, do not be vague. The customer obviously thinks you know more about wine than she or he does, so have the details of a few good wines ready so that you can recommend them to customers.

Never recommend only the most expensive wine, since the customer will think you want to sell that wine only because of its price.

If a customer should ask for a type of wine you don't have in stock, you should be able to suggest a similar wine which is on your wine list.

In the workplace

In relation to food and wine pairing, start with a single, simple concept - the wine should match the sauce of the entrée. If you want to do the job correctly, all the wait staff should have practical experience of which wines go with which dishes. (Goldstein, Evan: Five Star Service)
Wine promotes dining. Bottled wine turns food consumers into diners and diners into sophisticated diners. (Brown, Bob: The Little Brown Book of Restaurant Success.)

Unit 5:

Take drinks orders accurately

Take a drinks order as soon as customers are settled

Think about it

- Get it right: write it down. Accuracy is at the heart of great service.
  (Brown, Bob: The Big Brown Book of Managers' Success)

- Stand in the command position, which is across the table from the leader or buyer of any group. When you stand here and maximize eye contact, the leader looks strong, orders more, is happier and tips better.
  (Brown, Bob: The Little Brown Book of Restaurant Success.)

Serving drinks to customers

- Always present customers with the wine and drink list when they arrive, since they want to know what is available and the price.
- Have a thorough knowledge of all the items on the wine/drink list.
- When customers choose wines you will find that most people will choose wine from the middle of the list – not too cheap and not too expensive.
- Some wines have unusual names and some people have difficulty pronouncing them. Do not correct them obviously, but make sure you pronounce the name correctly when you are presenting it. If you are unsure of how to pronounce a name, you should ask your supervisor or perhaps the wine merchant or maker if you have contact with them.
- Present customers with the wine list when they are seated, but give them enough time to read the wine list before asking for their order.
- Do not delay in taking their order, but do not rush them.
- Approach the table and ask if they are ready to order.
- Never sit at the table or pull up a chair to take an order – always stand!
- Wine orders must be taken according to organisational requirements.
- Your establishment will have a set procedure for order taking, and this must be adhered to at all times.
- Generally, you will have an order pad with a section in which to write down the wine.
- Make sure you note who has ordered the wine.
- Make sure that you have written down the correct wine. Always repeat the order back to the customer; you may have more than one wine

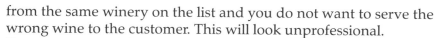

from the same winery on the list and you do not want to serve the wrong wine to the customer. This will look unprofessional.

- If customers are difficult to understand, ask them to repeat what they would like.
- If champagne has been ordered, record how many champagne glasses are needed.
- Once the order has been taken, take it to the service or dispensing bar immediately.
- One copy of your order will go to the bar and the other will probably be taken to the cashier. Your supervisor will advise you of this procedure.
- Make sure there are wine glasses on the table. White wine is always served in smaller glasses so that it can be drunk without getting warm. If you are serving red wine or champagne or sparkling wine, make sure that the correct glasses are on the table.
- If ice buckets or other utensils are required always make sure that these are in place before approaching the table to present and open the wine.
- You must serve the wine without any delay since most guests would like a glass of wine before the food is served. Guests will definitely be upset if the wine is served after their food has arrived.

To ensure customer satisfaction be ready to recommend that extra glass or bottle of wine to the customer to make his or her dining experience more pleasurable. Remember that this also means that you need to have a very good knowledge of the wines that complement certain dishes.

Learning Activity 1.4

Do this activity in groups of four.
Role-play the following scenarios making sure that you all have a turn to play the waiter, a customer and the manager. Your lecturer will assess your role-plays.

1. A customer orders a wine that is not available even though it is on the wine list. He is angry with the waiter.
2. A group of customers order three different wines for one table. The waiter gets two of these wrong.
3. The waiter doesn't know enough about how to pair food and wine and annoys a group of customers so much that they leave the restaurant.
4. A waiter recommends only the most expensive wine on the wine list but does not tell the customer how much it costs. The customer orders this and then cannot pay for it.

Your role play will be assessed using the following rubric:

Student Name:					
Activity:					
Criteria	**Outstanding 80-100%**	**Highly competent 70-79%**	**Competent 50-69%**	**Not yet competent 40-49%**	**Not achieved 0-39%**
Role	Student assumed both the role of being a waiter and the role of a customer accurately and appropriately.	Student was able to assume both roles required well.	Student was able to assume both roles.	Student was not able to assume both roles, but managed one of them.	Student was not able to assume either role on a believable way.
Responses	Student responded to their partner in a completely relevant way to both of the roles that they played.	Student responded to their partner in a partly relevant way to both of the roles that they played.	Student responded to their partner in a partly relevant way to one of the roles that they played.	Student responded to their partner with little or no relevance.	Student did not respond to their partner.
Listening skills	Student showed active listening skills by reacting appropriately and timeously to what their partner said or did.	Student showed active listening skills by reacting to what their partner said or did.	Student listened to their partner some of the time and usually reacted to what they said.	Student listened to their partner some of the time and occasionally reacted to what they said.	Student did not seem to listen to their partner at all.
Use of language	Student used language extremely effectively to portray a point of view.	Student used language effectively strategies to portray a point of view.	Student usually used language effectively to portray a point of view.	Student occasionally used language effectively to portray a point of view.	Student did not use language skills at all.
Speech	Student spoke clearly, accurately and in character.	Student generally spoke clearly and accurately.	Student occasionally spoke clearly or accurately.	Student never spoke clearly or accurately.	Student did not speak.
Body language	Student used body language (eye contact, posture, gestures) appropriately and effectively to enhance and support speech.	Student used most aspects of body language to enhance and support speech.	Student used some aspects of body language to enhance and support speech.	Student used a little body language.	Student used no body language at all.

Keep the rubric used to assess you in a safe place.

Unit 6:

The correct temperatures for wines

This unit will explain the importance of serving wine at the correct temperatures.

Wine temperature and flavor

Wine must always be served at the correct temperature. If wines are not served at the correct temperature, the flavour may not be at its best, and therefore you will not ensure complete customer satisfaction.

In your establishment, the temperature of your refrigerators and storage rooms should be consistent with the correct serving temperature of different wines. Customers expect to get their drinks at the correct temperature. Sometimes people want their wine colder than usual, but that is their right! If they want it colder you must be able to give them some ice.

It is extremely important to know at what temperature you should serve wines. In this table various wines are paired with the correct temperature.

Temperature °C	Type of Wine
18	top quality red wine such as burgundy or Bordeaux
16	sweet dessert wine, port, sweet sherry, Marsala
14	red wine
12	table red wine, aperitif wines, vermouth, dry sherry
11	rose and blanc de noir
10	top quality white wine
8	white wine
6	sparkling red wine
5	champagne and sparkling wine

The taste of a wine can change dramatically depending on the temperature at which it is served.

Maintain the correct temperature

Red wines can be removed from storage and kept at room temperature and chilled wines can be transferred to ice buckets or ice baths.

It is important not to subject wine to violent temperature changes because it affects the flavour and quality of the wine, and can result in the production of tartrates (crystals) which many guests mistakenly think are an indication of poor quality wine.

Unit 7:

Serve and clear bottled wines

Presenting wine correctly for tasting

Each bottle of wine served must be tasted by the host for approval before it is served.

- Fold a clean waiter's cloth and position it so that it covers the palm of your left hand, and your wrist.
- Place the wine bottle in your left palm with the base of the bottle resting against your fingers, the label facing forward and the first two fingers of your right hand resting gently on the neck of the bottle.
- Hold the bottle towards the guest for his or her approval. If the guest is at a table this is done from the guest's right hand side.
- Say the name, type and year of the wine to ensure that it is the wine that was ordered.
- Let the host (or person who ordered the wine) feel the temperature of the bottle if they wish.
- When the guest has approved the bottle, step back and open the wine.
- Drape your waiter's cloth over your left wrist so that it does not get in the way.
- Hold the bottle at a 45° angle by the neck, at waist height and open the knife of the "waiter's friend". If you are right-handed hold it in your left hand and in your right hand if you are left-handed.
- Carefully cut and remove the lead seal at the top ridge on the neck of the bottle and place this in your pocket.
- Close the knife.
- Open the corkscrew, and twist it into the centre of the cork, turning the corkscrew and not the bottle, until half a turn of the corkscrew remains visible.
- Drop the lever onto the top of the bottleneck and secure this with the forefinger of your left hand (or right hand if you are left-handed).
- Using your fingers, gently ease the cork out, making sure that it does not make a "popping" sound.
- Using your waiter's cloth, wipe the inside of the bottleneck to remove any residue.

In the workplace

The reason we have a customer taste the wine is not to see if he or she likes it or not. It is to check whether the wine is of the expected quality. Wine that is 'off' is referred to as being 'corked'. If wine is corked when the customer tries it, you must remove the tasting glass and the wine and bring the customer a new glass and another bottle of wine and go through the presenting process again. It is possible that the customer would prefer to choose a different wine, so you must bring the wine list again. This is a quite common occurrence. About 7% of wines are 'corked', because of bad storage, the cork not sealing correctly, the bottle not having been cleaned correctly, the wine being too old, or having been too hot or too cold in storage. Corking can occur with champagne and sparkling wines, too.

- If it is red vintage wine, place the cork on the table next to the host. A white wine cork may be placed in your pocket.
- Drape your waiter's cloth over your left arm and commence with the tasting and pouring.
- Hold the bottle in your right hand with the label clearly visible to the host.
- Approach the host to his or her right and pour a small quantity (a mouthful) of wine into his/her glass. Do not allow the neck of the bottle to touch the rim of the glass. To prevent spilling drops on the table, turn the bottle slightly as soon as you've poured the wine for tasting. Wait for approval before proceeding to serve the wine to the other guests.

Serving the wine

- When the wine has been approved, fill the glasses of guests first before filling the host's glass. Pour all glasses from each guest's right.
- Don't fill the glass up to the top! Fill it two thirds for white and half for red.
- Make sure you have enough wine for all the guests. There are 5 glasses of wine in a bottle, but if there are 6 people and only one bottle of wine, pour a little less into each glass so that everyone has a drink. The host may then wish to order another bottle.
- Fill the glass of the lady seated to the right of the host first and then – moving anti-clockwise around the table – fill all the ladies' glasses. When you've served the last lady – move clockwise back around the table and fill all the gentlemen's glasses. Fill the glass of the host last.
- Never allow the neck of the bottle to touch the rim of the glass and turn the bottle slightly as soon as you've poured the wine. This will prevent drops falling on the table cloth.
- When everybody at the table has been served, place the white, rose or sparkling wine bottle in the ice bucket and position it to the right of the host. Drape a waiter's cloth over the ice bucket. Red wine bottles are placed on the table in a basket or cradle – with the label facing the host – to his or her right.
- Refill the wineglasses as required. Check if the guests would like more wine – do not assume this.
- When a bottle is empty, ask the host if he or she would like another of the same or whether you should bring the wine list again.
- If the same wine is ordered, it is not necessary to change the glasses, unless this is requested by the host. You should still let the host taste the new bottle if he or she wishes to. It is still possible that there may be a problem with the new bottle, even if the first one was fine. If a new wine is ordered, all the glasses must be changed and you should repeat the opening and tasting process.
- If guests are seated at the bar, the procedure is the same except that you will be pouring from in front of the guest. The ice bucket will be placed on your service counter in front of the guest. Wine baskets (cradles) are not used for red wine at the bar.

Opening a wine bottle correctly

Think about it

Most opportunities to provide exceptional service happen very routinely. Too often we overlook these chances. So surprise your customers next time with exceptional service moments.
(Paz, Paul: Tips on Tips #44)

Nothing is worse than a mumbling server, except maybe a mumbling and clumsy server.
(Ross, Susie: "A Message for Wait Staff," Waiter Training Newsletter)

Selecting the appropriate glassware for serving wines

This table lists guidelines for serving different wines.

Wine	Bottle Quantity	Appropriate Glassware
White Wine	750 ml – approximately 6 glasses 250 ml – approximately 2 glasses	White wine glass
Red Wine	750 ml approximately – 4 glasses 250 ml approximately – 1 ½ glasses	Red wine glass
Dessert Wine	375 ml – approximately 6 glasses	Port glass
Sherry	750 ml – approximately 12 glasses	Sherry glass
Port	750 ml – approximately 12 glasses	Port glass
Sparkling Wine/ Champagne	750ml – approximately 6 glasses	Champagne flute

Champagne and sparkling wine

Champagne and sparkling wine are not the same!

The difference between champagne and sparkling wine

The difference between champagne and sparkling wine lies in the method of their making.
- Champagne is made using the traditional 'methode champenoise', and, because only producers in the Champagne region of France may call their product 'champagne', South African wines made in this way are called Methode Cap Classique (MCC).
- Sparkling wines are made using a completely different method which, while producing some elegant results, requires less time and patience.

Serving champagne and sparkling wine

- Ensure that the champagne glasses – flutes, or saucers (if these are requested) are on the table before you present the bottle.
- Follow the same method as outlined above for presenting a bottle of wine except for the following:
- If possible, champagne or sparkling wine glasses should be chilled.
- Point the bottle away from customers.
- The cork of champagne or sparkling wine bottles is covered with a safety wire and foil. These must be removed before the cork is extracted. Usually a small tag protrudes from the foil to facilitate its removal. Secure the top of the wire with the thumb of one hand and unwind the wire loop.
- Remove the foil and the wire cage (muselet), ensuring that you keep your thumb on the top of the cork to stop it from popping out of the bottle.

Words & terms

Muselet: The wire cage around the cork of a champagne bottle which attaches the cork to the bottle with a wire ring. This is used so that the cork cannot pop out of the bottle (because of the gas) during storage.

Punt: The indention at the bottom of a champagne or sparkling wine bottle.

- Put the foil and muselet in your pocket.
- Use a service cloth to cover and firmly hold the cork with the palm of your hand. Tilt the bottle to a 25 degree angle, away from you and your guests.
- Hold the base of the bottle with your left hand (or your right if you are left-handed) and twist the bottle and the cork in opposite directions to loosen the cork.
- The cork should ease out of the bottle gently without making a loud pop.
- Place the cork in your pocket.
- Unless the host requests it, it is not necessary for sparkling wine to be tasted. Slowly pour the sparkling wine into the glass, taking care that the foam does not overflow.
- It is acceptable to lift a champagne flute by the stem and to hold it at an angle when you are pouring to prevent the foam from overflowing.
  It is not necessary to lift a champagne saucer.

Opening a bottle of champagne

- Place the champagne or sparkling wine in an ice bucket with the service cloth over the ice bucket according to organisational requirements.
- When you are pouring champagne or sparkling wine you may hold the bottle with your thumb in the punt of the bottle and your fingers spread out to support the rest of the bottle. You may also pour the champagne or sparkling wine by holding the bottle the same way as you would any other bottle of wine.
- Never pour a bottle of wine, champagne or sparkling wine by holding the neck of the bottle.

? Did you know? ?

The term "Brut" that is printed on the labels of some champagne or sparkling wine bottles indicates that the wine is dry rather than sweet.

Unit 8:

Deal with customers in a polite and friendly manner

The way you greet a customer is important for creating a favourable first impression of yourself and your company. Here are three key points that you should always keep in mind.
- Whilst what you say and do is important, what really counts is your body language when you say and do it.
- The most powerful form of communication is behaviour.
- The tone of your voice shows what you feel and think.

Dealing with customers

Remember that the customer is the most important person and if you are doing things other than serving other customers, you must stop immediately to serve that customer.
- As soon as a customer walks in the door, he or she must be acknowledged, since there is nothing more off-putting than rude or indifferent staff. This has a direct impact on customer service.
- Greet customers as soon as they enter your establishment.
- If possible, open the door for them and assist with prams, wheelchairs, children, and elderly people.
- Take coats and excess bags and luggage if applicable.
- If you are busy and unable to meet the customers at the door, make sure you acknowledge them by smiling, nodding or greeting them. This is very important otherwise the customers will think that you are not interested in them and they will not feel welcome.
- If your establishment is only a bar, without a restaurant, it is still extremely important to greet the customers and make them feel welcome.
- You must follow establishment requirements regarding the order in which you perform all the customer related procedures.
- If the customers are having a drink at the bar while waiting for their table and they are still busy with their drinks when the table is ready, you may take their drinks to their table on a tray.
- Never spend too much time talking to one customer. If the customer engages you in conversation, you should excuse yourself politely at the appropriate time in order to carry out other duties.
- Serving the customer politely and correctly is part of the whole experience customers expect to enjoy when they are eating in a restaurant.

Presenting the wine list

As you now know, the host at the dining table is presented with a wine list once all the guests have been seated at the table. However, in the bar or lounge the wine list is presented when the guests request it as follows:
- Open the wine list to the first page, and hold it at the top in your right hand with your thumb down the inside of the spine and your first two fingers down the back of the spine.

- Approach the guest from his or her right hand side, and attract his or her attention by saying something like: "Excuse me, Sir/Ma'am. Here is the wine list."
- Tell the guest of any wines on the wine list that are out of stock.
- Allow the guest to examine the wine list without interference. Pay attention to the body language of the guest: he or she will close the wine list and probably look up when ready to place the order.

Learning Activity 1.5

Do this activity in pairs.
1. Write out the details of three or four possible customer interactions with waiters in a restaurant.
2. Write out the details of three or four possible customer interactions with waiters in a bar or a lounge.
3. Role-play these interactions making sure that you all get a chance to play both roles.
4. Choose the best of your role plays and present this to the class as a whole.

Unit 9:

Working within prescribed time limits

This unit will ensure that you understand the impact on customer service of working within prescribed time limits.

> Peter Granoff of Virtual Vinyards describes his experiences as the sommelier at Square One, an exclusive San Francisco restaurant:
>
> Each table was different. I needed to size up the customer before helping them select a wine. If a customer had a business dinner in progress, I would be in and out quickly, and ask how we might make their evening more productive. If, on the other hand, we had a couple in for a romantic dinner, I might linger a bit to give them the story behind a vineyard or answer their questions about a bottle of wine.

Time management in dealing with customers

- Customers must be dealt with promptly at all times.
- Never assume that customers have all the time in the world. They may be in a hurry, so do not delay attending to them.
- Your guests expect reliable and prompt service. If they do not get it from you they will take their business elsewhere. This could jeopardise your job in the organisation.
- Tardiness is not tolerated well by most guests; show your respect for them and for their time by always being punctual and working quickly.
- Developing efficient and organised work habits will help you to not only be able to carry out your duties more efficiently and effectively, but will also make you enjoy your job more.
- When you are able to carry out duties easily and in an organised manner, you will be able to enjoy the customers whom you are serving. You will be able to chat with them with confidence and inform them of interesting things regarding wines and other types of drinks.
- This shows the customers that you are a professional and will not only make you look good to them, but they will establish a high opinion of the establishment, which in turn will bring more business.

How to work within prescribed time limits

- Always work within specified areas to avoid disturbing the workflow of others.
- Plan your work to avoid unnecessary movement, e.g. if you are going to the bar or kitchen, never go empty handed – there is always something that needs to be removed from the main bar.
- Organise your work area to establish an efficient workflow. Always have all equipment and stock ready for use to avoid unnecessary trips.
- Always clean as you go and go as you clean, as this will avoid unnecessary cleaning and time wasting at the end of your shift

- All preparation areas should be kept clean at all times and all new wine deliveries should be put away to avoid people tripping over boxes and cartons that have been delivered, and therefore avoid injuries and accidents.
- Working together with your colleagues as a team will ensure that everyone knows what the others are doing so there is no doubling up of tasks which waste time. This will also ensure that you do not go to the same customers with the same questions.

Unit 10:

Explain how customer service could be improved

Improving customer care

Always strive to improve on the customer care you give your guests by considering the factors below:
- Understand what the guests like about what you do and plan to do more of it.
- Understand what the guests are less happy about in how you are delivering your service and plan to improve this.
- Be open to the cultural differences of your guests and try to familiarise yourself with information regarding the various cultures of your guests.
- Be tolerant of the different values, attitudes and beliefs, as well as the different ways of behaving, of your guests.
- Be responsive to your guests' needs.

Training of wine service staff

Remember to improve customer service in relation to the serving of wine by ensuring that all staff is equipped with the following knowledge:
- how to pronounce the names of the wines
- what type of wine each is
- which foods they complement
- what the price of each wine is
- the availability of each wine.

The manager/head waiter should use the pre-service briefing as an opportunity to test the wine knowledge of the service staff, and to provide them with necessary information.

He or she should provide support to service staff when necessary. This is particularly important if they experience problems with dissatisfied guests, or with the quality or availability of wine products.

Coaching should be provided discreetly if staff members are unsure of themselves or if they are making mistakes.

The head wine waiter should assist staff by making recommendations on the handling of various situations. If staff members have problems with the availability of wine, she or he should make recommendations

Give accurate information and advice

When guests ask for assistance with selecting a wine, the following points will assist you:
- What will the guests be eating? Perhaps they should look at the menus first. If guests decide to choose food first, use the guidelines provided in the section on "Wines and Food" in Unit 4 of this topic.

- Does the guest prefer a white or red wine?
- If white, does the guest prefer still or sparkling?
- Does the guest prefer dry, off-dry or semi-sweet?
- If the guest prefers red wine, does she or he prefer a medium or full-bodied wine?

Make two or three choices, ensuring that you include at least one less expensive wine in the choice.

Learning how to recommend wines to give guests a choice

Ensure that you are able to give guests appropriate information about the wines you recommend.
- There are ways to gain knowledge on all the aspects of wines such as courses on wine tasting and courses on which wines complement which foods. There are also courses on the wine making process.
- The responsibility lies with you to attend courses that will enable you to give customers the correct information and advice. Customers will give larger tips to a professional waiter who is interested and who knows her or his job.
- Suggest to your manager that she or he sponsor wine courses for waiters.

What you should know about wine

As a wine waiter, you should know:
- the name and type of wine
- the vintage of the wine
- the characteristics of the taste of the wine
- the alcohol content of the wine
- the price of the wine
- which wine goes with which food item
- the country and region of origin of the wine
- the grape variety or varieties used in the wine.

In the workplace

People will return to your restaurant if your food is just "ok" or just "good," but the service always makes them glad they chose your restaurant and they feel they got the best value for their money. Their repeat business is the ultimate compliment to your service quality.
Source: adapted from Ross, Susie: "Customer Service: Fact or Myth?" Waiter Training Newsletter
The only difference between average customer service and winning service is a hair's breadth of preparation and anticipation.
(Paz, Paul: Tips on Tips #4)

Attending to detail in taking an order and in serving the wine

- When you notice that the guest is ready to order, approach and stand to her or his right and ask whether she or he is ready to place an order.
- When the guest has placed the order, repeat it to confirm that you have understood correctly. If it is a particularly good wine, you may want to say something like: "Meerlust Rubicon. An excellent wine, Ma'am/Sir." Or you might say something like, "Boschendal Le Pavillon Blanc. One of our most popular wines."
- Write the order in your order book, ensuring that the table number is clearly noted and that the name of the wine is clearly and correctly written down.
- Pick up the wine list from the table. If the guest is still holding it, ask if you may take it.
- Once you have taken the order you may process it at the bar.

A guest re-ordering the same wine

- When a second bottle of wine is ordered, the wine must be of the same vintage.
- If the second bottle of wine is the same as the first, only one clean glass should be brought to the table for the host to taste the wine.
- If the second bottle is not the same as the first one (either another vintage or another wine) clean glasses should be brought for all the guests.

A guest re-ordering a different wine

Guests often enjoy different wines during an evening out.
- If the host indicates that he or she would like to order another bottle of wine, offer the wine list. Take the order in the same way as described above for the first bottle.
- Before serving the wine the correct glasses must be placed on the table.

Suggestive selling

This is the most popular form of selling in hospitality establishments. It involves recommending that extra glass or bottle of wine to the customer to make her or his dining experience more pleasurable.

But it does mean that you need to have a very good knowledge of the wines that complement certain dishes.

The benefits of using this selling technique include:
- providing a better service to the guest by offering a range of service options and facilities
- increased guest satisfaction because they appreciate your thoughtfulness
- increased profits from sales.

Some examples of suggestive selling

Here are three examples of suggestive selling.

- Customers have finished a bottle of wine. You could say, "Would you like another of the same wine or shall I bring you the wine list?"
- Customers are celebrating a special occasion. You could day, "We have a fine selection of champagne available by the glass and by the bottle. Shall I bring you the list?"
- Customers have finished their wine, but have ordered dessert. Here you could say, "We have a wonderful dessert wine available, including a 1996 vintage Gewurztraminer that would complement your chocolate tart wonderfully well".

Learning Activity 1.6

Work on your own.

Basing your answers on the organisational procedures of the restaurant or bar where you are doing your in-service training, answer the following questions. Justify your answers.

1. To whom would you refer a difficult situation in your unit?
2. Who should you contact if a guest's behaviour is likely to cause harm or offence to other guests and/or staff members?
3. If an incident occurred that was outside the authority of the manager in change to whom would you report it?

Use the following grid to assess your ability to complete written tasks:

Student Name:				
Activity:				
On Task Time	I can write for at least a half hour without stopping. I would enjoy writing longer if time allowed.	I can be focused while writing up to a half an hour.	I can write for a half hour, but I have to stop and get refocused a few times.	I write very slowly.
Distractions	I am able to ignore noise and other distractions while I'm working.	I am able to ignore noise and other distractions while I'm working most of the time.	I am bothered by distractions and I often talk to others, move from my seat, or fidget.	I am bothered so much by distractions that I must be sitting alone before I can start writing.
Sentence Structure	I use clear and complete sentences in correct paragraph form.	I use clear and complete sentences, but I do not always have correct paragraph form.	I use complete sentences most of the time. I am not able to put paragraphs into my work.	I am not able to use complete sentences or paragraphs.
Mechanics	My spelling and punctuation are extremely good.	My spelling and punctuation are adequate.	My spelling and punctuation are inconsistent, but it does not affect the comprehension of my story.	My spelling and punctuation are unsatisfactory. The errors prevent the reader from understanding what I wrote.
Clarity	I communicate my ideas clearly and effectively in writing. My writing is very interesting and understandable.	I communicate my ideas clearly in writing. My writing is understandable.	I have difficulty communicating in writing. It may be unclear, hard to follow, or boring.	My writing only makes sense to me. I am unable to communicate my thoughts to others in writing.

Save your completed rubric somewhere safe.

License requirements

This unit will ensure that you understand the license requirements and the consequences of serving alcohol to customers under the legal age.

The Liquor licence

When you are starting work at a new establishment, it is of vital importance to find out about the type of liquor licence that the establishment has. You need to know how it will affect you in your work and what responsibilities it will give you. Knowing how to deal with all types of situations in regard to the serving of wine and other alcohol is very important.

Service times

This refers to the times during which liquor may be served. These are established once the establishment acquires a licence. Your supervisor will advise you of the organisational requirements regarding service times. This will be according to the licence given to the specific restaurant or bar.

You must never serve wine or alcohol to anyone outside these times.

Bring your own (BYO)

Some establishments have a dual licence that allows them to sell alcohol as well as allow customers to bring their own. You must check with your supervisor if this is the case and follow organisational requirements regarding this arrangement. Sometimes there is a charge associated with customers bringing their own wine. This is called corkage. Other rules still apply regarding hours of service and in relation to preventing under-age people from consuming alcohol on the premises.

Age limits

Most countries have a minimum age at which persons may be served wine or other alcohol. You must know what this limit is before you serve anyone wine or alcohol. The age limit in South Africa is currently 18 years. If you are unsure of a person's age, you must ask for identification. Your organisational requirements will tell you what forms of identification are acceptable.

You must also be aware of when and under what circumstances under-age persons are permitted to be on your premises. For example, this may be acceptable when they are having a meal or when they are accompanied by a parent, spouse or guardian.

You must also be aware when under-age people are permitted to consume alcohol on your premises. This may be acceptable, for example, when such persons are having a meal with a parent or a guardian.

Dealing with intoxicated persons

If you suspect that a person is drunk, you must not serve them wine or any other alcohol.

Some of the symptoms of intoxication include:
- slurred speech
- bleary eyes
- smelling of alcohol
- staggering, swaying, falling, tripping or stumbling
- spilling drinks
- dropping money
- bumping into things
- becoming annoying
- loud speech, inappropriate singing and swearing
- becoming inappropriately emotional
- becoming overly friendly
- getting abusive.

Do not serve a customer you suspect is drunk

Unit 12:

Unexpected operational situations

This unit will help you in dealing with unexpected operational situations as they occur.

Dealing with damaged or broken service equipment

If the refrigerator is not holding the correct temperature, make an alternative arrangement for ensuring that wines are kept at the correct temperature for service. For example, store wines in ice baths or ice buckets or in another refrigerator. Remember that damaged or broken service equipment is never an excuse for bad or slow service. The customer pays for the product so you will have to make a plan.

Report all equipment problems, and particularly problems with the refrigerators, to the Maintenance Department immediately so that they can be repaired.

Breakages and spillages

If the neck of a bottle breaks while you are opening the wine, return the bottle to the bar with an explanation.

Details of the bottle must be noted in the Ullage Book and it must be set aside until the next stock take.

Record should be kept of the cost of replacing drinks. This may be in the form of getting a receipt signed by your supervisor for the replacement drinks or entering the spillages and breakages and their cost into the spillage book.

You should report any breakages and spillages to your supervisor as soon as possible for the following reasons:
- It may be necessary for your supervisor to record any breakages or spillages so that staff members cannot be accused of theft.
- Replacing spilt or broken stock affects the stock control procedures of the establishment as well as its profits since more stock will have been used than is recorded by the amount of cash received
- It may be possible to recover some of the cost of breakages and spillages if adequate records are kept.
- There may be legal implications if customers have been injured or if their property, including clothing, has been damaged
- Replacement stock or equipment may need to be ordered.

Words & terms

Ullages: Any drink product which is not fit to be served. Typical examples are:
- Bottled beverages and minerals which are flat, infected or which have an off taste or odour when poured.
- Damaged bottles or leaking bottles of wine that suggest deterioration of the wine.

A broken cork

If the cork breaks while you are removing it, place the broken piece in your pocket, and screw the corkscrew into the remainder or the cork. Remove it carefully.

If a little cork has fallen into the bottle, go to your side station and strain the wine into a glass to remove it.

Availability and quality of products

Remember that you should have checked stock levels before service, and that you should know if wines are out of stock or if only a limited supply of certain wines is available.

When wines are out of stock, make a note so that you can inform service staff at the briefing immediately before service. Where stocks of wines are low (for example, if there are only one or two bottles of a particular wine left) make a note of this so that service staff can be informed. Find out when stocks of these wines are expected. If the Bartender has been waiting for stocks, contact the Store personnel or the Purchasing Department to find out when deliveries are expected.

If a guest orders a wine that is in limited supply (three bottles or fewer), tell her or him so that she or he can decide whether to go ahead and order or select another wine. Such a guest should also be given the opportunity to ask that you reserve the remaining bottle(s) for her or his table.

Serving the incorrect wine

If you do this, apologise immediately to the customer and ask whether you should bring a bottle of the correct wine.

Sometimes the customer will agree to keep the incorrect wine.

Should the customer want to change it, replace the wine right away and ensure that it is recorded in the Ullage book and that the manager is made aware of this

Quality of a wine poor

If a guest returns a wine, saying it is unacceptable, ask the guest if he or she would like to try another bottle of the same wine or if he or she would prefer to make another choice.

Return the rejected wine to the bar with an explanation, and obtain the requested replacement.

The returned bottle should be noted in the Ullage Book and set aside until the next stock take.

Remember that if a little cork gets into the wine it does not mean that the wine is corked. Wine becomes corked only when the cork dries out and the quality of the wine is spoiled.

If the labels on the wine bottles are damaged, return the bottles to Stores, ensuring that the Stores person issues a credit note.

Under-age guests ordering wine

When you are confronted with guests who are under the legal age of consumption attempting to order wine, bring the legislative requirement to the guest's attention.

Should the guest insist that he or she is over the minimum age, politely ask to see documentation

Make the guest aware in a polite manner that there are certain laws which the establishment needs to abide by and that you cannot compromise on this.

Unruly guests

Staff must not get involved with unruly guests and must continue with serving the other guests. The consequences of staff getting involved could lead to the other guests feeling uncomfortable.

In the event of guests becoming violent and disruptive it is recommended that wait staff not get involved but that they call the manager immediately.

Assessment Activity 1.1

Assignment

Question 1

Describe in your own words what you understand by customer care. (3)

Question 2

Get a copy of your unit's Customer Service Manual. Hand it in with this assessment. If the restaurant or bar where you are doing your training doesn't have a Customer Service Manual, find one from another restaurant or bar.

List problem areas in the manual's approach to customer service and make suggestions on improving the customer service skills. (10)

Question 3

It is part of our job in the hospitality industry to make sure that we do everything we can to make the guest's experience a happy one. It is not enough to have merely 'ok' service: the service must be excellent so that the guest will keep coming back.

Read the following case studies and answer the question on each.

Case study A

Waiter John has a headache after a party the previous evening and greets an old gentleman pushing his wife in a wheelchair, by saying, with a frown on his face, "Howzit Uncle?" He goes on to say, "I don't feel well today, but since all these other waiters are so lazy, I will have to serve you otherwise our horrible mean manager who is so lazy himself, will fire me. You can go and sit at the table in the right hand corner at the back of the restaurant so that you don't upset other guests by talking too loudly and spilling food. I will not be able to help you to your table because I am very busy.'

While placing his order, the gentleman wants to know if they stock small bottles of wine or if they serve wine by the glass since his wife does not drink alcohol. John doesn't have proper knowledge of the stock available and he replies, "I don't know, but in any case I think you will find wine too expensive so rather take some Cola."

a) Write down six customer service rules that John did not follow. (6)

Case study B

A couple with their teenage daughter are received by Peter, a young waiter. While escorting them to their table he puts his arm around the girl and says, "Where did such plain looking parents get a beautiful daughter like you?"

While waiting for their drinks to be served, the guests start discussing the play they are going to see after their meal. Peter, storming to their table immediately says, "The wine you have ordered it out of stock, order something else."

When they eventually are drinking their wine, the daughter suddenly starts blushing and in reply to a question by her father about why this is happening, she looks in the direction of Peter and two other giggling waiters.

b) Write down four customer service rules that were broken here. (4)

Case study C

A guest, who is clearly not in a good mood, complaints that the type of wine he prefers is not on the wine list. The waiter serving him, answers by saying, "'You are welcome to leave and look for another restaurant with a wider variety."

The guest throws down his serviette and storms out of the restaurant while shouting, "This place will never see me or any of my friends ever again!"

c) How will this incident influence the restaurant's business and how could it have been prevented? (5)

Question 4

Write down the guidelines for superior guest care by discussing each of the points below in two or three sentences.
a) The importance of teamwork
b) Projecting the right image
c) Respecting cultural differences
d) Keeping your promises
e) Being reliable
f) Listening to your guests (12)

Question 5

When you are assisting guests to make a choice of wine, you should make sure that you are able to give them the correct information about the wines you recommend.

Do some research and write about 200 words on the different ways available to you in which you, as a waiter, can gain knowledge about all the different aspects of various types of wine. (10)

Assessment Activity 1.2

Simulation

Complete a simulation exercise on the service of wine. Your lecturer will complete an observational checklist to assess your work.

Assessment Activity 1.3

Assessed practical

Provide a wine service in a live situation. Your lecturer will complete an observational checklist to assess your work.

Topic Summary

This topic focused on serving bottled wine and included how to assist customers to select wine and how to serve it in an appropriate manner.

Unit 1 looked at service equipment and glassware and discussed in details the shapes of various wine glasses. Other service equipment was displayed and discussed. Unit 2 introduced you to the wine making process and Unit 3 covered the characteristics of various wines and how these may help with the pairing of wines and foods. This unit also looked at the different kinds of wines available on the market.

Unit 4 provided enough information to enable you to provide customers with accurate information about wines as well as to be able to promote certain wines and offer alternatives if necessary. Unit 5 covers the skills you will need to take drinks orders accurately and Unit 6 ensures that you know how each kind of wine should be served.

In Unit 7 you learned how to actually serve and clear the bottled wine and in Unit 8 how to deal with customers was covered. Unit 9 explained the very important aspect of working within prescribed time limits. Unit 10 explained how customer services could be improved and focused on training and knowledge. Unit 11 briefly looks at the license requirements of an establishment that sells alcohol and the consequences of serving alcohol to someone under the legal age. The topic ends with Unit 12 which help you deal with unexpected operational situations.

The following are important to remember:

- In order to deliver a professional service you have to use appropriate service equipment and glassware. Revise Level 2, Topic 1: Cleaning and storing glassware.
- The wine making process has an impact on the end product. Visit the library and read as much as you can on the internet and in books and magazines about wine making.
- Attend wine tasting courses and events. These teach you how to identify different wine varieties and their basic characteristics. If you develop a sense of the taste of different wines, you will start to realise which wines will complement which food items.
- The size of your tip will be influenced by providing customers with accurate information on wines, your knowledge of the promotions and specials offered by your establishment and your ability to offer alternative options if your establishment does not stock the specific wine asked for.
- If you do not take drinks orders accurately you may have to pay for a wrong order as the drink will be wasted if the customer sends it back. Repeat the order back to the customers as this will ensure that you serve the correct drink professionally.
- The taste of wine is influenced by the temperature it is served at. Make sure you know these temperatures and always serve wine at the correct temperatures. It is no excuse when you are serving white wine at room temperature, for example, that your refrigerator is broken. During mise en place you should have put the wine in a bath or basin with ice.
- Practise serving and clearing bottled wines with your fellow students, using a wine bottle with water in it. Don't see it as a time to play around and make jokes: if you are in the real situation and don't know what to do it will not be in the least bit funny!
- Deal with customers in a polite and friendly manner since it is not enough to have merely 'ok' service: the service must be excellent so that the guest will keep coming back.
- Pick up signals that guests may be in a hurry. You may lose their business if you are slow with your service.
- Make suggestions at staff meetings on how customer service could be improved. During these discussions staff may come up with very good ideas since they are working with different customers every day.
- Understand the licence requirements and the consequences of serving alcohol to customers under the legal age. Never breach these requirements because your business can lose its license or be made to pay a fine.
- Develop a way of thinking that there is no problem that cannot be solved. The problem should be solved in such a way as to affect the customer in the smallest way possible. Deal with unexpected operational situations as they occur and do not always rely only on management to solve problems. Follow organisational procedures when you are solving problems.

Assess yourself

Assess your understanding of the information covered in this Topic by completing the following table:

	Yes	Partly	No
I am able to identify and explain the uses of appropriate service equipment and glassware.			
I understand the wine making process and its impact on the end product.			
I can identify different wine varieties, know their basic characteristics and the appropriate food items with which to serve with.			
I have the skills to provide customers with accurate information on wines, promote certain wines and offer alternative options.			
I can take drinks orders accurately.			
I am able to explain the importance of serving wine at the correct temperature.			
I can serve and clear bottled wines.			
I am able to deal with customers in a polite and friendly manner.			
I understand the impact on customer service of working within prescribed time limits.			
I am able to explain how customer service could be improved.			
I understand the license requirements and the consequences of serving alcohol to customers under the legal age.			
I am able to deal with unexpected operational situations as they occur.			
I can identify and explain the uses of appropriate service equipment and glassware.			
I understand the wine making process and its impact on the end product.			
I can identify different wine varieties, know their basic characteristics and the appropriate food items with which to serve with.			
I am able to provide customers with accurate information on wines, promote certain wines and offer alternative options.			
I can take drinks orders accurately.			
I can explain the importance of serving wine at the correct temperature.			
I am able to serve and clear bottled wines.			
I know how to deal with customers in a polite and friendly manner.			
I understand the impact on customer service of working within prescribed time limits.			
I can explain how customer service could be improved.			
I understand the license requirements and the consequences of serving alcohol to customers under the legal age.			
I am able to deal with unexpected operational situations as they occur.			

If you answered no or partly, then you need to revise that section again, or ask your lecturer for help.

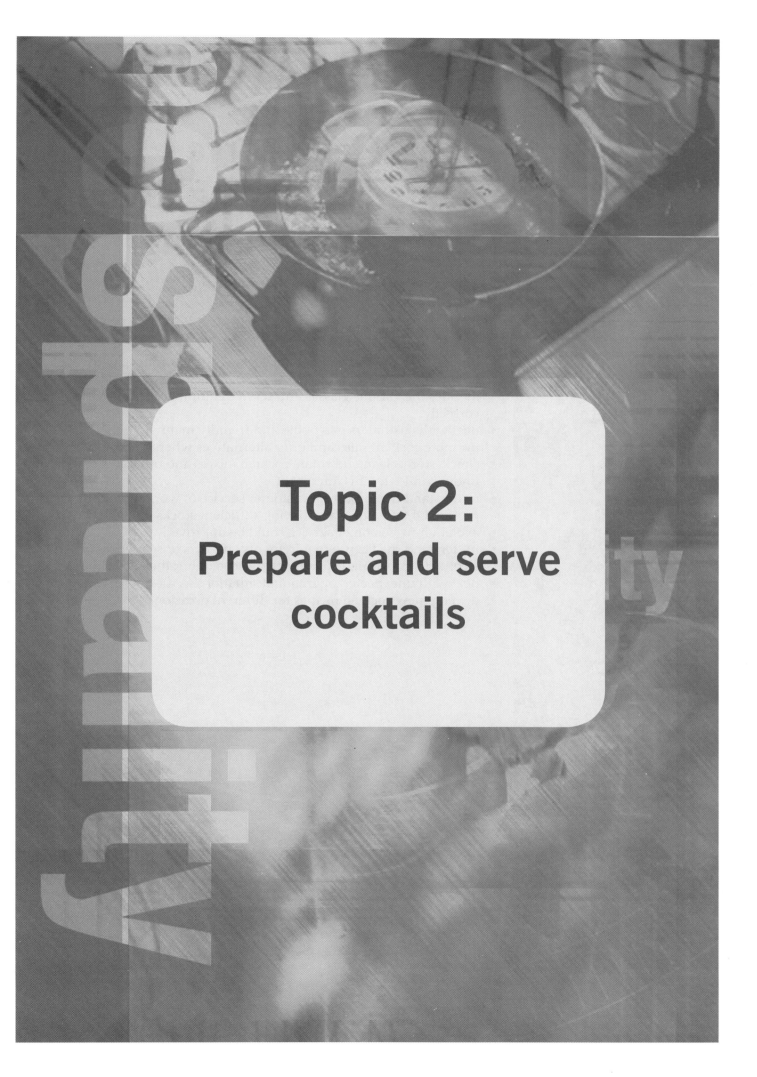

Topic 2:
Prepare and serve cocktails

Module 2

Prepare and serve cocktails: keeping to the recipe and satisfying customers

In this module you will ...

- prepare and present a variety of cocktails in accordance with organisational procedures
- identify the various glasses and service equipment and use this correctly
- deal with customers in a polite and friendly manner
- promote cocktail sales and offer alternatives where appropriate
- check, store, clean and rotate cocktail mixers and other ingredients and understand why this important
- understand the impact on customer service of working within prescribed time limits and having sufficient stocks on hand
- explain how customer service could be improved
- understand the license requirements and the consequences of serving alcohol to intoxicated customers or those under the legal age
- deal with unexpected operational situations as they occur
- develop new cocktail recipes for different occasions.

Unit 1:

Preparing and presenting cocktails

This unit will cover how to prepare and present a variety of cocktails in accordance with organisational procedures.

Cocktails

These can be divided in two main categories:
- spirit based cocktails
- non-alcoholic cocktails

Spirit based cocktails

A spirit-based cocktail refers to any cocktail that uses a spirit for its base.

Spirits

A spirit is a fermented alcoholic beverage that has been distilled to separate the alcohol from the water. Many spirits are made from grains such as rye, barley or corn. Others, such as brandy, are produced from grapes.

The main spirit groups are:
- whisky and bourbon
- gin
- vodka
- brandy
- rum.

Non alcoholic cocktails

Recently there has been an increase in demand for non-alcoholic cocktails (called mocktails). (They can be made using the blend, shake, stir or build method of making cocktails, as described under the next heading.)

These cocktails are usually served over ice in a long glass with a straw and the appropriate garnish.

Some of the ingredients suitable for non-alcoholic cocktails include:
- fruit juices – pineapple, orange, lemon, lime and tomato
- coconut cream

- ice
- cola
- ice-cream
- cream
- strawberries

Preparing cocktails

Not all cocktails are prepared in the same way. Just as the ingredients can vary, there are several ways in which to mix a cocktail. The four most frequently used methods are:

Shaking

The cocktail is mixed by hand in a cocktail shaker. The shaker is first filled three quarters with ice, preferably ice cubes since crushed ice will melt and dilute the cocktail. (Nobody likes a watery cocktail.)

The ingredients are then poured on top of the ice, in order of alcohol content beginning with the highest. For example, vodka will be added before a liqueur.

When you are shaking a cocktail, hold the shaker in both hands, one hand on the top and the other supporting the base of the shaker, and shake vigorously. When water has begun condensing on the outside of the shaker, the cocktail is sufficiently chilled, and the cocktail should immediately be strained into the glass. In general, shaking creates a colder cocktail than stirring does, but a shaken cocktail is also always cloudier.

A cocktail shaker

Always strain the liquid, unless told otherwise. Never shake fizzy ingredients. These are always added last.

Stirring

The cocktail is stirred with a glass or metal rod in a mixing glass, and then strained into a glass. As with the shaking method, crushed ice should not be used, and water condensing on the outside tells you when the cocktail is ready for straining.

Blending

An electric blender is used to mix fruit juices, alcohol, fruit and so on. Blending is an excellent way of mixing ingredients which do not blend easily in any other way. Blend the cocktail till it has reached a smooth consistency. If the recipe requires ice, add crushed ice last, but be careful not to add too much since the cocktail may then be watered down. Blending is a much disputed method of mixing a cocktail, and in general, blending should be avoided unless the recipe demands it.

A blender

Building

When you are building a cocktail, pour the ingredients into the glass in which the cocktail will be served. Usually, the ingredients are floated, one on top of the previous one, but occasionally a swizzle stick is put into the glass, allowing the ingredients to be mixed.

Tips on preparing cocktails

- Measure consistently. Provided the measure used is kept constant throughout the recipe, the finished cocktail will have the correct flavour, texture and colour. Use small or large measures depending on the number of drinks required.
- Use real fruit juice. Juice extracted from fresh fruit is the best. To extract as much juice as possible from the fruit, soak it for a few minutes in hot water before squeezing, or rub it between the hands.
- Keep slices of orange, lemon or lime fresh by covering them with a damp cloth or plastic wrap and storing them in the refrigerator.
- Use a twist of citrus fruit peel as a garnish. Using a very sharp knife, slice or shave off strips of the zest (or coloured part) of the peel. Be sure to leave behind the white pith since this tastes bitter. Twist a strip of peel over the surface of the drink and then drop the end of the twist into the cocktail.
- Wrap ice cubes in a clean, dry tea towel and bash these with a mallet if no crushed ice is available.

Cocktail glasses are usually garnished

Table 1: Recipes and mixing methods for popular cocktails

Drinks	Ingredients and Serving
Brandy Alexander	25 ml brandy 25 ml creme de cacao (liqueur) 25 ml cream Shake. Serve in a martini glass. Sprinkle nutmeg on top.
B 52	Use equal parts Kahlua, Grand Marnier and Baileys Irish Cream (or Cape Velvet). Layer in a liqueur glass – first the Baileys, then the Kahlua, then the Grand Marnier.
Black Russian	25 ml vodka 25 ml Kahlua Build into an old-fashioned glass filled with ice.

Bloody Mary	25 ml vodka 200 ml tomato juice a dash of lemon juice 2 dashes of Worcestershire Sauce a dash of Tabasco salt and pepper to taste. Shake, stir or build in a highball or zombie glass. Garnish with a lemon slice and/or a stick of celery.
Caribbean Sunset	20 ml gin 20 ml creme de banana (liqueur) 20 ml fresh cream 20 ml blue curacao 20 ml fresh lemon juice a dash of grenadine Shake all the ingredients except the grenadine. Strain into a large cocktail or pilsner glass. Add the grenadine. Garnish with cherries, an orange slice, pineapple leaves and an umbrella. Serve with a straw.
Fuzzy Navel	50 ml peach liqueur 200 ml orange juice Build into an ice-filled highball glass. Garnish with a slice of orange.
Golden Cadillac	25 ml Galliano 25 ml white creme de cacao 25 ml fresh cream Shake and strain into a champagne saucer or martini glass. Garnish with cherries.
Golden Dream	25 ml Galliano 25 ml Cointreau 25 ml orange juice 25 ml cream Shake and serve in a martini glass or champagne saucer. Garnish with cherries and an orange slice.
Grasshopper	25 ml white creme de cacao 25 ml creme de menthe 25 ml fresh cream Shake and serve in a martini glass or a champagne saucer.
Harvey Wallbanger	25 ml vodka 200 ml orange juice a dash of Galliano Build all but the Galliano into an ice-filled highball glass. Top with the Galliano. Garnish with an orange slice and serve with straw.
Kir	a dash of creme de cassis 200 ml dry white wine Pour the wine onto the creme de cassis in a white wineglass.
Kir Royale	a dash of creme de cassis 200 ml dry sparkling wine Pour the sparkling wine onto the creme de cassis in a white wineglass.
Mai Tai	25 ml Bacardi 25 ml dark rum a dash of curacao a dash of sugar syrup a dash of grenadine a dash of fresh lemon juice (or preferably fresh lime juice) Build into a large old-fashioned glass filled with ice. Garnish with a slice of lime (or lemon), a slice of pineapple, a sprig of mint and a cherry. Serve with a straw.

Manhattan	40 ml rye whiskey a dash of sweet vermouth a dash of Angostura bitters Stir and serve in a martini glass with a cherry. Variation: Use dry vermouth for a dry Manhattan, and garnish with a twist of lemon peel.
Margarita	40 ml tequila 20 ml triple sec 25 ml fresh lemon juice Shake. Rim a martini glass with salt, and garnish with a lemon slice.
Martini	50 ml gin (or vodka) a dash of dry vermouth Stir. Serve in a martini glass with a twist of lemon or a stuffed green olive.
Old fashioned	1 small sugar lump Angostura bitters 50 ml rye whiskey Place the sugar in an old-fashioned glass, saturate with Angostura bitters and add enough soda water to dissolve the sugar. Fill the glass with ice. Add the whisky. Garnish with a half slice of orange and a cherry. Serve with a swizzle stick. Variations: Can also be made using Scotch whisky or bourbon.
Pink Lady	50 ml gin a dash of grenadine 1 egg white Shake and serve in a martini glass with a cherry.
Planters Punch	50 ml golden rum 100 ml fresh orange juice a dash of fresh lemon juice Shake and serve in a martini glass with an orange slice and cherries.
Rusty Nail	25 ml Scotch whisky 25 ml Drambuie Serve in an ice-filled old-fashioned glass with a twist of lemon.
Screwdriver	50 ml vodka 200 ml orange juice Build into an ice-filled highball glass. Garnish with an orange slice.
Singapore Sling	25 ml cherry brandy a dash of fresh lemon juice 100 ml pineapple juice a dash of grenadine a dash of triple sec a dash of Benedictine Shake and strain into a large cocktail glass with crushed ice. Fill with soda. Garnish with a pineapple slice and cherries, and serve with a swizzle stick and a straw.
Tequila Sunrise	50 ml tequila 200 ml fresh orange juice 2 dashes of grenadine Build the tequila and orange juice into an ice-filled highball glass. Splash in the grenadine. Garnish with a slice of orange and a cherry. Serve with a swizzle stick and a straw.
White Russian	25 ml vodka 25 ml Kahlua Cream Build into an ice-filled old-fashioned glass. Float the cream on top.

Zombie	20 ml Bacardi 20 ml golden rum 20 ml dark rum 2 dashes apricot brandy 50 ml fresh pineapple juice 50 ml fresh lime juice a dash of sugar syrup Shake or mix and strain into a large cocktail glass filled with crushed ice. Garnish with fruit in season and mint. Serve with an umbrella, a swizzle stick and a straw.

Table 2: Recipes for popular non-alcoholic cocktails (Mocktails)

Acapulco Gold	Shake together six parts pineapple juice, one part grapefruit juice, two parts coconut cream, two parts fresh cream and a scoop of crushed ice. Serve unstrained.
Appleade	Chop up two large apples and pour a pint of boiling water over them. Sprinkle in about a teaspoon of sugar and leave to stand for a few minutes. Strain the liquid and leave to cool. Serve with plenty of ice and garnish with a wedge of apple and a slice of lemon.
Barleyade	Pour equal quantities of lemon barley and lemonade into a tumbler; add ice and a slice of lemon. Serve with a straw.
Capucine	Shake together one part peppermint cordial and four parts fresh cream. Strain and add crushed ice. Finely grate a little plain chocolate over the top.
Cardinal Punch	Over ice cubes pour four parts cranberry juice, two parts orange juice, one part lemon juice and ginger ale to top up. Garnish with fruit and serve with a straw.
Cinderella	Shake together equal parts pineapple juice, orange juice and lemon juice. Strain over ice cubes, top with soda water and splash in a little grenadine. Garnish with a slice of pineapple, or a pineapple chunk and a cherry on a stick. Serve with a straw.
Godchild	Place four or five ice cubes in a glass and fill three-quarters full with lemonade. Add a squeeze of lemon juice and gently pour a measure of sirop de cassis on top. Garnish with a slice of lemon and serve with a straw.
Grapefruit Ice cream Soda	Put two tablespoons of fresh grapefruit juice in a glass with two teaspoons of sugar and stir until sugar has dissolved. Fill the glass two-thirds full with soda water and top with a large scoop of vanilla ice cream. Serve with a straw and a spoon.
Grecian	Blend together four parts peach juice, two parts orange juice, one part lemon juice and a scoop of crushed ice. Pour unstrained into the glass, add a squirt of soda water and garnish with fresh fruit.
Lemonade (Fizzy)	Pour the juice of a lemon into the glass and add two teaspoons of sugar. Stir until the sugar is dissolved, add four or five ice cubes and top up with soda water. Garnish with a slice of lemon.
Lemonade (Pink)	Shake together two scoops of crushed ice, the juice of a lemon and two teaspoons of sugar. Pour unstrained into a glass and top up with water. Stir in a tablespoon of sirop de framboise.
Lemonade (Still)	As above but leave out the sirop de framboise and garnish with a slice of lemon. Serve with a straw.
Lemon Ice cream Soda	Put two tablespoons of fresh lemon juice in a glass with two teaspoons of sugar and stir until the sugar is dissolved. Fill the glass two-thirds full with soda water and top with a large scoop of soft vanilla ice cream. Serve with a straw and a spoon.
Limeade	Shake together the juice of three limes and sugar to taste. Strain over ice cubes and add water or soda water. Garnish with fruit.
Nursery Fiz	Pour equal parts orange juice and ginger ale over ice cubes. Garnish with a slice of orange and a cherry and serve with a straw.
Orange Ice Cream Soda	Put two tablespoons of fresh orange juice in a glass with two teaspoons of sugar and stir until the sugar is dissolved. Fill the glass two-thirds full with soda water and top with a large scoop of soft vanilla ice cream. Serve with a straw and a spoon.
Princess Margaret	Blend together five or six strawberries, a slice of pineapple, the juice of half a lemon, juice of half an orange, a couple of dashes of sirop de fraise and a scoop of crushed ice. Garnish with a strawberry on the rim of the glass.

Queen Charlie	Over ice cubes pour a measure of grenadine and top up with soda water. Garnish with a slice of lemon and a cherry on a stick, serve with a straw.
Redcurrant and Lemon	Heat one tablespoon of redcurrant jelly with two tablespoons of water to dissolve. Add the juice of a lemon and stir. Pour over ice cubes and top up with either soda water or water. Garnish with a slice of lemon.
Rosy Pippin	Stir a wine glass of apple juice with a dash of grenadine and a squeeze of lemon juice. Top up with ginger ale and garnish with a wedge of apple.
Saint Clements	Stir equal parts of orange juice and bitter lemon with plenty of ice. Serve garnished with slices of orange and lemon.
Shirley Temple	Pour ginger ale over ice cubes and add a little grenadine. Stir and garnish with a cherry.
Southern Belle	Crush a sprig of mint with a teaspoon of sugar at the bottom of a glass to extract the mint flavour. Add a squeeze of lemon juice and lots of ice. Top up with ginger ale, garnish with a sprig of mint and serve with a straw.
Summertime Soda	Stir the juice of an orange, a lemon and a grapefruit. Pour over ice cubes and add soda water and a scoop of soft vanilla ice cream. Serve with a straw and a spoon.
Tomato juice cocktail	Shake together tomato juice, a good squeeze of lemon juice, a couple of dashes of Worcestershire sauce, a couple of drops of Tabasco, a pinch of celery salt and a shake of pepper. Strain and serve on ice cubes. Garnish with a slice of lemon and a stick of celery.
Ugly	Pour equal amounts of grapefruit and orange juice over plenty of ice and serve with a straw.

Measuring

Never short-tot – this is against the law. If you are dispensing the spirit from an optic, push the top of the glass firmly up against the optic, and allow the full tot to empty into the glass. Wait until the measure has emptied properly.

In order to meet Liquor Licensing laws, measures of alcohol must be precise. Illegal measures can result in fines. The system used to measure spirits and liqueurs, such as a glass or a measure, must be approved by the Government to ensure that the quantity is accurate. There are two main reasons for this:
- It stops establishments serving less than the amount designated.
- It enables staff and customers to have an accurate guide to the amount of alcohol that has been consumed.

Standard measures are used to determine the cost of the drink and the profit that can be made from it.

Using an optic

Hold the glass under the optic and push firmly to release the spirit. The amount will be printed on the optic. The liquor licensing commission determines the amount.

For a double, let the optic refill and push the lever a second time.

Using an optic helps to ensure that you do not short-tot

Garnishes that may be used to finish a cocktail

The range of garnishes that may be used to finish a cocktail includes:
- lemon
- orange
- fruit
- ice
- sugar
- salt.

When you are choosing an optional garnish you should take into consideration these points:
- the flavour of the drink to be garnished
- the colour of the drink
- the concept of the drink.

Handling garnishes

- Always use clean utensils when you are preparing garnishes.
- Always check fruit to ensure that it is of good quality. Poor quality fruit will only detract from the presentation of the drink.
- Dispose of fruit that has spoiled or dried through exposure to air.
- In the powdered condiments such as coconut, salt, sugar, powdered chocolate always look for foreign particles.
- Never re-use swizzle sticks, umbrellas or fruit.
- Always keep the garnish preparation areas clean and tidy.
- If a garnish stains the cutting board make sure it is cleaned thoroughly.
- Do not forget that bacteria lurks wherever food is being prepared. Clean up as you go and use hot soapy water.

Table 3: Garnishes and appropriate drinks

Examples of garnishes	
Garnish	**Drinks**
Lemon slice (in the drink)	Soda, Lemonade, Tonic Water, Squash, Diet Coke, Gin and tonic (G&T), Whisky Sour, Margarita
Lemon wheel	Bloody Mary, Margarita, Missouri Sour
Lemon and cherry (cherry on the side)	Singapore Sling
Lemon and cherry (on top)	Lemon or Standard Daiquiri
Lemon twist (in the drink)	Martini, Vodkatini
Orange slice (in the drink)	All fresh Orange Juice drinks, Cointreau on ice
Orange slice	Freddie Fudpucker, Harvey Wallbanger, Blue Lagoon
Orange slice and cherry	Golden Dream, Tropical Zone, West (on the side) Indian Yellowbird
Orange slice and cherry (cherry on top)	Fluffy Duck
Lime slice	Gimlet
Lime wheel	T.Q. Tornado
Lime wedge	Vodka, Lime and Soda
Lime wedge and cherry (cherry on top)	Tom Collins, Cuba Libre

Olive (in the drink)	Martini
Maraschino cherry (in the drink)	Japanese Slipper
Maraschino cherry or nutmeg dusted over the top in a cross effect	Brandy Alexander, Grasshopper
Pineapple wedge	Midori Colada
Pineapple wedge and cherry	Blue Hawaii, Midori Illusion, Midori Splice, Pina Colada, Pine/Coconut Mocktail, Mixed Mocktail
Banana wheel (with skin), Banana wheel (skinless), Banana and cherry	Banana Bender
½ Strawberry	Bananarama, Champagne, Baileys on Ice
¼ Strawberry	Glass of Champagne
Opened strawberry (lips)	Strawberry/Banana/Mango Mocktails, Summer Breeze
Honey (inside glass)	Toblerone, Smoothies
Chocolate topping (inside glass)	Bananarama
Rimmed glass – salt	Margarita
Rimmed glass – sugar	Brandy Crusta, Jitterbug Juice
Rimmed glass – coconut	Coco Lush
Rimmed glass – grenadine/coconut	Strawberry Shortcake
Chocolate flakes (on the drink)	Blueberry Delight, Bananarama, Cherry Ripe
Sugar cube (dipped in bitters)	Champagne Cocktail
Grenadine and cream (hearts that float)	Field of Hearts
Float cream	Midori Splice, Blue Hawaii
Float whipped cream	Liqueur Coffee, Chocolate

Table 4: Drinks: Ice and/or garnish?

Drink	Ice	Garnish
Gin	yes	lemon
Vodka	yes	lemon
White Rum	yes	lemon
Cane	yes	lemon
Brandy	usually	none
Cognac	no	none
Whisky	usually	none
Whisky	usually	none
Vermouth	yes	lemon
Campari	yes	orange
Sherry/Port	no	none
Liqueur	no	none
Schnapps	no	none
Tequila	no	salt shaker and lemon
Dark Rum	yes	lemon
Pimms No. 1	yes	cucumber skin, lemon slice, orange slice, cherry

Presenting cocktails

To present or serve cocktails always hold the glass by the stem or the base to avoid leaving fingerprints on the glass. This will also prevent unnecessary warming of the drink. Never fill the glass to the brim and remember to leave room for a garnish if you are adding one.

Almost any glass can be used for cocktails. However, as a rough guideline choose stemmed glasses for cocktails which are not served on ice (stemmed glasses will stay cooler longer) and tumblers for drinks served on ice. Short cocktails look best in traditional cocktail glasses, while goblet shaped glasses are generally used for drinks incorporating egg yolks, such as eggnog.

It is essential that all cocktails be served very cold and, ideally, the glasses should also be chilled. They can be kept in the refrigerator for an hour or two or, alternatively, ice can be placed in a glass while the drink is being prepared to help cool the glass.

In the workplace

Frosting is often used to decorate cocktails. Frosting leaves an edge of sugar, salt, cocoa, or any other fine powder on the rim of the glass. Rub the rim of the glass with a slice of orange or lemon, then submerge the rim in sugar or salt (or any other powder) just so that it lines the top of the rim. Other methods use egg white to glue the powder to the glass. For a more colourful frosting, use small drops of food colouring in the powder. With some cocktails, such as the Margarita, frosting is a standard decoration.

In the workplace

Decorations either complement the flavour of the drink, such as pineapple and cherries on a pina colada, or contrast with the colour. Sometimes it will do both, such as a stick of celery served with a Bloody Mary. Avoid making the drink look like a fruit salad or like a Christmas tree.

Work in accordance with organisational procedures

- Staff must be well trained and extremely knowledgeable about the drinks they are selling and what is available in their establishment.
- Make sure that your hands, especially your nails, are always clean.
- Never smoke behind the bar.
- Always handle glasses by the stem or base, and never put your fingers inside the glass or near the rim.
- In order to deal correctly with customers, staff must also be honest, loyal to their establishment and trustworthy. If you say you will do something, follow it through.
- Staff must be capable of their job and hygienic in their appearance.

- Staff must be able to correctly describe to customers how drinks are prepared and what is in them.
- Customers may also want to know the amount of alcohol that goes into each cocktail. This is vital information that you must know. You will find the exact amounts of each ingredient in the cocktail recipe book used by your organisation. Follow the recipes precisely so as to be in accordance with organisational procedures.
- One part of the work area in a bar should be reserved specifically for the preparation of cocktails, and it should always be kept spotlessly clean.
- Always break an egg into a separate glass to test its freshness when you are preparing a cocktail with egg as an ingredient.
- Never put fizzy ingredients into a shaker, mixing glass or blender.
- In a mixed order of drinks, always make the cocktails last so that they are served fresh – a cocktail will separate if it is left standing too long.
- Always prepare your cocktails in the same manner and with the same garnish since cocktails tend to be remembered by guests, and they are often disappointed if they are presented with a cocktail that is different from the last one they had.
- An establishment usually has specifications for the recipes, mixing methods and way in which cocktails are to be garnished. This may depend on the image being presented and the price being charged for the cocktail. Always garnish in accordance with these organisational procedures.
- Alcohol is expensive so take care when you are working with it to avoid breakages and spilling.

Dealing with waste drinks

Sometimes a drink that has been made becomes a 'waste drink'. There are several reasons for this:
- You made the wrong drink.
- The customer changed his or her mind.
- The wrong mixer was used in the making of a drink
- A foreign object such as a fly was in the drink.
- The drink was 'off,' or, in the case of wine, corked.

When you are disposing of waste drinks you must always follow organisational requirements concerning this process. Most establishments will state that waste drinks must be reported and then disposed of in the sink. Staff may not drink the waste drinks.

Sometimes it may be possible to give an extra free drink to a regular customer in the interests of good customer relations, but this must be approved of by your supervisor.

Assessment Activity 2.1

Assignment

Do this assignment on your own.

Write a full description of the preparation and presentation of 6 different alcoholic cocktails and 6 different mocktails.

Include detailed notes on the different types of cocktails and mocktails and their ingredients.

Describe the glasses that are used for serving these various cocktails and mocktails.
Describe the appropriate garnishes for them.

Assessment Activity 2.2

Assignment

Question 1

Visit a liquor store to gather information and then also use the cocktail recipes in your text book to copy and complete this table.

Name of cocktail ingredient	Colour of the bottle and details shown on the label of the bottle	% alcohol and ingredients listed	Names of two cocktails in which this ingredient is used	Garnish and appropriate way to serve
Drambuie				
Bacardi				
Kahlua				
Tequila				
Grenadine				
Benedictine				
Angostura bitters				
Galliano				
Triple sec				
Cointreau				
Blue curacao				
Grand Marnier				

(24)

Question 2

Describe the purpose of garnishes and serving methods in relation to any four cocktails. (8)

Question 3

Cocktails fall into three broad categories:
* Pre-dinner cocktails – usually acidic or dry
* After dinner cocktails – usually richer, sweeter and creamier
* Long drink cocktails – usually made with fruit juice, a soft drink or milk

From the recipes given in this Unit, choose 3 cocktails which fall in each of the above categories. Justify your choice of category for each cocktail. (18)

Unit 2:

Glasses and service equipment

This unit will identify the various glasses and service equipment and explain to you how to use them correctly.

Glasses used for Cocktails

Brandy snifter, champagne flute, cocktail glass

Brandy Snifter Glass
This is a glass with a large bowl and a stem. The design induces the heat from your hand to warm the brandy or cognac in the bowl. It is also called a cognac glass.

Champagne Flute
This glass is primarily used to serve champagne, but is also the glass of choice for many mixed drinks. The slim opening at the top prevents the carbonation (gas bubbles) from fading away too rapidly.

Cocktail Glass
Often called a martini glass, the cocktail glass is designed to keep your mixed drink mixed. The shape prevents the ingredients from separating, and when it is held by the stem, your drink stays chilled.

Collins glass, Cordial glass, Highball glass

Collins Glass
This tall, narrow glass is named after the Tom Collins drink.

Cordial Glass
Drinks served in this glass are generally served after the meal. Its capacity is usually very small, around 60ml.

Highball Glass
Highball (or Hi Ball) glasses vary in size and height. Generally, this is a tall glass holding about 350ml. It is the glass used for many classic drinks, such as Manhattans and Rusty Nails.

Irish coffee glass, Old fashioned/Lowball glass, Pousse café glass

Irish Coffee Glass
Similar to a mug, this glass also has a stem. It is used to serve many hot beverages and cocktails, most notably Irish Coffee.

Old-Fashioned/Lowball Glass

This glass is used in many drinks. It is a shorter version of the highball glass. It is also called a rocks glass.

Pousse-cafe Glass

This is a very fancy glass and is used only for very few cocktails.

Shot glass, Whisky sour glass, Wine glass

Shot Glass

Shot glasses range in size from 30 – 90ml. This is a very small glass, and the drink is intended to be "shot", or thrown into the back of the throat and swallowed immediately.

Whisky Sour Glass

This is a mix between a champagne flute and a wine glass. This glass looks like an egg sitting on a stem. It is mostly used for sour drinks (whisky sour, rum sour.).

Wine Glass

There are several varieties of wine glass, but they all share common properties. They are all stemmed glasses holding 180ml or more.

Examples of Cocktails served in a Martini or Cocktail Glass

Marl: Made from dark rum, sweet vermouth and a lemon twist
Margaret: Made from Anejo Rum, lime juice, Grenadine and light cream
Margarita: Made from Tequila, triple sec, lemon juice and salt
Martinez: Made from gin, dry vermouth, triple sec, orange bitters and a cherry
Martini Cocktail: Made from gin, dry vermouth and a lemon twist or from Gin, Dry vermouth, Lemon-lime soda and Lemon twist
Martini, Dry: Made from gin, dry vermouth and a cocktail olive
Martini, Sweet: Made from gin, sweet vermouth and a cocktail olive
Martini, Traditional (2-to-1) Cocktail: Made from gin, dry vermouth and a cocktail olive

Examples of Cocktails served in a Highball Glass

Apricot-Screwdriver: Made from vodka, apricot brandy, Cointreau and orange juice

Atman-Cocktail: Made from vodka, Grand Marnier Rouge and 7-Up or Sprite

Babar-Drink: Made from vodka, Passoa, Guanaba juice, cranberry juice and 7-Up or Sprite

Bacardi-Highball: Made from Bacardi White Rum, Cointreau, lemon juice and Club soda

Bacardi-Lime-Red-Bull: Made from Bacardi Limon and Red Bull

Back-to-Back-Drink: Made from rum, Xante, Passoa, cranberry juice and 7-Up or Sprite

Baguz-Drink: Made from vodka, Passoa, passionfruit juice, lime and bitter lemon

Examples of Cocktails served in a Champagne Flute

Freska-Nova: Made from Mandarine Napoleon, orange juice, syrup and cream

Frozen-Daiquiri: Made from light rum, triple sec, lime juice, sugar, crushed ice and a cherry

Frozen Pineapple Daiquiri Cocktail: Made from light rum, pineapple chunks, lime juice and sugar

Examples of Cocktails served in a Shot Glass

01555-Shooter: Made from Kahlua, Sambucca and Bailey's

After-Twelve-Shot: Made from Dark Creme de Cacao and Creme de Menthe

Alice-in-Wonderland-Shot: Made from Tequila and Mandarine Napoleon

Apple-Cake-Shooter: Made from apple liqueur, vanilla vodka and cinnamon

Examples of Cocktails served in a Wine Glass

After-Ski-Relaxer: Made from Creme de Menthe, Cognac or brandy, hot cocoa and whipped cream

Alex-Coffee: Made from Scotch Whisky, brown sugar, vanilla ice cream and strong coffee

Amaretto-Coffee-Cocktail: Made from Amaretto, espresso and whipped cream

Eggnog: Made from whisky, rum, sugar, egg yolks and cream

Examples of Cocktails served in a Brandy Snifter Glass

Black-Maria: Made from coffee, brandy, light rum, coffee and powdered sugar

Jamaican-Banana: Made from light rum, White creme de cacao, Creme de Bananes, vanilla ice cream, half-and-half milk, banana, nutmeg and strawberry

Kentucky-BandB: Made from Bourbon and Benedictine

Examples of Cocktails served in an Irish Coffee Glass

American-Coffee-Cocktail: Made from Bourbon, brown sugar, hot coffee and whipped cream
Arctic-Warmer-Cocktail: Made from vodka, Creme de Menthe, orange juice and hot water
Barrier-Breaker-Cocktail: Made from dark rum, Galliano, Dark creme de cacao, coffee and crushed ice
Irish-Coffee-Cocktail: Made from coffee, Bailey's Irish Cream, half-and-half and sugar

Examples of Cocktails served in an Old-Fashioned/ Lowball Glass

Rum-Toddy-Cocktail: Made from Light rum, powdered sugar, lemon peel twist and water
Rusty-Nail-Cocktail: Made from Scotch, Drambuie and lemon twist
Scarlet-OHara-Drink: Made from Southern Comfort, Roses lime and cranberry juice

Examples of Cocktails served in a Collins Glass

Original-Singapore-Sling-Cocktail: Made from gin, Cherry brandy, lime juice, Benedictine and brandy
Papaya-Sling-Cocktail
Made from gin, lime juice, papaya-syrup, bitters, club soda and pineapple stick
Peach-Treat-Cocktail: Made from Peach brandy, orange juice, champagne and peach

Service equipment used in a cocktail bar

- Pourer: This is inserted into the neck of the bottle, either to make pouring easier or in some cases to measure drinks.
- Blender: This is ideal for blending fruit and frozen cocktails, such as Daiquiris and Margaritas.
- Squeezers: Electric as well as manual squeezers are available; they are used to squeeze out fresh lemon and orange juice.
- Drip trays: These are a deep trays covered with a slotted top. If glasses with drinks are carried on a drip tray the spills are caught in the bottom part of the tray.
- Soda siphon: This uses water in a special container coupled with a carbon dioxide gas canister to create fresh, sparkling water.
- Cocktail shaker: This is also known as a cobbler shaker or a three piece shaker. It contains a metal tumbler, a strainer and a lid. Some times the strainer is attached to the lid.
- Boston shaker: This consists of a mixing glass and a larger, flat bottomed metal cone. The cone is then placed over the glass to shake the cocktail. The Boston has two purposes: it can be used as a shaker or the glass alone can be used for stirring drinks or muddling.

There is a vast array of service equipment used in a bar

- Strainer: When you are transferring the cocktail to the prepared glass, the strainer separates ice or unwanted fruit and so on from the liquid. It is shaped to fit in a beverage shaker or tumbler. Typically made of stainless steel, a Bar Strainer may have a handle for ease of gripping that is connected to a strainer plate with 2 or 4 extended prongs that rest over the opening of the shaker or tumbler. In addition to the prongs, the strainer plate also has perforations and a spring that allow the mixture to be strained while the spring acts as both a strainer and a lid gripper to keep the strainer in place over the shaker opening. The springs on the strainer can be removed for ease of cleaning.
- Measures can be found in different sizes: 25ml (single measure), 50ml (double measure) and 175ml (small glass of wine), 250ml (large glass of wine). There are also measuring tools that have a single measure on one end and a double measure on the other.
- Optic: Most popular spirits – for example, gin, scotch, brandy, vodka, rum – hang upside down from brackets fitted to a shelf in the bar. At the neck of each bottle is an optic, which measures and dispenses the correct amount of the spirit.
- Ice bucket: This keeps ice clean and cold to avoid rapid melting. Most ice buckets are metal but you can find acrylic ones. It is useful to have a removable container that the ice sits in so that the excess water can be easily drained into the lower compartment.
- Bottle coolers: These can be used not only for wine, but also for spirits that have to be kept cool.
- Ice tongs and ice scoop: The ice tongs are used to serve and add ice cubes or cracked ice, while the scoop is useful to handle crushed ice.
- Corkscrew and bottle opener: These are very handy to keep on you at all times when you are preparing and serving drinks.
- Sifter: This is used for sprinkling sugar and spice and so on onto drinks.

Did you know?

Fresh juice always tastes better than processed juice.

- Salt saucer: Check that the saucer is larger than the top diameter of the glass that needs to be salted (normally a cocktail glass used for serving a Margarita, for example). The glass can then be turned upside down into the salt filled saucer.
- Grater: This may be needed to grate nutmeg over the top of a cocktail. On a standard grater, the finest side can be used.
- Cocktail sticks: These are used for spearing slices of fruit, olives, cherries, and so on as cocktails decorations. Cocktail sticks are made of both wood and plastic. Wooden sticks are most often used, and are suited for just about any kind of cocktail, but they cannot be reused. Plastic sticks, however, should be carefully used, because they give the cocktail a somewhat artificial appearance. Unlike wooden sticks, plastic ones can be reused, but should be carefully washed and boiled first.
- Straws: These can be used for additional reasons such as for decoration or to stir a drink.
- Swizzle sticks: These are used to stir drinks. They come in a variety of unusual and attractive designs that look good in cocktails.
- Cocktail parasols: These are typical of holiday cocktail decorations.
- Tablespoons and teaspoons: These are ideal to use for measuring.
- Chopping board: This is used for chopping fruit.
- Sharp knife: This is used for chopping fruit.
- Mixing glass: This is used for mixing cocktails and can also be used for muddling.
- Muddler: This is made of wood or metal and is used to mash ingredients at the bottom of the glass. For example, you may be asked to muddle the mint in preparation for making a Mojito.
- Cloths and towels: These are used to keep your work area tidy and clean.

In the workplace

Remember to dry glasses with a clean towel, and, before using wipe them, again with a clean towel to remove any smears and fingerprints that may be on them.

Checking the equipment

There is a large amount of equipment used in bars. It is important for you to be familiar with the correct use of all this equipment. This may also include assembling and dismantling it.

Always check that you know the following:
- where the equipment connects to the power source
- how to assemble the equipment
- the correct running temperature of the equipment, such as fridges, glass washers and espresso machines
- any safety procedures relating to the piece of equipment for example, a blender.

It is important never to use equipment that is damaged or broken. Tell your supervisor about the faulty equipment as soon as possible. Not doing so may mean placing yourself and others at risk of injury.

Unit 3:

Deal with customers in a polite and friendly manner

Dealing with customers

Customers visit an establishment for a number of reasons and most of these have to do with customer relations.
- the location of the establishment
- the fact of its being licensed or unlicensed
- the prices charged
- the quality of the drinks and the variety of the wine list
- the entertainment offered such as, for example, live music or dancing
- the service on offer – bar, table, cocktail
- its suitability for a special occasion or for everyday use
- the style of the drinks on offer – international, cocktail bar, wine bar
- the specific theme of the hospitality establishment as represented in its décor and menu, for example, Hawaiian, Italian or Chinese
- the friendliness of the staff
- the courtesy of the staff
- the helpfulness of the staff.

Being polite and friendly

Good customer relations are vital to the success of any hospitality establishment. If the staff members are grumpy and rude, or if they ignore the customers, the customers will not return.
- In order to identify customer requirements correctly, it is important that you listen carefully to the customer's order.
- Repeat the order back to him or her to check that you have heard correctly. If you are not exactly sure what it is that the customer requires, don't be too embarrassed to ask for further information. It is better to clarify the order at this stage, rather than mix the wrong cocktail and waste money and your customer's time.
- Each person ordering a cocktail will have different tastes so it is important to find out individual preferences.
- You must serve the type of cocktail exactly as requested by the customer. Also, if a customer asks for a particular brand of spirit to be used in their cocktail, you must prepare the drink using that brand. If that brand is not available, you must offer the customer an alternative brand before you prepare the cocktail.
- Also, if the customer requests that a particular type of garnish, such a salt, for example, not be used you must make sure that this requirement is met.

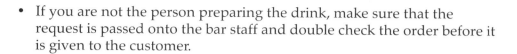

- If you are not the person preparing the drink, make sure that the request is passed onto the bar staff and double check the order before it is given to the customer.

Being helpful and knowledgeable

Customers expect all hospitality establishment staff to be well informed about what they are serving.

You must know all about:
- the measures that are used at the bar
- the relative strengths of various kinds of alcohol
- the ingredients used in different cocktails and mocktails
- the price of all the items served.

Meeting customer expectations

When customers visit a hospitality establishment, they expect a certain level of service, no matter what the style or kind of place it may be. These expectations include:
- The venue must be clean and hygienic.
- Staff must be friendly at all times, even if they are having a bad day – personal problems should not be taken to work.
- Staff must always speak to them in a clear voice and in a calm manner – not too loudly or softly, but with a certain amount of energy and enthusiasm.
- They should be treated equally, but at the same time feel that they are all special.

It is vital to 'read' your customers – their mood and possible requirements. If they arrive with a small child, get them a highchair immediately. If they walk in with a packet of cigarettes, get them an ashtray.

As soon as a customer walks in the door, he or she must be acknowledged:
- Greet customers immediately as they enter.
- If possible, open the door for them and assist with prams, wheelchairs, children, and elderly people.
- Take coats and excess bags and luggage if applicable.
- If you are busy and unable to meet the customers at the door, make sure you acknowledge them by smiling, nodding or greeting them. This is very important otherwise the customers will think that you are not interested in them and will not feel welcome.
- Even if your establishment is only a bar, without a restaurant, it is still extremely important to greet the customers and make them feel welcome.

You must follow establishment requirements regarding the order in which you do all the procedures.
- If the customers are having a drink at the bar, you may take their drink to their table on a tray.

- Remember that the customer is the most important person and if you are doing things other than serving other customers, you must stop immediately to serve that customer.
- Never spend too much time talking to one customer. If the customer engages you in conversation, you should excuse yourself politely at the appropriate time in order to carry out other duties.
- Being served politely and correctly is part of the whole experience.

In the workplace

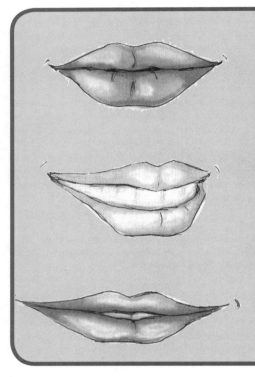

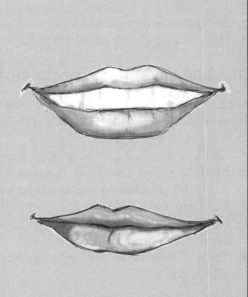

You will often come across grumpy patrons, or a customer who is in a bad mood. Don't let them put you in the same frame of mind. Keep smiling and be friendly. Pretend that they are not in a bad mood. Don't ask them what is wrong but think of some positive things to say, like, "What a lovely day it is" or "What a great special we have available for you to try today.". You will find that it is very difficult for someone to stay in a bad mood if other people around him or her are being friendly and pleasantly friendly and helpful.

Unit 4:

Cocktail sales and alternatives

This unit will equip you with the skills to promote cocktail sales and offer alternatives where appropriate.

In the workplace

Remember that the reason for using a garnish is to enhance the overall presentation of the drink to be served. This should ultimately increase sales through "visual selling".

Promote cocktail sales

- Sometimes when a customer approaches the bar, they will already know what drink they wish to order. However, on other occasions the customer is not sure and will ask your advice. This is your chance to promote the sale of cocktails including any special or promotional offers that the establishment may have.
- It is useful if you have a photo or display card to help describe the cocktail to the customer.
- Customers will often order cocktails that they perceive to be good value. You should try to guide them towards a speciality drink or creative cocktail that gives them good value for money.
- Remember that a good bartender is also a good sales person. Sell or promote the cocktails that you know you make well. This will ensure that your guests will return
- When you are promoting cocktails to customers, remember that they will want to know:
  - the price of the drink
  - the ingredients used to make the drink
  - the relative strength of the alcohol contained in the drink.

Customers may also want to know the amount of alcohol that goes into each drink. This is all vital information that you must know.

If a customer requests a cocktail that is not on your establishment's list, it may still be possible for you to prepare that cocktail, if you are allowed to according to your organisation's requirements. Make sure you have the required ingredients and a reliable cocktail recipe book before you offer to mix such a cocktail.

If new staff members do not know enough about cocktails to make suggestions and answer guests' questions, ask the head bartender or head waiter to assist. The new staff member should carefully listen to the handling of the situation so that he or she can learn.

Suggestive selling

A customer is looking at the drink list and cannot decide what to have. She goes backwards and forwards though the list and begins to look frustrated. A waiter sees this and goes up to her and says, "Today we have a special cocktail available. It's made from fresh strawberries, strawberry liqueur and white rum. We are offering it especially to refresh you on such a hot summer's day." The customer is delighted with this response to her uncertainty and she orders the cocktail.

You should use every opportunity possible to promote particular drinks. The first opportunity to promote drinks is when customers arrive. This gives you the chance to tell them about the house specials, or, possibly, the cocktail of the week or of the month.

Presenting the customers with the drinks list is also a form of promotion. When customers have finished a drink, recommend another.

If customers have not been drinking alcohol at all, then you should suggest a non-alcoholic cocktail (mocktail) or fruit juice. Mention if it is, for example, made from freshly squeezed oranges.

Promoting drinks to customers will increase the amount they are spending, and will, therefore, increase the revenue for the business, and also, if customers tip a certain percentage, you may get a higher tip.

If promotional material, such as tent cards, drinks lists and posters are used, they must be clean, accurate and up to date.

Sometimes drinks are promoted by way of specials such as "two for the price of one", or prizes that can be won depending on how many drinks customers buy. Make sure you find out before service starts which "specials" are available. It will look very unprofessional if a customer asks you about a special offer and you don't know about it.

Offer alternatives

If customers appear to have had enough alcohol to drink, do not suggest more alcohol. You might suggest coffee, or some food or a non- alcoholic drink. If you know that a customer has to drive, this gives you the opportunity to promote low alcohol drinks.

If the occasion appears to be a special one, you may wish to promote champagne to celebrate the occasion.

If you see that a customer likes a particular cocktail you could suggest that she or he try a different one that uses similar ingredients or that has a similar taste.

Unit 5:

Cocktail mixes and other ingredients

This unit will show you how to check, store, clean and rotate cocktail mixes and other ingredients and understand why this is important.

Check, store, clean and rotate stock

The storage, cleanliness, arrangement and rotation of stocks and accompaniments is extremely important in order to be cost effective and because it can have an impact on the quality of the drinks. This must all be implemented rigorously.

Stocks include the following:
• bottled and canned beers
• wines
• spirits
• liqueurs
• cold drinks and other soft drinks
• hot drinks such as tea, coffee, hot chocolate
• cocktail mixes
• sundry items such as coasters, straws and napkins.

Accompaniments include the following:
• ice and water
• cordials and juices
• food garnishes for drinks such as cocktails and mixed drinks
• decorative items for drinks
• nuts, chips or other snacks that you may serve with drinks.

When an order arrives, it must be checked in according to organisational requirements and then be arranged in the allocated area. Each item that is delivered will have a particular area assigned to it. This is to make it easier for everyone to locate items when needed. It will also allow for easy reordering, as it is possible to see how much is still available.

When an order arrives, it is very important to always put the new stock behind the old stock. This is so that the older stock is used first. This is called stock rotation or FIFO (first in first out). If you don't do this you will find that the stock at the back is never used and it will therefore spoil and cost the company money.

The same procedure must be followed in the bar when you are stocking it up. Never just put the new stock in front of the older stock. Always check for 'use by dates' as you are restocking to ensure that a good quality level is always maintained.

All stock should be packed away neatly so that you and the customers can see what is available. This will make counting easier and you will know how much stock you are going to need for re-stocking.

All food accompaniments, such as garnishes, sugar, nuts and other snacks and biscuits or chocolates that may be served with coffee or tea, must be stored in the refrigerator, if necessary, or in their appropriate place. The stock levels on these must be carefully monitored, since they perish a lot faster that bottled drinks do. Never over-order these types of items.

Remember that too little stock is not good, and that having too much stock is not good either, since you may waste unused stock or have no place to pack it away.

It is extremely important to follow all relevant hygiene, health and safety principles. (Refer to Topics 1 – 6, Hospitality Generics, Level 2.) All preparation areas, storage areas, equipment and stock such as bottles with spirits and liqueurs should be kept clean at all times and all new deliveries should be put away to avoid people tripping over boxes and cartons that have been delivered.

Unit 6:

Time limits and stocks

This unit will help you to understand the impact on customer service of working within prescribed time limits and having sufficient stocks on hand.

Working within prescribed time limits

Customers must be dealt with promptly at all times. Never assume that customers have all the time in the world. They may be in a hurry, so do not delay in attending to them.

Your organisational procedures will include reference to the maximum time that should be taken in dispensing drinks orders. Keep to these times. Customers do not have limitless patience and no one likes to be kept waiting for unreasonably lengthy periods of times. You do not want your hospitality establishment to get a bad name and keeping people waiting is a sure way of making this happen. Satisfied customers mean return business.

Stock on hand

Stock is kept behind the bar, on the shelves, and in the drink cabinets to help serve orders quickly and efficiently. It is also kept in storerooms.

Stock in the bar

In the bar you will also have a level that must be maintained (par level). When this is low the shelves must be stocked up from the main storeroom. All stocking up is usually done at the beginning or end of a shift.

You must avoid running out of necessary items during service since this wastes time. You will have to go and get things instead of serving customers and this is not the best use of your time. The only time that you should have to get more stock or accompaniments during service is when you are very busy and you do not have enough storage space in the bar. In this case, you must be prepared to go and collect these things – they should be ready for collection in a convenient place in the storage room.

Food garnishes must be prepared in advance to avoid keeping customers waiting while you cut up fruit or prepare your garnish, but you should only prepare as much as you think you will need to avoid wastage.

Stock visible to customers

If the stock is kept in cabinets with glass doors, the customers can also see what is available. It is extremely important to keep stocks and accompaniments at high and professional levels according to organisational requirements. You do not want customers to see empty shelves and poor stock levels. This will destroy their confidence in your hospitality establishment.

Stock in storerooms

Some stock and accompaniments are kept in storerooms and collected when needed in the bar. If any stocks or accompaniments are running low, you must report this to your supervisor so that more can be ordered.

Have sufficient stock on hand

You must ensure that you have sufficient stock before service begins.
- To avoid running out of items during service, it is essential that stocks be thoroughly checked before service.
- Running out of items during service will lead to customers having to wait a long time for their drinks and therefore, to customer complaints.
- Your establishment will get a bad name because of unprofessional service.

Learning Activity 2.1

Do this activity on your own.
1. Fetch a stock list from the bar in your workplace and find out what the par stock is for all the items.
2. Enter all this information in a two-column table with the left column headed Stock Item and the right column headed Par Stock Level.
3. Compare your table with that of another student.
4. Discuss any differences.

Unit 7:

Customer service

This unit will explain how customer service could be improved.

How can customer service be improved?

Deliver superior customer service and you will achieve major benefits in competitive advantage and profitability. The key to growth in an organisation lies in having a caring attitude towards all customers, even the difficult ones. Good customer service must therefore be a part of an organisation's very reason for being, and not seen simply as a tool to prevent customers from going elsewhere. For example, sometimes it may be possible to give an extra free drink to a regular customer. This is part of good customer relations but remember that any such action must be approved of by your supervisor. Knowing about current trends in consumption and sharing this knowledge is an excellent way to improve customer relations. Effective staff working relations are also important in this regard.

Improved service

There are a few things to remember in the interests of improved customer service.

- Cocktails should be served as fresh as possible and should never be prepared in advance. This is because almost all cocktails are drunk cold.
- Carry them carefully to avoid spilling them or dislodging the fruit or other garnishes.
- Name each cocktail to the customer as you serve it.
- Since condensation will develop on a cocktail glass, they should be placed on coasters or drip mats.

Be informed and knowledgeable

It is important that you have the knowledge to provide customers with correct information about what is available and that you keep up to date on the trends of consumption. Know what new types of cocktails are in fashion.

Effective staff working relationships

It is important that staff treat each other in a polite and helpful manner at all times. If a positive interpersonal relationship exists among all staff members it will be clearly noticed by customers. This will ensure that a positive image is reflected to the outside world of customers.

Appropriate division of responsibilities and the sharing of workload in a co-operative team will ensure maximum efficiency and will, therefore, contribute to greater productivity and to improve customer relations. Staff morale is a very noticeable yardstick of an organisation's efficiency.

It is important to support each other in the performance of your work since as staff you are all dependant on one another and you cannot perform well in isolation.

Anticipate your customers' needs

Anticipating your customers' needs could eliminate unnecessary time and irritation. Pay attention to their needs and decide how your hotel or restaurant's service can benefit them. If you identify appropriate products and/or services that the guest has not requested, offer to provide the service without requiring the guest to ask for it.

To anticipate the needs of your guests, you should ask yourself the following questions:
* Have I considered all of the guest's needs?
* What is the guest likely to need or want next?
* How can I improve the service for the guest?

Learning Activity 2.2

Do this activity in pairs.
1. Visit a local hospitality establishment that specialises in cocktails.
2. Research what the popular trends in consumption are among their clientele.
If you are unable to do this for religious, age-related or other legitimate reasons, ask your lecturer for an alternative assignment.

Use the following checklist of questions to assess your own ability to work with a partner.

Student Name:			
Partner's Name:			
Activity:			
Statement	**Yes**	**No**	**Sometimes**
I like working with a partner.			
I learn more with a partner than I would working alone.			
Working with a partner gets in the way of my learning.			
I think working with a partner to complete projects is a good idea.			
I dislike working with a partner.			
I run into problems with my partner not cooperating with me.			
My partner won't work out solutions with me when we need to work something out or plan our next step.			
I don't know my partner very well, but we are learning to work together.			

I think my partner would rather work alone.			
I think I would rather work alone than work with a partner.			
When we run into problems or have to figure something out, my partner and I are able to find a solution.			

Keep your completed checklist in a safe place.

Unit 8:

License requirements and serving alcohol

This unit will unsure that you understand the license requirements and the consequences of serving alcohol to intoxicated customers or those under the legal age.

License requirements

There are many different types of establishment that serve drinks. These are divided into licensed and unlicensed premises. Licensed premises are permitted to serve and sell alcohol and unlicensed premises are permitted to sell only non-alcoholic beverages.

When you are serving drinks in licensed premises, you must be aware of a number of issues including customer requirements, compliance with licensing legislation, correct service of all drinks and adherence to organisational requirements. It is extremely important to have a very good understanding of all these different things, especially the licensing legislation.

Service times

These are established once the establishment acquires a license. The days and hours that you are allowed to serve alcohol are outlined in the license. There are restrictions that apply to public holidays, Sundays, and holidays like Christmas Day.

You must never serve wine or alcohol to anyone outside these times.

Your supervisor will advise you of the organisational requirements regarding these times of service.

Age limits

You must know what this limit is before you serve anyone alcohol. The age limit in South Africa is 18 years of age. If you are unsure of a person's age, you must ask for identification. Your organisational requirements will tell you what forms of identification are acceptable.

Some establishments will have someone at the door checking identification. You should also check at the bar if you think an under-age person got in without being checked.

When you are checking identification, you must be aware of the following:
- Check carefully that the person on the ID document is the one in front of you.
- Pay close attention to the match between the physical features, such as the shape of the nose, for example, between the photo and the person.

- Check the photo section for bumps:a different photo may have been inserted and glued in.
- Check the date of birth carefully to make sure that it has not been changed by someone using liquid paper, scratching or letra-setting.

You must be aware of when and under what circumstances underage persons are permitted to be on your premises, for example, when they are having a meal or are accompanied by a parent, spouse or guardian.

You must also be aware when underage people are permitted to consume alcohol on your premises, for example, with a parent or guardian and with a meal.

In the workplace

You will often have to refuse customers drinks, especially if you are working in a bar. This is not an easy thing to do. There are certain steps that should be taken in order to do this properly and to diffuse a situation before it becomes a problem. Remember the phrase TAKE CARE

T – Tell early - recognise the signs of intoxication and take action early.
A – Avoid put-downs – don't blame or belittle the customer.
K – Keep calm – do not raise your voice, if you remain calm they will too.
E – Ever courteous – always be polite.

C – Clarify refusal – explain simply why you cannot serve the customer.
A – Alternatives – suggest low or non-alcoholic drinks.
R – Report – always inform other staff and your supervisor of the situation.
E – Echo – reinforce the message, especially if the customer is a regular.

Intoxicated persons

If you suspect a person to be drunk, you must not serve them wine or any other alcohol. If there is a person on the door of your establishment who is checking for identification, then they will also be monitoring the entry of people into the establishment and should not allow intoxicated persons onto the premises.

Intoxicated persons can be recognised by:
- slurred speech
- staggering, swaying, falling, tripping, stumbling
- spilling drinks
- dropping money
- bumping into things
- becoming annoying
- loud speech, singing, swearing
- getting emotional
- getting overly friendly
- getting abusive
- bleary eyes
- smell of alcohol on the person
- falling asleep.

Learning Activity 2.3

Role play

Do this activity in groups.
Role play the following scenario in front of the whole class.
A very drunk customer is being loud, offensive and unmanageable. A waiter tries to deal with him but has to call a supervisor for help. The supervisor has to get help from the security staff.

Learning Activity 2.4

Do this activity on your own.
Answer the following questions in writing.
1. How can you tell if someone is drunk? Give at least six ways of doing so.
2. If you are unsure of someone's age, what should you do?
3. What is a mocktail? Give at least six examples.
4. What is suggestive selling? Explain your answer with a short example of how suggestive selling could be carried out

Unit 9:

Unexpected operational situations

This unit will help you to deal with unexpected operational situations as they occur.

Unexpected operational situations

Unexpected situations do occur. For example, service equipment and glassware gets broken or damaged. Customers become rude and unruly or they order unknown cocktails. Accompaniments run out and under-age people demand alcohol.

In the event of any of this happening the establishment should ensure that support to service staff, especially new staff, is provided when necessary. This is particularly necessary if they experience problems with dissatisfied guests, or with the quality or availability of drinks, for example, liqueurs and spirits.

A new waiter should be observant of how these problems are handled. A professional waiter should be able to handle problems by himself or herself, but remember it should always be done in accordance with organisational requirements.

Remain calm when you are handling difficult customers especially during a busy service period.

In the workplace

You must be very careful if people come to the bar to get drinks but do not want to pay for them immediately. The best way of making sure that the drinks are paid for is to inform other staff of the situation. If the person wishes to pay with a credit card, take the card from him or her and put it in with the order. Generally, most people will not leave without their credit card.

Damaged or broken service equipment

The best way to prevent this from happening is to carry out preventative maintenance. The objective of a preventative maintenance programme is to take care of equipment on an ongoing basis so that breakdowns are avoided and safe conditions are maintained

But if you do have a problems with any equipment apologise at once and remove the damaged or broken item immediately. Stay calm and work efficiently.

The incident must be reported immediately or as soon as possible to either the Maintenance or the Duty Manager. If equipment continues to go unattended to, despite having reported it, inform the Head of Department.

Chipped or broken glassware

Any glassware that is chipped or cracked must be thrown away. Inform your supervisor and keep a record of all breakages according to organisational requirements.

Should you have a situation with broken or chipped glassware having been given to a customer, apologise immediately and replace it as quickly as possible.

Requests for unknown cocktails

Ask the customer if he or she more or less knows the ingredients used for the cocktail. There should be cocktail recipe books available in each bar. Look for a recipe using the ingredients, show it to the customer and ask if he or she would like you to mix the suggested cocktail.

You could also promote one of your cocktails that is more or less the same.

Unruly guests

When you are dealing with drunk and disorderly guests, politely ask them to quieten down since they are disturbing other guests. If they continue to be disturbing, do not get into an argument. Call your Duty Manager who is trained to handle such situations.

Under-age persons ordering drinks

If you are unsure of a person's age, you must ask for identification. Your organisational requirements will tell you what forms of identification are acceptable. Under no circumstances should you sell alcohol to under- age persons; suggest a nice mocktail.

Make the guest aware in a polite manner that there are certain laws which the establishment needs to abide by and say that you cannot compromise.

Shortage of accompaniments

This should not happen if mise en place was done properly. But if it does, deal with this professionally and efficiently.

These days, super markets are open until late so when you realize that you are going to run short, immediately send somebody to go and buy what is needed. Use tinned or frozen fruit if this is available and appropriate.

If you cannot obtain the accompaniments apologise to the customer and offer her or him some compensation such as a free drink or a free meal either then or later. Make sure, though, that you adhere to organisational rules and procedures.

Unit 10:

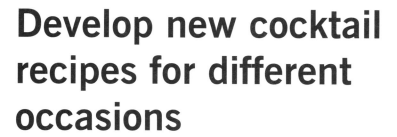

Develop new cocktail recipes for different occasions

Develop a new cocktail recipe

Cocktails can be served before or after meals. Many aperitif cocktails are wine-based, while after dinner cocktails are based on spirits such as brandy and whisky. Depending on when the cocktail is to be served, think about how well different appropriate ingredients would mix.

In the workplace

Although it is usual to serve certain combinations either before or after meals, remember that there are no hard and fast rules about what cocktails must be served at a specific time. The customer is always right.

Start developing new recipes at parties with friends. Select your preferred base ingredient (the main type of liquor you want to use) and take it from there by experimenting with different taste combinations. Ask for feedback from your friends.

It will take a lot of practice and experience to be able to invent new recipes. Try to find a cocktail bar where you can start by performing basic duties like cleaning up (even without pay) and learn as you watch, then practise. Mixing cocktails is an art that needs a lot of practice.

To develop a recipe for a specific occasion, choose a base liquor that will represent the atmosphere of the occasion and starts working from there. For example, if it is a Spanish themed function, start by using a traditional liquor of Spain and experiment with what blends nicely with it. If it's for a celebration think about using champagne as your base liquor.

Assessment Activity 2.3

Simulation

Work on your own

1. You will be given six different cocktail and mocktail recipes and instructions.
2. Select two of the recipes and complete the order within 45 minutes.

This simulation will be assessed using the following checklist:

Practical checklist – Drink service

Topic 2: Prepare and serve cocktails

Student's name: _____

Assessor's name: _____

Date: _____

	Yes	No	Comments
1. Hygiene:			
1.1 Correct dress code			
1.2 Personal hygiene			
1.3 Cleaning preparation area			
1.4 Cleaning all equipment			
1.5 Cleaning during preparation			
1.6 Cleaning after preparation			
1.7 Contamination threats and hygiene procedures			
1.8 Prepare and store garnishes hygienically			
1.9 Safe disposal of waste			
2. Poured/build/layer preparation method			
2.1 Pour the ingredients in the order they are given on recipe directly in serving glass			
2.2 Use the back of a bar spoon to gently disperse (or float) the ingredient on top of the ingredients already in the glass			
2.3 Ingredients forms layers and does not mix			
2.4 Use correct glass			
3. Shaking preparation method			
3.1 Measure ingredients correctly.			
3.2 Know how to handle tot measure and pourer.			
3.3 Know how to use shaker			
3.4 Use ice scoop to handle ice cubes			
3.5 Shake only until sufficiently cooled			
3.6 Use correct glass for service			
3.7 Strain cocktail correctly into glass			
3.8 Garnish neatly according to recipe			
4. Stirring preparation method			
4.1 Measure ingredients correctly.			
4.2 Know how to handle tot measure and pourer.			
4.3 Use ice scoop to handle ice cubes			
4.4 Use correct mixing glass			
4.5 Use correct stirring equipment			

4.6 Stir only until sufficiently cooled			
4.7 Strain cocktail correctly into glass			
4.8 Garnish neatly according to recipe			
5. Blending preparation method			
5.1 Correct use of knives, chopping boards and squeezers for fruit/ fruit juice			
5.2 Correct use of electric blender			
5.3 Know how to crush ice			
5.4 Add only enough crushed ice			
5.5 Use correct serving glass			
5.6 Fill glass to correct height (Don't Over-/Under fill)			
5.7 Garnish neatly according to recipe			
6. Serving cocktails			
6.1 Handle glasses by the stem			
6.2 glasses on a drip-tray to customers.			

Assessment Activity 2.4

Assessed practical

You will provide a cocktail service in a live situation. Your lecturer will assess your performance. The same assessment checklist will be used as was used in Assessment Activity 3.

Topic Summary

This topic focused on the preparation and serving of cocktails. Unit 1 extensively covered the processes of preparing and presenting cocktails and provided many examples of both cocktails and mocktails. Unit 2 looked at the glasses and service equipment you would need to use and explained how to use them properly.

Unit 3 focused on dealing with customer and Unit 4 on promoting cocktail sales and offering alternatives. Unit 5 discussed the importance of the correct treatment of cocktail mixes and other required ingredients. Topic 6 would have helped you to understand the impact on customers of working within prescribed time limits and of having stock available immediately on hand. This unit led to Unit 7 which looked at how customer service could be improved.

Unit 8 looked at the very important license requirements and the consequences of serving alcohol to intoxicated customers or underage people. Unit 9 looked at how to deal with unexpected occurrences and the topic ended with Unit 10 which looked at how new cocktail recipes are developed.

Assess yourself

Assess your understanding of the information covered in this Module by completing the following table:

	Yes	Partly	No
I can prepare and present a variety of cocktails in accordance with organisational procedures			
I am able to identify the various glasses and service equipment and use this correctly			
I have the skills to deal with customers in a polite and friendly manner			
I am able to promote cocktail sales and offer alternatives where appropriate			
I can check, store, clean and rotate cocktail mixers and other ingredients and I understand why this important			
I understand the impact on customer service of working within prescribed time limits and having sufficient stocks on hand			
I am able to explain how customer service could be improved			
I understand the license requirements and the consequences of serving alcohol to intoxicated customers or those under the legal age			
I have the skills to deal with unexpected operational situations as they occur			
I am able to develop new cocktail recipes for different occasions.			

If you answered no or partly, then you need to revise that section again, or ask your lecturer for help.

Topic 3:
Provide a silver service

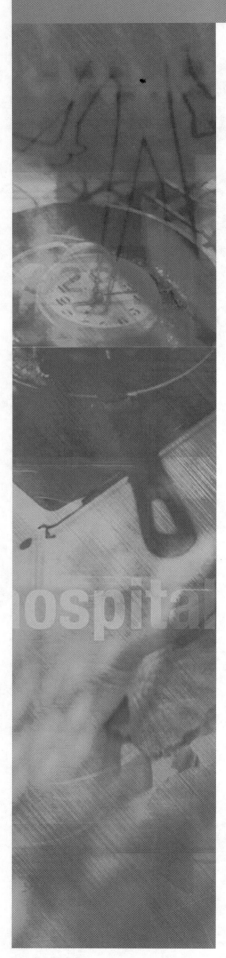

Module 3

Provide silver service and understand the importance of professionalism

Provide silver service in an efficient manner and understand the importance of completing tasks in a professional manner in order to attract repeat business

In this module you will:

- meet and deal with customers in a polite and friendly manner
- take accurate orders and advise customers on appropriate menu choices
- locate and use appropriate service items and equipment and understand why it is important to keep sufficient equipment stocks available
- serve food according to organisational procedures
- portion, serve and attractively arrange food using the appropriate service equipment
- clear tables and demonstrate the appropriate timing and method of clearing of tables
- check and store food service items and equipment according to organisational procedures
- recommend ways of improving service to customers
- describe decisions made and give reasons for actions taken in response to unexpected situations
- develop ways and methods to train new staff in the delivery of silver service.

Unit 1:

An introduction to silver service

What is silver service?

Silver service is a formal table service. It is a ceremony in which you present the food to your customers on a service platter and then transfer it to hot plates that have been placed in front of them. Silver service is used to make an occasion more formal and more elegant. If it is done well your customers will be impressed and think very highly of your establishment.

To become good at silver service, you must practise it often. You can only provide this kind of service to your customers once you know exactly how to do it. A good place to practise silver service, and any other hospitality service skills, is at home. You can serve dinner to your family following the silver service requirements every evening to become comfortable with, and efficient at, this technique. The better you are at silver service the less nervous you'll be in front of paying customers.

Silver service in a restaurant

In a restaurant, silver service starts with your placing hot dinner plates on the tables, one for each customer. Once the hot plates are in place you can take the food to your customers' table on a serving platter called a flat. The food is then transferred from the presentation platter to the dinner plates using a fork and spoon, or two forks and two spoons, depending on the type of food being served.

Some restaurants don't always do a full silver service; they may only serve some food this way, such as the bread or maybe the vegetables that accompany the main dishes.

One of the challenges of silver service is to serve the food while the plates and the food are still hot. You never want to serve cold food to your customers.

Think about it

To help you while you are working with this topic, revise what you learnt about providing table service in Level 3. You covered this in Topic 3: Provide a table service.

In the workplace

When you provide silver service at a banquet, it is very important to work quickly. In a banquet situation you will be serving 10 to 12 people at a table and each of them expects to eat hot food.

A variation of silver service is called Gueridon service. In this method of service a trolley is placed next to the customer's table and food is served onto their hot plates from the trolley. Gueridon service can also include cooking at the guests' table. This means that the cooking of some dishes is done next to the customer using a portable cooking trolley.

Popular Gueridon dishes include Crepes Suzette and Steak Tartar.

For both these types of service it is extremely important to follow all the relevant health and safety and food hygiene principles. It is also important for you to be comfortable with silver service techniques in order to provide service that meets your customers' expectations.

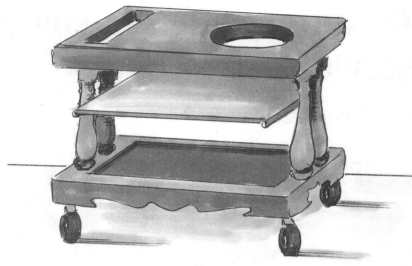

The Gueridon trolley is fitted with a gas burner. The top of this trolley is stainless steel so it is easy to clean. In the trolley is a drawer with extra service cutlery and a cutting board that is used during cooking. The bracket on the lower tray holds bottles of spirits and liqueurs and the indentation on top of the trolley holds the accompaniments.

A gueridon trolley

In the workplace

Food served by Gueridon service may be carved, filleted, flambéed or prepared (for example, a Caesar salad) at the guest's table before it is served. This form of service is normally found in higher-class establishments. It is expensive because it requires skilled labour, expensive equipment and a large room area for trolleys to be moved around easily. The first claimed flambé dish was Crepes Suzette served in Monte Carlo.

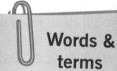

Words & terms

Gueridon Service: Food service in which a movable service tray or trolley is used.

Learning activity 3.1

Do this research activity in groups.
1. Find out which restaurants in South Africa offer Gueridon service and what dishes they prepare in front of their customers.
2. Write a report in which you document the information you have gathered.

Your research and report writing skills will be assessed using the following rubric:

Student Name:					
Activity:					
Criteria	**Outstanding 80-100%**	**Highly competent 70-79%**	**Competent 50-69%**	**Not yet competent 40-49%**	**Not achieved 0-39%**
Question	Student posed a thoughtful, creative question that engaged them in challenging or provocative research.	Student posed a focused question involving them in challenging research.	Student relied on questions from the lecturer or developed a question requiring little creative thought.	Student posed an unrelated question.	Student did not pose a question to guide their research.
Information Gathering	Student gathered information from a wide variety of quality electronic and print sources.	Student gathered information from a variety of relevant sources – print and electronic.	Student gathered information that lacked relevance, quality, depth and balance.	Student did not gather any relevant information.	Student did not gather any information at all.
Analysis	Student carefully analysed the information collected and drew appropriate conclusions.	Student made a good effort to analyse the evidence collected.	Student reached a relevant conclusion and did analyse some of the information gathered.	Student conclusions simply involved restating information.	Student did not reach any conclusion or analyse the information gathered.
Document-ation	Student documented all sources. Documentation is error-free.	Student documented sources with some care. Few errors noted.	Student need to use greater care in documenting sources.	Documentation was poorly constructed or absent.	Student clearly plagiarized materials.
Product/ Process	Student effectively and creatively communicated their conclusions and demonstrated thorough, effective research techniques. Report displays creativity and originality.	Student effectively communicated the results of research to the audience.	Student need to work on communicating more effectively.	Student showed little evidence of thoughtful research.	Product does not effectively communicate research findings.

Unit 2:

Meet and deal with customers in a polite and friendly manner

Greeting and taking care of customers

Taking good care of your guests is a skill. You must always strive to make sure your guests receive the best service and assistance possible. Part of this is to communicate with them in a way that is caring and efficient.

It is the Manager or Supervisor's role to ensure that everyone in the department is skilled in handling and assisting all types of guests in a wide variety of situations. If you cannot do this you will lose customers, and without customers you have no business.

You only have one chance to make a first impression, so you must make sure that you are polite and genuine when you greet customers. Your establishment may have a set greeting that they wish you to use or, if not, you should practise a greeting that sounds warm, honest and professional. A sincere greeting will put the customers at ease and start the service on a positive note.

When customers make purchases or use services and are spending their hard-earned money, they want to be, and like to be, treated properly, no matter what sex, age, race, colour or creed they are. They can always take their business somewhere else if they do not think they are getting what they are paying for.

A good rule to follow is to create a friendly atmosphere before any guests approach you. Look friendly and available to them. By doing this you are sending out warm, positive signals to each guest before the start of any interaction. If you look too busy or seem to be focusing on something else they might avoid coming up to you. Take notice of customers in your reception area and look at them, try to make eye contact and smile. This will invite them in and make them feel cared for and welcome.

Dealing with customers with communication difficulties

When you are dealing with customers who have communication difficulties, always do your best to communicate with them. If you feel that the customer does not understand you, call on someone with more experience to help. If you know what language the customer speaks, find out if another staff member may be able to help. Keep your language simple, and if appropriate, point to a menu or drink items to find out if that is what they are looking for. Be patient and speak slowly. Many foreign visitors may come into your restaurant so it is important that you

Think about it

Using people's names when you greet them or talk to them is a powerful and genuine way to achieve the "recognition factor", and this is always top on your guests' list of important expectations.
Source: adapted from Five Star Service by Evan Goldstein

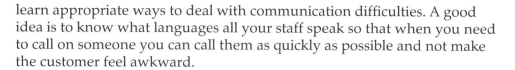

learn appropriate ways to deal with communication difficulties. A good idea is to know what languages all your staff speak so that when you need to call on someone you can call them as quickly as possible and not make the customer feel awkward.

What not to do

There are some annoying habits that irritate customers that you must never do. Look at the following list to see what behaviours annoy customers:

- ignoring and not greeting your customers
- appearing false by smiling insincerely at a guest
- not calling guests by their name
- yelling at guests or at other staff in the presence of guests
- keeping guests waiting in long, slow-moving queues
- not paying attention to what the guest is saying
- keeping guests waiting, without acknowledging them, while you are busy with something else, on the phone or talking to another staff member
- giving guests unhelpful monosyllabic answers, especially "No!"
- smoking or chewing while you are serving guests
- using negative body language
- running out of stock, such as drinks that are on the menu
- having confusing signs or directions around your establishment
- not thanking a guest when they leave your establishment.

> **Learning activity 3.2**
>
> Do this activity in pairs.
> 1. Discuss the importance of meeting and dealing with customers in a polite and friendly manner during a class discussion.
> 2. Take turns greeting each other and answering each other's queries in a polite way.
> 3. Assess each other and offer constructive criticism.

Unit 3:

Taking orders and advising customers

This unit will equip you to take accurate orders and advise customers on appropriate menu choices.

How to take orders and process them

In a silver service situation, the waiter will take the orders for the entire table through the host. When you take the orders, you must stand to the host's left and be ready to offer any suggestions, advice or explanations of dishes on the menu. In some instances you may need to translate the foreign names of certain dishes. This is your chance to promote sales of signature dishes and to encourage your customers to buy a good variety of your best dishes on offer, both starters and main courses.

The written copies of the order, called the food checks, should be written using the same language and names in the menu and during the first food ordering phase you should take all the orders up to and including the main course.

A second food ordering phase can be done after the main courses have been eaten, to find out what desserts, called 'sweets', or coffees or other drinks the customers would like.

When food is served at the table, you cannot ask who ordered which dishes. You must know who ordered which dish and where to place each plate of food, as well as the correct plates and cutlery for the meal. To help you remember this, remember the position at the table where you started taking orders and write the orders down in a clockwise direction. This will help you to serve the correct dish to the correct guest without having to ask. In this way you will create a more professional impression.

Politely guiding customers to an appropriate choice

Some customers, who have visited your establishment before, will be familiar with your menu, and may not need your help when selecting their meal. However, other customers may be visiting your restaurant for the first time and would like, or need, help or guidance about what to choose. In order to help them properly you need to find out what they like and dislike. To do this you can ask them questions such as:
- Do you prefer meat, fish or poultry?
- Do you like your food to be spicy?
- How hungry are you?
- Are you in a hurry?
- Do you prefer vegetables or salad?

The more information that you have about them, the easier it is for you to suggest what they might like to eat.

It also helps if you are very familiar with the menu – customers will not be impressed if you tell them that a particular dish is not spicy and when they order it they find out that it is.

There are some basic selling skills that will help you when you are taking orders.
- If appropriate, use your hands to demonstrate the size of a dish.
- Try to describe each dish as accurately as possible, including the main ingredients and the cooking methods used.
- If you know that guests are in a hurry, suggest dishes that are quick to prepare.
- If there are children at the table, ask if they would like their meals served earlier – possibly at the same time as the entrées.
- Be patient when customers are indecisive or change their minds. Offer further information or possibly make a suggestion.
- Always try to increase the sales of your establishment, for example, by suggesting sour cream, side salads, extra bacon or cheese or French fries.

Orders from the carving trolley

The carving trolley helps to sell meals. It a useful aid that lets customers see what is on offer and might tempt them to buy something that had not thought of ordering. Usually when a waiter takes orders, the customers have to rely on the descriptions of the food given by the waiter, and this might not be enough to sell a meal. The carving trolley supplements the waiter's sales pitch by showing the customers what the food looks like. The trolley is taken to the table as the waiter takes orders so that he or she may suggest and show off particular items to the guest. The carving trolley should always be pushed and not pulled.

Service items and equipment

This unit will explain how to use appropriate service items and equipment and keep sufficient equipment stocks available.

Service items and equipment

There is a wide range of service items and equipment that you need to learn about. Look at the table below.

Service item	Description
Trays	A tray is an open receptacle that is either round or square. It holds, displays or serves food. It can be made from fibreglass, stainless steel or plastic. Tray sizes range from small to medium to large, depending on what they are needed for.
Service Salvers	These are round silver trays, that are about 35 cm in diameter, and are covered with a clean serviette when they are being used.
Dishes	These are any type of dish that food will be served in, such as bowls for soup or semi flat dishes for vegetables.
Service cutlery (Silverware)	This is the cutlery you will use to serve the food. The cutlery is made up of a fork and a spoon, or two forks or two spoons, depending on the type of food you are serving.
Silverware	All types of dishes, cloches (the domes that are put over food to keep it warm), sauce boats, etc. made from silver.
Crockery	This includes all the non-silver items, such as the plates, bowls and other items that food is served on.
Glassware	You learnt all about glassware in Level 2. If you refer back to Topic 1 in your Level 2 book you can read all about the types of glassware and which glasses are appropriate for serving different types of drinks.
Liners/flats/ under flats	These are the large, generally oval dishes that the food is presented on to the customers. They are usually made of stainless steel.
Service cloths and other linen	These are used under the flat or platter you are carrying to stop it from slipping and to protect your hands from the heat generated from the platter, or to cover the servers and make them look attractive. Before you use these items you must check that they are all clean and don't have any holes or tears in them.
White cotton gloves	These are worn to give a more professional look to the service and for hygienic reasons. All waiters should wear white cotton gloves and never plastic or rubber ones.

A cloche

Checking and using serving items and equipment

All service items and equipment must be inspected before they are used to check that:

- they are clean
- they are free from chips, cracks and other damage
- they are polished. This applies to the silverware; it must never be used if it is tarnished. All silver must be cleaned properly on a regular basis in order to keep it shining.

Other important points to remember about using service items are:

- Linen must not be torn, stained, frayed, or have holes in it and all items must be neatly ironed.
- All service items and equipment must be placed correctly.
- Make sure you have enough of each item to last throughout the service. Most items are stored on a sideboard or service station near you so you can keep track of availability.
- Items such as silver service cutlery may be kept in the kitchen, near where you will collect the food. Make sure you know where these are and that there is clean set of service cutlery ready for you each time you take a platter of food into the restaurant.
- Make sure you have enough hot plates ready. They are usually kept in the kitchen or you may have a plate warmer situated next to your waiter's station.
- Make sure that you have enough waiter's cloths and that they are folded and ready to use, according to organisational requirements.

Unit 5:

Serve food according to organisational procedures

In the workplace

Accompaniments are highly flavoured seasonings served with different kinds of dishes and there is a large variety of them. The purpose of accompaniments is to bring out the flavours of certain dishes and so to improve the taste of the food or to counteract the richness in the food, for example, applesauce offered with roast pork. There are standard accompaniments for some dishes and waiters must know all these so that when he or she serves a particular dish, the correct accompaniments will be offered automatically. This is all part of the service a waiter should provide and shows that a waiter is thoughtful and efficient in anticipating and providing for all the guests needs.

Serving food in the correct order

Look at the list to see the different kinds of foods that are served in a silver service restaurant and the order in which they are served:
• Hors d'oeuvres
• Soups
• Fish
• Entrées
• Sorbets
• Roasts
• Vegetables
• Salads
• Sweets
• Cheeses
• Beverages.

During silver service, it is important to serve food in the correct order, as shown in the list above, and that you serve one course after the other. The only orders that are served together are the roast or meat dish together with the vegetables and/or the side salad. Together these form the main course.

How to use the service cutlery

To use the service cutlery correctly:
• Hold the spoon and fork in your right hand, or your left hand if you are left-handed, with the fork positioned in the spoon and both of them facing upwards.
• The palm of your hand and all your fingers must be over both handles; this must feel comfortable.
• Insert your first finger between the spoon and the fork handles, halfway down the handles, so that your first finger can lever open the fork and the spoon. You use this finger to open and close the gap between the fork and the spoon so as to be able to lift and serve food.

- To serve larger items such as bread rolls, stuffed tomatoes and roast potatoes, you should turn the fork around. This will give you a better grip. The cutlery will also curve around the food so it will be more secure when you are serving it.
- If you are serving large soft items such as an omelette or large whole fish or fillet, then you should use two fish knives. Hold the fish knives in the same way as you hold the spoon and fork, and splay them out to give you better support for the item.

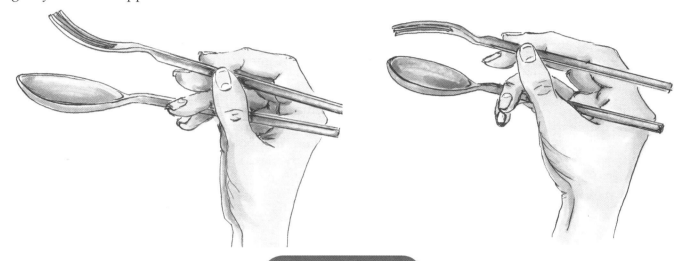

In the workplace

Remember that silver service has to be practised over and over to ensure perfection!

Learning activity 3.3

Do this activity on your own.
1. Practise using the service cutlery to lift and serve food. You can practise with raw vegetables or similar items.

Placing the plates

As a rule, if the food served is hot, the plates must be hot. If the food served is cold, the plates must be cold.

To serve and place the plates:
- hold the pile of plates on the palm of your left hand, on a service cloth; one end of the service cloth should be wrapped around and over the top of the plates
- approach the customer on their right hand side, take a plate by the rim and place it in front of them. Make sure you don't touch the plate or put your thumb on the rim of the plate.
- if there is a logo on each plate, make sure it is at the top of the setting facing the customer.

Presenting and serving the food

When you receive the food from the kitchen it is usually covered with a cloche, which is a dome-shaped food cover. Once you get to the sideboard or waiter's station you should remove the cloche, and be careful to tilt it slightly so that any condensation caught under the lid will not drip onto the tablecloth or the food.

Make sure that your service cloth is folded and laid along your arm under the whole dish. You will carry the platter in your left hand, and your service cutlery in your right hand. (You will do this the other way around if you are left handed.) Present the entire dish to the table of customers before serving, so that all the customers can admire the dish.

When doing silver service, always serve food or present items from the left side of each customer. To do this you must stand to the left of the customer you are serving, and then step towards the customer with your left foot between the customers. Bend forward so that the platter just overlaps the customer's plate. It must not touch the plate; keep it about 2 to 3 centimetres above the plate. It is best to bend your knees, not your back, while serving.

There are particular points to know about serving each course, and these are explained below.

Serving the hors d'oeuvres (starters or appetisers)

The correct cover for an hors d'oeuvre is a large side plate (also called a sweet plate) that is 18 cm in diameter or a fish plate that is 20 cm in diameter as well as a side, dessert or fish knife and fork.

During silver service the hors d'oeuvre is usually served from a tray carrying a number of small dishes, generally six in number, each with its own particular variety of hors d'oeuvre. Each dish should have its own service spoon and fork.

The tray should be rotated on the waiter's hand so that the item being served is in the dish closest to the guest's plate.

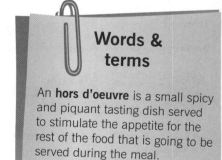

Words & terms

An **hors d'oeuvre** is a small spicy and piquant tasting dish served to stimulate the appetite for the rest of the food that is going to be served during the meal.

There are many different kinds of hors d'oeuvres and some examples are:
- fruit, for example, grapefruit or melon
- oysters
- snails
- prawns
- caviar
- mousses, for example, ham, biltong or smoked fish
- smoked salmon or trout
- asparagus
- artichokes
- patês, for example, goose or chicken liver.

Serving the soup

Soup can be dished up and served in two ways, either from a side table or gueridon, or from a tureen at the guests' table.

- Serving soup from a side table or Gueridon: This is one of the best ways to serve soup. On the side table make sure you have the soup tureen, a soup ladle and enough soup plates and under-plates to serve all the guests at the table. Hold the soup plate in your left hand and the soup ladle in your right hand. Gently spoon the soup into the plates and garnish appropriately. Then gently place the soup plate with the under-plate in front of the customer.
- Serving soup from a tureen at the guests' table: The individual portion of soup will be in a soup tureen that must be served on a silver salver. Hold the hot soup plates, with their under-plates, between your forearm and third and fourth fingers. You must then move the hot soup plate and under-plate from your right hand, which is the holding hand, and place it in front of the guest using your left hand. Now you will dish up the soup.

To do this, stand sideways at the table, so that you don't bump or inconvenience other guests at the table and so that the soup tureen on the service salver is held away from the table, thus reducing the risk of accidents. Position the service salver so that the rim of the service salver just overlaps the rim of the soup plate. Make sure the salver is kept level and not tilted. You don't want to mess soup on your guests. Lift the soup tureen to the edge of the service salver then tilt it slowly to pour the soup. Make sure you pour the soup away from the guest and into the soup plate.

Offer any accompaniments, depending on what soup it is, after the soup has been served. Examples are croutons or grated Parmesan cheese.

If you have to serve, for example, two individual portions of soup at the same table, then you can serve them the same way as described here. The only difference is that the second hot soup plate and under-plate will initially be held in your 'serving' hand. You will then first set both soup plates on their under-plates in front of the guests and then serve the individual portions of soup from the service salver followed by any accompaniments.

Serving the fish

The correct cover for a fish dish is a fish knife and fork and a hot fish plate. Make sure you have this ready before you serve the fish. If the fish is part of the main course and will be accompanied by potatoes and vegetables, then replace the fish plate with a hot joint plate.

Make sure you have a neatly folded service cloth on the palm of your left hand with a hot under-plate. You will then put the plate with the fish on the under-plate. Present the dish to the guest and then, using two service forks, serve the fish from the left-hand side of the customer.

Hold the service flat so that it is a little above the fish or joint plate and overlap it slightly. This is to avoid messing. Serve the head of the fish detached from the body using the back of one of the 'serving' forks. When you serve soft fibred meats such as fish, you are less likely to break the meat if you use two serving forks to serve the fish. You do this by holding the two serving forks apart and lifting the portion of fish from the flat and presenting it neatly and attractively onto the hot fish or joint plate. Once you have served the fish, you can rest the two forks on the under flat and then use the serving spoon, that you keep in your left hand underneath the under flat, to pour sufficient sauce over the fish, if the fish that you have served has sauce over it.

You can use a slice instead of the two forks if you find it easier to use.

Serving the entrée

How you serve an entrée depends on what type of food it is. For example, if it is a fish, meat, or vegetable dish you will serve it using the method described for these dishes.

Did you know?

Entrees that can be cooked using a gueridon are: Steak au Poivre (steak with pepper), Steak Diane (for this dish a waiter sears a steak, cooks a rich cream sauce and flames the finished product) as well as lobster curry.

In the workplace

In a restaurant, an entrée is a smaller course that precedes the main course. In the United States and English Canada the entrée is the first course, appetizer, or starter. Some restaurant menus will offer the same dish in different-sized servings as both an entrée and a main course. If there is not a fish course on the menu, certain fish dishes can also be served as an entrée.

There are many different kinds of dishes that can be served as an entrée.

Meat entrées:
- Chicken medallions filled with spinach and feta Cheese
- Carpaccio of veal with rocket, radicchio, fried capers and virgin olive oil
- Smoked beef fillet with fig and walnut dressing; shaved parmesan and rocket salad
- Shaved prosciutto with twice-cooked feta and hazelnut soufflé
- Smoked breast of chicken with soft dried tomato, baby spinach and red onion
- Duck confit on mushroom and pearl barley risotto; cabernet sauce
- Braised chicken on brown lentils with grilled pancetta and radicchio
- Steamed pork belly with bok choy, tofu and seaweed scallops

Vegetable entrées:
- Fresh asparagus and feta with tomato salad; black olive paste and frisse salad
- Chargrilled mushrooms, with cress and onion salad; fig vincotto dressing
- Caramelised onion and slow roasted tomato tart, rocket salad with grilled mushroom

Pasta entrées:
- Penne pasta with tomato sauce; parmesan, pesto and chilli
- Steamed salmon on pasta; herb and cream sauce; garlic toast
- Spinach and ricotta cannelloni with tomato sauce, chilli, pesto and parmesan
- Goat's cheese gnocchi with grape tomatoes; basil and rocket salad

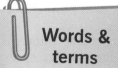

Words & terms

The word **entrée** is a French word that literally means entry or entrance.

Fish entrées:

- Freshly cooked Tiger prawns; cress and tatsoi with pear and ginger dressing
- Smoked Atlantic salmon, with baby potatoes, Swiss chard and gonfretts
- Chargrilled prawns on Asian greens with orange curry and steamed Jasmine rice
- Panfried snapper on sweet potato mash; chardonnay vinegar dressing.

Serving the sorbet

Sorbets are often served either as a palate refresher between courses or as a dessert. Sorbet is sometimes distinguished from sherbet by the fact that it never contains milk and it is usually of a softer consistency. Sorbets can be savoury or lightly sweetened. They're sometimes also called ices or granitas, though both of these mixtures are generally more granular in texture than a sorbet.

Unlike ice cream, sorbet has no air whipped into it, so it is a dense and very flavourful product. Sorbet is often served as a non-fat or low-fat (sometimes 3% fat) alternative to ice cream.

Take sorbet out of the freezer 15 minutes before serving and serve it garnished with 3 to 4 mint or lavender leaves.

To serve it, follow the rules for silver service. Place chilled dessert bowls or champagne saucers in front of the guest and then serving from the left, with the sorbet presented on a service flat, scoop the sorbet into the bowls.

Serving the roasts and other meat dishes

Before serving meat, make sure you have the correct cover laid out and ready. This is a joint knife and fork and a hot joint plate.

Roasts can be carved beforehand and presented to the guest on a serving platter or they can be brought to the table on a carving trolley and sliced in front of the guests. Other meat dishes are to be presented to the guests so that they can see the complete dish as it has come from the kitchen. This is to show off the chef's artistry in the presentation.

To serve the meat, cover the palm of your hand with a service cloth to protect your hand against the heat. Place the serving spoon and fork on the under flat next to the serving dish with meat. Position the serving dish a little above the joint plate so the rim of the serving dish holding the meat overlaps the rim of the hot joint plate slightly. Serve from the left-hand side of the guest and serve the portion of meat nearest to the hot joint plate. To make sure that you have a firm grip on the meat, turn the service fork. This will give you more control in your serving technique. Place the portion of meat on the joint plate in the '6 o'clock position'. That is the position nearest to the guest.

When you move on to serve the second portion of meat, rotate the under flat on the service cloth, so that the next portion of meat to be served will be nearest to the hot joint plate.

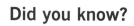

Did you know?

According to folklore Nero, a Roman Emperor, invented sorbet in the first century, when he had runners along the Appian way collect buckets of snow from the mountains to his banquet hall where it was then mixed with honey and wine. The Chinese have also made a sorbet-like food for thousands years from mixing snow, juice, and fruit pulp.

Words & terms

A **roast** is a large piece of meat cooked by roasting it. It is then sliced and the slices are served as appropriate individual portions.

Serving the potatoes and vegetables

The general rule is for potatoes to be served before vegetables. When you are serving either potatoes or vegetables, the vegetable dish itself should be placed on an under flat that is covered by a napkin. This is for presentation and to prevent the vegetable dish from slipping about on the under flat while you are serving.

Use a separate service spoon and service fork for each different type of vegetable and potato dish served. You must never mix foods since this can mix flavours and cause food contamination.

To serve potatoes and vegetable, place a service cloth on the palm of your hand to protect it and to allow you to easily rotate the vegetable dish on its under flat. Hold the serving dish in the correct position and serve the potato dish nearest to the hot joint plate each time.

Place the potatoes or potato dish on the far side of each hot joint plate so that you can work towards yourself when you serve the vegetables. This makes placing the remaining vegetables easier and helps to ensure the food is presented in an attractive way. Once the potato dish is served, rotate the vegetable dish on the service cloth so that the second vegetable dish may be served with a clean service spoon and fork. The second vegetable dish is positioned neatly next to the vegetables already served.

Serving the accompanying sauces

Sauces are presented in a sauceboat on a doily on an under plate and with a sauce ladle. Remember to always cover the palm of your hand with a service cloth to protect it from the heat of the dish you are serving.

When you serve sauces, ask each guest where he or she would like the sauce poured, such as on their meat. Serving from the left, and holding the ladle in your right, fill the ladle by moving it across the sauceboat towards you, lift the ladle full of sauce clear of the sauceboat and run the underside of the ladle along the edge of the sauceboat to avoid any drips falling on the table cloth or over the edge of the hot joint plate. Pour the sauce over the portion of meat already served, or where requested, by moving the spoon away from you. Let the sauce glide over the food. Do not cover more than 1/3 of the food with sauce.

Learning activity 3.4

Do this activity in pairs.
Your lecturer will divide the class into pairs for the practical activity.
1. Practise doing silver service by following the instructions given above, step-by-step.
You can use water as the soup and raw vegetables as the food that will be served.

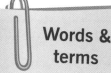

Serving the salads

A green or Greek salad is generally offered as an accompaniment to a main course dish such as chicken, duck or grilled steak. All salads should be served chilled, crisp and attractive.

The cover for a salad that is offered with a main course dish will be a crescent-shaped salad dish, a side plate or a small wooden bowl and a small fork or dessert fork.

When you serve the salad, ask which salad dressing the guest would prefer, if any, and then on the gueridon or sideboard, lightly toss the dressing and salad together in a glass salad bowl just before serving it. You will serve the salad on to the salad crescent, plate or bowl and place it at the top left-hand corner of the guest's place setting before serving the main dish.

Serving the sweets or dessert

Traditionally, sweets and desserts were offered as two separate courses on the menu. This still happens today, but most modern establishments consider sweets and desserts as the same type of dishes and serve them in the same course.

The appropriate way to present the cover for this course is to set the dessertspoon to the right, and dessert fork to the left, on the dessert plate and to place the cover, correctly laid out, in front of the guest. Once you have placed the plate you will position the dessertspoon on the right of the plate and the dessert fork left of it.

Flambéd dishes are very popular desserts to serve during silver service or gueridon service. For these dishes, fruit or pancakes are served from the pan, in which they are flambéed, onto the hot sweet plate that was placed in front of the guest earlier.

Serving the cheese

Cheese may be served and eaten either as a separate course after the sweet and dessert course, or as an alternative to the sweet and dessert course.

Before your serve cheese you must prepare the correct cover, which is a side plate and side knife. You must also replace the wine glass on the table with a Port glass. Port is an alcoholic beverage that commonly accompanies cheese. While you are laying out the cover, you can also place all the appropriate accompaniments on the table, such as a fresh dish of butter, celery, radishes and the cruet (salt and pepper pots).

Words & terms

Dessert includes all types of fresh fruits and nuts dressed up in a fruit basket and used as a central piece on a cold buffet until required.

Sweets (also called **entremets**) are hot or cold sweet dishes, such as soufflés; crepes; baked puddings; flambéed pears, peaches, bananas, cherries; ice creams and mousses.

Flambé is a French word that means flamed or flaming. This dramatic way of presenting food involves sprinkling food with alcohol, such as brandy, kirsch or rum, and setting it aflame just before serving the dish. Examples of dishes that are served this way are Bananas flambé, Peach flambé and Cherries flambé.

To serve the cheese you present the cheese board showing the selection of cheeses on offer. As with all silver service, serve the cheese from the left-hand side of the guest. Make sure that you have a service cloth between your palm and the cheese board to enable you to rotate the board more easily. Once the guest has made his or selection, cut an appropriate sized piece of the selected cheese and place in onto the guest's plate using the double-pronged tip of the cheese knife.

You can now offer a selection of dry cheese biscuits to the guest, again from the left-hand side.

A cheese knife

Serving the beverages

After all the food courses are served you can take order for and serve warm beverages such as tea or coffee. Some guests may want to order some other after dinner drinks such as whisky or sherry, but for now you are going to learn about serving tea and coffee using the silver service method.

Serving coffee

Coffee that is served after either lunch or dinner, while guests are still seated at the table, is usually served in a demi-tasse, which is a small coffee cup. The coffee service consists of a demi-tasse on its saucer, placed on a side plate and with the coffee spoon resting in the saucer and at right angles under the handle of the cup.

Did you know?

Dinner and a show: Tableside service add flair

Order a cheese plate at some up market restaurants and you'll be treated to a bit of a ceremony. The server will wheel over a cart with rotating domes containing six cheeses, explain the selections, carefully slice the cheese for your plate and offer accompaniments such as apricots poached in Champagne or candied nuts. And he can reach into an accompanying basket to pair a dessert wine, port or sherry with your cheese and pour it at table.

This is example of one kind of cheese service at upmarket restaurants.

Before serving the coffee, place the coffee service on the table on the right hand side of each guest who ordered coffee.

Before you serve the coffee, place a neatly folded service cloth on the palm of your hand, and on that you can place the service salver from which the coffee will be served. This allows you to rotate the service salver. On the salver, place the coffee pot, the jugs for the cream and the milk and the two sugar basins, one with white sugar and the other with brown sugar, along with their teaspoons, and all in a way that is easy for you to serve the coffee.

To serve the coffee:
- Position the silver salver just above the coffee service and rotate it so that the hot coffee pot and cream jug are in their correct positions for serving.
- Ask the guest if they would like sugar. This is always offered first. You can then place the desired amount of sugar in the demi-tasse.
- Once the sugar is in the cup, ask the guest if they would like black coffee or coffee with cream or milk.
- Then, keeping the service salver level, tilt the hot coffee pot and pour the coffee. If the gusts want milk or cream, rotate the salver so that the cream or milk jug is in the serving position, and again keeping the service salver level, tilt the jug and pour the milk or cream.

Once you have served coffee to a guest, gently place the coffee service in the centre of the place setting for their convenience. You must do this each time you have served a guest coffee.

Make sure that you return to the table at the appropriate time, to see if the guests would like more coffee.

Serving tea

Serving tea is done much the same as serving coffee, but some items that must be presented on the silver salver are different, such as:
- have a jug of cold milk on the salver; hot milk and cream are never served with tea
- along with the tea pot, also provide a pot with boiling water in it, to dilute the tea if it is too strong
- have a bowl or side plate with lemon wedges or slices and a pair of tongs to use if a guest prefers black tea with lemon
- have one sugar basin on the salver, with white sugar in it.

Unit 6:

Portion, serve and arrange food

This unit will equip you to portion, serve and attractively arrange food using the appropriate service equipment.

Portioning

When you serve food it is important to know what portions to serve guests and how to serve these so that they look attractive on the plate.

Before you start serving, you must know what size portions to give each customer. The portion sizes are determined before service by the chef according to organisational requirements. There will be a set amount of each vegetable and meat per person. For example this may be 2 spoons of peas, 3 carrots, 2 slices of meat, and 1 roast potato per person. The meat will generally be grouped and served with a piece of garnish.

You will get better at judging how much you should give people and you should know each of the customer's requirements before you start serving. Make sure that you have enough food for the number of customers and never decrease portions as you move around the table.

Learning activity 3.5

Do this research activity in groups.
1. Research the average portion sizes of the following items: meat, fish, chicken, rice, potatoes, vegetables, sauces.
2. Create a poster in which you illustrate the portion sizes.
3. You will assess each other's poster using the provided checklist.

Checklist for assessing a poster:

Information included	Did the group include enough relevant points to make the poster valuable?
Labeling	Is the poster clearly and accurately labeled?
Graphics	Are all the graphics used relevant?
Visual appeal	Is the poster is visually appealing and pleasing?
Language	Is all the language on the poster is appropriate including legibility, grammar and spelling?
Balance	Has the group achieved a balance between graphics and written information on the poster?

Assign a mark out of 5 for each of the criteria using the following scale:
5 – Outstanding
4 – Highly competent
3 – Competent
2 – Not yet competent
1 – Not achieved

Add the marks allocated for each criterion together to result in a total score out of 30 for the poster you are assessing.

Serving the food

The way you serve food in silver service is very important. As you already know, you always serve the food on the left-hand side of each customer. Learn the following points on how to serve food correctly.

- Always serve the main item first and place it closest to the customer, on the lower centre of the plate. The main item may be meat, fish, poultry or a vegetarian item.
- Serve the potatoes next and place them on the top right of the plate.
- Serve the vegetables next and place them on the top left of the plate.
- Serve the gravy or sauce last.
- Make you serve each item of food using the correct techniques as you learnt in Unit 5.
- Other accompaniments such as mustard and apple sauce are served to the left of the main item.
- Do not serve food so that it is placed on the rim of the plate.
- Position the food for all your gusts in the same way. You must work out what positioning you will do beforehand so that what you do will work.
- When you are serving a pastry dish, portion the pastry first, then spoon the filling onto the plate. Finally you will place the pastry crust on the dish.
- When you serve sweet or savoury flans, always place the point of the flan towards the customer.
- You should always ask the guest if they would like sauce, gravy, cream or any similar accompaniment. Do not assume they would like it.
- Always keep the serving cutlery above the serving dish to avoid drips.
- Move to the right around the table.
- Always serve the host last.

A plated meal

Learning activity 3.6

Do this activity on your own.
1. Draw a plate of food consisting of sliced meat, roast potatoes, cauliflower, carrots and sauce.
2. Place the items in the manner you would silver serve them.
3. Submit your drawing to your lecturer for comment.

Unit 7:

Clearing tables

This unit will cover the process used to clear tables and will demonstrate the appropriate timing and method of clearing of tables.

Clearing after each course

After each course is served and eaten it must also be cleared away. How you clear the tables and when you clear each course is just as important to know as how and when you serve each course. The courses that you need to clear away are:

- the soup
- the starters
- the main course
- the dessert.

Only when everyone at the table has finished eating do you to clear the table. People show that they have finished eating by placing their cutlery together on their plate. Once you can see the last person do this, then you can start clearing the course away. If you notice that someone is not eating, but not all the cutlery is placed correctly, then check with the customer if he or she has finished.

Start clearing with the person on the host's left and move around the table to the right, finishing with the host. When you clear stand to the guest's right, lean forward and pick up the plate with your right hand. Move away from the guest and transfer the plate to your left hand.

How to clear away plates

There is a particular way to hold plates that you are clearing away:

- With your left hand, grip the plate with your thumb on the rim and your first and second fingers underneath.

- Point your third and fourth finger upward to form a platform.
- To stop the cutlery from sliding around, place your thumb on the end of the fork handle.
- Place the knife under the fork pointing in the opposite direction.
- Move onto the next guest and pick up his or her plate with your right hand.
- Transfer the plate to your left hand onto the platform created by your third and fourth fingers and forearm.

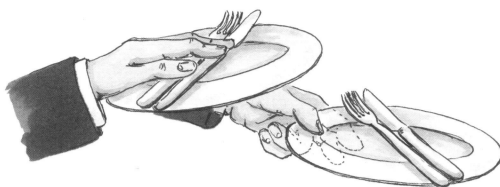

- Place the next fork next to the first fork.
- Use the second knife to scrape the food scraps onto the first plate. Then place the knife under the forks next to the other knife.
- Clear the rest of the table the same way.
- When you have finished, take the dirty dishes to the kitchen or wash-up area.

How to clear away side plates

Side plates must be cleared at the same time as the main plates and using the same technique as you used for the main pates.
- Continue around the table a second time and pick up the side plates and knives with your right hand.
- Place all the side plates on the pile of plates that are supported by your left hand and arm.
- Use the knives to move leftover food onto the first dinner plate and then place the knives on the first plate with all the other knives.
- Continue until you have finished clearing the table.

After you have cleared away all the dinner plates and taken them to the wash-up area, return to the table with one clean dinner plate. Hold and use this plate in the same way as you did the first clearing plate.

If you are clearing away odd shaped plates, clear only what you can carry in two hands. Do not try to stack plates since they may fall.

Clearing soup bowls and under plates

Soup bowls can be quite awkward to clear, because of their unusual shape and because there are usually also under-plates that need to be cleared. To clear these follow this procedure:
- The first bowl and under plate are held like the dinner plate.
- The next bowl and under plate are place on the platform created by your fingers and forearm.
- Place the spoon from the first bowl into the second bowl.
- Place the second bowl with the spoons into the first bowl.
- The under-plate from the second bowl stays on your forearm.
- Continue around the table until you have finished.

Clearing the table

After clearing each course you must clear all the crockery and cutlery that the customer no longer needs.
- After the entrée remove the entrée cutlery that has not been used.
- After the main course, make sure that all the side plates have been cleared.

- Remove the cruets and other condiments.
- Remove all the other crockery that may have been used such as finger bowls, extra plates and butter plates.
- Remove breadbaskets if they have been used.
- Remove any main course cutlery that may not have been used.
- If the dessert cutlery is not already on the table, then set the table for dessert.
- Carry the cutlery on a plate and place the cutlery on the table according to organisational requirements, with the fork on the left and the spoon on the right.
- Do not lean in front of guests when laying down the cutlery. Go to both sides of the customer to place the dessert cutlery.
- Make sure that ashtrays are also changed when there is a maximum of two butts in the ashtray. This must be done continually during service. Some people may wish for you to take the ashtray away during the courses.
- Once the dessert plates have been cleared you should remove everything from the table except for glasses that are being used, the decorative items and the ashtrays.
- At this point you should 'crumb down'. You do this by using a folded napkin to brush all the crumbs from the table onto a plate. When you do this you should also remove any other food debris and waste such as cigarette packets and wrappings from the table.
- Once everything is cleared after dessert, you can serve the warm beverages.
- All tableware, crockery, cutlery and service items should be removed, replaced and checked according to organisational requirements.

Unit 8:

Check and store food service items and equipment

This unit will show you how to check and store food service items and equipment according to organisational procedures.

Clearing service equipment

After you have finished a busy shift, you may be tired, but your work is not yet done. For this next stage in the clearing all the waiting staff should work together to make sure that all the service equipment is cleared away correctly. In order to avoid repeating tasks that someone has already done, it is a good idea to work in a logical order.

Your supervisor may instruct you on what sequence to follow when clearing service equipment but a good system is as follows:

- Make sure that your waiter's station has been cleaned and is well organised. This will make it easier when you replace unused service equipment in the station for storage.
- Using a tray, clear dirty service items from tables. Take all dirty crockery, cutlery and glassware to the kitchen to be washed. Stack the crockery carefully in the kitchen to avoid breakages. Some establishments soak cutlery at the end of the night.
- Return wiped condiment containers and unused service equipment to the correct storage area and refrigerate any condiments if necessary.
- Gather up all dirty linen and ready it for laundering.
- Empty all ashtrays. At the end of the night, these should be washed thoroughly. For hygiene reasons, wash ashtrays separately from other dirty equipment.
- Place all food waste into the appropriate waste bins.
- Empty and clean all the waste containers. Some establishments sanitise their waste containers at the end of every night, so if you need to do this then it must be done at this stage.
- Wipe all bench tops, tables, chairs, trays and trolleys, make sure they are clean and sanitise them if you are required to do so.
- Wipe menus, tent cards and table numbers and make sure they are clean.
- Discard any dead floral arrangements or unsatisfactory table decorations.
- If it is your workplace policy, reset the tables for the next service period.

Clearing condiments and accompaniments

Once you have removed food items, condiments and accompaniments from the table at the end of the shift, you should follow these guidelines:

- When you have finished serving food, you may have food left over on the server. This may be because there was more food on the platter than was needed or a guest did not wish to have the full portion allocated to them. Whenever there is food left over, return it to the kitchen as soon as you have finished serving the table and then follow the organisational requirements regarding the disposal of the surplus food.
- Any food items or condiments that need to be refrigerated should be covered with plastic wrap or a lid. Before putting them in the refrigerator, make sure you have cleaned the outside of the containers properly. Any milk or cream that has been taken from the tables should be discarded.
- It is a waste of time to place dirty and empty condiment containers back in the storage area. You must clean and refill the condiment containers to ready them for the next service. This will save a lot of time for all staff. It is very important to always keep containers and surfaces clean since dirty containers will attract pests and provide places for bacteria to grow and spread.
- Some condiments and accompaniments must be poured back into their original containers for storage. Check what the workplace policy for this is with your supervisor.
- If the condiment is to be stored in the service container, make sure that the outside of the container is wiped with a clean damp cloth to remove any spills or marks.
- Remove lumps from sugar bowls and check them for ants or other pests. Refill the containers, if necessary.
- Remember to store all food items, condiments and accompaniments in their designated storage area. This will make it easier for the next shift when they set-up the dining area again.

Turning off equipment

It is very important to turn off dining room equipment at the end of the day. Equipment that might need to be turned off may include:
- plate warmers
- hot cupboards
- drink chillers
- urns and coffee machines
- sound systems
- air-conditioning and heating systems
- lights.

Turning off equipment after service saves energy and reduces company costs.

Do this activity in two large groups.

Each group must discuss the following questions and write the group's answers on a piece of paper. Try not to use your textbook to find the answers.

1. Explain the following term "Gueridon Service".
2. What kind of items may be cooked using Gueridon service?
3. What do you understand by the term "mise-en-place"?
4. In what order do you serve guests at a table?
5. What do the following types of people eat:
   a) vegetarians?
   b) vegans?
   c) lactose intolerant people?
   d) gluten intolerant people?

Submit your answers to your lecturer for assessment. Your lecturer will announce which group got the highest mark.

Unit 9:

Recommend ways of improving service to customers

Special requirements

The main aim of the hospitality industry is to provide great service to customers. In all areas of the industry the customer comes first, and they expect nothing less. If customers are not treated properly, they will not return to your establishment, and neither will they recommend your establishment to anyone else.

Most customers will be happy with, or only need the standard service or menu that you offer, but some people may have special needs or requirements. In a restaurant, for example, most customers will order from the menu they are presented with and not have any other requests, but you will always come across someone who wants an item that is not on the menu for a variety of reasons, such as:
* they have special dietary requirements
* they are vegetarian
* they are vegan
* they are lactose intolerant
* they need to eat a low fat diet
* they need to eat a gluten free diet
* they have a particular food allergy, such as being allergic to nuts
* there is nothing the person likes on the menu
* the customer has a craving for an item not on the menu
* the customer is very fussy.

It is important to try and meet the special requirements that customers may have at all times. You will generally always be able to do this, but it takes a little patience and time on the part of the waiting staff. Always make sure that you know exactly what the customer wants.

If a customer has a special requirement, you do not want to risk getting the order wrong, so make sure you know what they want or need and then talk to your supervisor and the chef in the kitchen. If, for example, someone has a food allergy it can be very dangerous if you don't make sure that the food you will serve him or her is free from the allergen. If it is not your customer could become very ill and possibly die.

Whenever you make arrangements for a special need or order, you must let your supervisor know. You need to know whether or not they will be charged extra for what they want and if the chef is able to make what they have asked for. Don't promise to do something for a customer than you don't know can be done. Tell them you first need to make sure that it can be made, to avoid disappointing them.

Other kinds of special requirements might not be food related. A customer might need one of the following, for example:
- a quiet table for a romantic dinner
- a quiet area for a business meeting
- a table where there is room for a wheelchair or pram
- a birthday cake
- a smoking or non smoking table
- a window table
- a round table.

When you are providing silver service to customers, it is important to take special note of the customers' requests, and listen to them as you work around the table serving. Not all the customers will want everything that you are serving. For example, they may not want as much as has been portioned out to them. If they require more, then you may have to check with the kitchen about availability.

You should try to satisfy the customer's requirements at all times, and if there is an extra cost involved, the customer must be informed about it at the time of the request.

Ways of improving service

One way of knowing how to improve your service is to ask customers is to give you feedback or to fill in a questionnaire. It is a good idea for all establishments to have a guest questionnaire to fill in, since no matter how well you think you are all serving the customers, there is always room for improvement.

The guest questionnaire is one of the most important formal quality control systems in an establishment. Once a customer has filled a copy of the questionnaire in, it must be read and responded to by the General Manager. The feedback gathered from the questionnaire must then be passed on to the departments mentioned so that they can see what they do well or what they can improve or change. It is good for all feedback to be read, not only the negative feedback. Getting good feedback is very motivating and encouraging to all staff.

All negative feedback must be handled in a constructive manner. If a particular staff member's actions were mentioned, this should be handled privately. If the entire department or a group of people was mentioned, give the feedback in the context of either a department meeting or a special meeting. The intention of getting and acting on feedback is not to highlight weaknesses but to identify areas that need improvement. This is a constructive process and should not be one in which people are singled out or departments are made to look bad.

It is important to take a problem solving approach to any negative feedback.

Remember, too, that customers like to know if their feedback has been read and acted on or not. Someone might not come back to your establishment if they think that something they didn't like has not been changed. Reply to your customers, thank them for taking the time to give you feedback and let them know what you have done in response to the feedback they gave you.

Unit 10:

Decisions made and actions taken

This unit will describe decisions made and give reasons for action taken in response to unexpected situations.

Dealing with unexpected situations during silver service

There are many different kinds of unexpected situations that can happen during silver service. Below are examples of some kinds of unexpected situations and how they can be handled.

Damaged or broken service items or equipment

The best way to avoid this situation is to prevent it by ensuring that all equipment is well maintained. If you find equipment that is broken or damaged, you must take action quickly and report the problem to your supervisor. This is important because:

- Using damaged equipment can cause further problems that are more expensive to fix or result in the piece of equipment having to be completely replaced. Damaged equipment, especially electrical appliances, can cause damage to other equipment or infrastructure and hurt people using it or standing near it.
- If damaged equipment injures a guest then that guest, and other with him or her, are unlikely to come back to your restaurant. Losing business this way is expensive and is a huge cost to the company. The guest can also sue your company.
- Damaged equipment can mean that certain work can't be done. This 'down time' costs the company money.

If ever you find any damaged equipment you must report it immediately and then call any technicians needed to repair it. Remember that you might need to make an alternative plan while the equipment is being repaired.

A customer complains about the food

If a customer complains about the food or drink served, always:
- listen without interrupting
- acknowledge the complaint
- respond by offering a replacement or alternative drink or dish
- apologise
- check later that the new drink or dish is satisfactory
- report the incident to your supervisor.

An incorrect order

Check with the service staff and kitchen staff what the customer's order was. If the incorrect order was processed, apologise to the client and come to an amicable arrangement to solve the problem and that is satisfactory to the customer.

Food is not the correct temperature

Determine what the correct temperature should be and if the service and kitchen staff did not maintain the correct temperature and food was cooked incorrectly, apologise to the customer and ensure that the customer gets his or her food prepared and served correctly.

There is a delay in the service or a problem with the service

Establish what the delay is and assist with the service if it is because of business pressure.

A customer complains about the service

The waiter should always have a pleasant manner, showing courtesy and tact, an even temper and good humour, while serving customers. You must never show displeasure even though at times things may be difficult and you must never argue with a guest.

If a customer complains about the service and you cannot deal with the situation on your own then you must inform a senior member of the team, who, because of greater experience, should be able to calm the guest and correct the problem. Remember that the longer it takes to deal with a problem or complaint, the worse the situation gets.

An accident in the restaurant

As soon as you witness an accident, such as a guest slipping on the stairs, or someone feeling ill, you must report it to a person of authority and they must be called to the scene of the accident.

The person in authority must ask if the guest needs any assistance and at the same time decide how serious the accident or illness is. If it is possible, it is best to move the guest to another room to see if they are able to recover in a few minutes. But if the injury or illness is serious, and the person is unable to move him or herself, then it is better to wait for someone with medical training to give permission to move them or to treat them. In any serious accident you must immediately call for a doctor or nurse who will be able to tell you if you need to call an ambulance. Then try to screen off the area.

When an accident happens, place the person's meal on a hotplate until they return. If, after a short period of time, the guest returns and continues with their meal, then a fresh cover will be laid and the meal returned from the hotplate.

Although accidents can be difficult situations to deal with in front of other guests and staff, it is important that you react calmly and efficiently and to try and make as little fuss as possible. This is to reassure the rest of your guests, to keep an atmosphere of control, and prevent any further problems.

If the guest who has fallen ill or has had an accident is a woman, then a woman member of staff should attend to her. If the guest is male, a man should attend to him.

The guest may have had a sudden stomach upset and wishes to leave without finishing their meal. If the guest is alone at the restaurant, then you must call a taxi for them to get home safely. The payment for the meal and the taxi fare will be dealt with according to the policy of the establishment.

It is important that all accidents, both minor and serious, are recorded, in detail, in an accident book. This is in case of a claim against the establishment at a later date.

Unit 11:

Training staff in the delivery of silver service

This unit will give you the skills to develop ways and methods to train new staff in the delivery of silver service.

Silver service training

It is essential that service staff members receive regular training in service skills. To do this, follow the procedures below:
* make sure staff know what the expected level of service is
* ensure that regular short training sessions are held
* communicate to staff what the organisational goals are
* help staff in handling difficult situations and make sure that they are present when you deal with these situations so that they can learn from you.

Silver service demands much practised skill on the part of the waiter in handling and manipulating a service spoon and fork and in organising his or her service so that all the meals are served quickly and efficiently.
* The waiter must ensure that the food is served on to the guest's plate in an attractive and presentable manner and that all the chef's hard work and preparation skills are not spoiled by incorrect service methods.
* It is important to practise silver service in simulated circumstances over and over until it is perfected. Only then can a waiter start serving real guests.
* It is a good idea to let new staff observe how an experienced waiter does silver service.

A guide for training new staff to do silver service

Use the table below as a guideline to train a new waiter in the delivery of silver service. Your session can be planned and conducted as follows:

Stage	Trainer activities	Trainee activities
1. Introduction	Explain the purpose of the task. Ask questions that enable you to assess how much the trainee already knows.	Answers questions from the trainer.
2. Demonstration	Demonstrate the task. Explain what you are doing, how it should be done and why it should be done that way. Ask questions to involve the trainee. Ask if the trainee has any questions.	Observes. Answers questions. Asks questions.
3. Practice	Ask the trainee to do the task and explain what he or she is doing and why. Ask questions when the trainee does not explain. Correct the trainee if a mistake is made. Allow the trainee to practise until he or she gets the task right.	Trainee practises the task and explains what is being done and why. Trainee answers questions from the trainer.

4. Summary	Summarise the task and what was taught. Ask questions to check that the trainee understands the task completely. Ask if the trainee has any questions. Tell the trainee what will be taught in the next training session.	Trainee answers questions and asks any final questions he or she may have.

Assessment Activity 3.1

Assignment

Provide a silver service

Complete a short question assignment on the improvement of customer service and selling techniques.

Question 1

What do you understand by "suggestive selling"? Give an example of how you would use this technique. (6)

Question 2

Increased sales of food and beverages have a positive impact on turnover and increases profitability, which is the purpose of any business. For this reason it is important that the manager encourages and rewards waiters to promote sales through the skill of up-sell, on-sell, specials and promotions. Explain the following terms:
a) Up-selling
b) On-selling
c) Promotion
d) Specials (8)

Question 3

Discuss five guidelines that you think are the most important in terms of providing customer care. (10)

Question 4: Case study

A few years ago, a colleague of mine was travelling for business. It was towards the end of a long trip and he was weary from multiple nights in different hotels. As he checked in to a particular hotel the front desk attendant noticed that he looked tired and distracted. The hotel employee asked if he was OK, to which he responded, "You know how you feel when you're really exhausted from working hard and all you want to do is go home and have a peanut butter and jam sandwich with a glass of milk? Well that's how I feel."

So he checked in, took his bags up to his room, and sat on the bed watching the television. There was a knock on his door claiming "room service". He was puzzled since he had not ordered anything. When he opened the door, the waiter was holding a tray on which there was a peanut butter and jam sandwich with a glass of milk. The waiter simply said, "Compliments of the hotel management. Enjoy your stay."

Guess what he talked about for months afterwards? Guess what his hotel of choice is now? And it happened because one person noticed the customer, listened to him and responded. That's all it took. Seems simple, doesn't it?

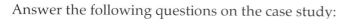

Answer the following questions on the case study:

a) All customers have basically the same needs when it comes to the type of service that they expect from you. Name four of the guest's needs that were fulfilled. (4)
b) Name three ways in which the hotel as well as the staff will benefit from the front desk attendant's and waiter's actions. (3)

Question 5

Discuss three ways in which an establishment could improve their customer service. (9)

Assessment Activity 3.2

Simulation

For this assessment activity you are to simulate providing silver service to a customer. Your lecture will observe you and assess how well you perform silver service using a checklist during the simulation. Before you do this assessment, practise all the steps as explained in your textbook

Topic Summary

This topic focused on providing silver service.

Unit 1 was a brief introduction to silver service and Unit 2 started the process with how to meet and deal with customers in a polite and friendly manner. Unit 3 looked specifically at taking orders and advising customers while Unit 4 examined the service items specific to silver service.

Unit 5 explained in detail how to serve food according to organisational procedures while Unit 6 looked at the skills of portioning, serving and arranging food. Unit 7 explained how to end a meal by clearing tables appropriately.

Unit 8 explained how to check and store food service items and equipment. Unit 9 looked at ways to improve service to customers and the topic ended with Unit 10 which described decisions made and reasons for actions taken.

The following are important things to remember:
• Before attempting to silver service you must be prepared. All your service items and equipment must be clean, undamaged and positioned ready for service.
• Providing silver service in a restaurant requires staff to be very organised and efficient. You must have a work plan, know all the procedures and the organisational requirements and be comfortable carrying them out.
• Gueridon service is the most advanced form of food service and demands dexterity and skill from the waiter as the preparation of the dishes has to be completed at the table on a trolley or side table.
• In the case of gueridon and silver service, you must be careful not to spill or drop any of the food that you are serving on the customers.

- It is also important that you disturb the customers as little as possible during silver service. You are working very close to them and you must not lean on or over them or hover near them for too long.
- The longer you take to perform silver serving the greater the chance is that you will serve cold food. To avoid this you must work quickly and efficiently at all times.
- If you work in a polite, efficient and organised way and follow organisational requirements you can be sure to keep your customers satisfied. Satisfied customers mean good business as they will most likely visit your establishment again and give you good advertising by telling others how they enjoyed your restaurant.
- After you have completed your service you need to clear way all the service equipment. This equipment must be returned to the kitchen or wash up area. You should not leave any dirty or used dishes in the restaurant and in view of customers. Your sideboard or waiter's station should always be clear of all used equipment. This will make the whole restaurant look neat and tidy. Remember that the overall appearance of the establishment is very important.

Assess yourself

Assess your understanding of the information covered in this Module by completing the following table:

	Yes	Partly	No
I have the skills to meet and deal with customers in a polite and friendly manner.			
I am able to take accurate orders and advise customers on appropriate menu choices.			
I can locate and use appropriate service items and equipment and I understand why it is important to keep sufficient equipment stocks available.			
I am able to serve food according to organisational procedures.			
I can portion, serve and attractively arrange food using the appropriate service equipment.			
I know how to clear tables and can demonstrate the appropriate timing and method of clearing of tables.			
I have the skills to check and store food service items and equipment according to organisational procedures.			
I am able to recommend ways of improving service to customers.			
I can describe decisions made and give reasons for actions taken in response to unexpected situations.			
I am able to develop ways and methods to train new staff in the delivery of silver service.			

If you answered no or partly, then you need to revise that section again, or ask your lecturer for help.

Topic 4:
Maintain a drinks service

Module 4

Maintain the drinks service and communicate with staff

Maintain the drinks service and communicate with staff to ensure high service standards and customer service

The information in this topic is aimed at waiters who are in the position of supervisor or head waiter.

In this module you will…

- implement the procedures for the maintenance of a drinks service
- describe the legal requirements for the operation of a licensed premise
- explain the consequences of selling alcohol to under-aged or intoxicated persons
- understand why staff needs product knowledge and should comply with service standards
- devise ways to motivate staff in increasing sales
- discuss ways to deal with violent or disruptive customers and identify the guidance that should be provided to staff in this area
- understand why equipment should be maintained safely and hygienically
- implement the fault and maintenance reporting procedures and complete all the necessary paperwork
- complete all set-up procedures required prior to service delivery including cleaning; clearing and restocking the drinks service area and preparing all equipment ready for service
- communicate with customers in a polite and friendly way
- learn to be able to handle unexpected operational situations.

Unit 1:

Implement the procedures for the maintenance of a drinks service

Monitor service standards

- Ensure that guest do not wait longer than necessary for service.
- Check that the service staff are presenting and serving drinks in the correct manner.
- Monitor feedback from customers (both positive and negative).
- Observe the manner in which staff speak and interact with customers.
- Check personal hygiene and appearance of staff.

Maintaining cleaning and clearing

- Supervise the clearing and cleaning of the drink service area in a logical and orderly fashion. It is critical to do this in order for the drinks service to begin on time.
- Allocate staff to the cleaning areas.
- Communicate cleaning requirements in terms of the expected standard, cleaning agents to be used and the time frame in which the cleaning must be completed.

Inspecting the drink service area

Inspecting the drink preparation area is essential and must always be done from the guest's point of view.

Begin your inspection at the entrance to the drinks service area by standing at the entrance and then move around the drink service area paying attention to:
- lighting
- temperature
- volume of music
- appropriateness of the music
- any odours.

Check the following:
- the appearance of the bar counter and the bar chairs
- the appearance of the displays, flower arrangements and plants
- the arrangement of tables and chairs
- any promotional material that is out
- the freshness and attractiveness of snacks.

Ensure that any special guest areas are clearly demarcated:
- Non-smoking areas must have appropriate signs
- Private party areas must have an appropriate notice
- Eating areas should be clearly separated from the rest of the drink service area.

If you are checking the preparedness of the area for a function, ensure that all the requirements of the client have been met by referring to the function sheet. (Revise Level 2, Topic 4: Prepare, service and clean function rooms.)

Maintain drinks service procedures

Throughout the service period, observe proceedings in the drinks service area to ensure the following:
- all areas are kept tidy and clean
- dirty glasses and ashtrays are removed
- empty bottles and cans are discarded
- snacks are cleared and replenished
- service stations and counters are kept clean and tidy
- ice is replenished regularly
- bar counters are cleaned and cleared of dirty glasses
- fridges are restocked and optics are functioning to ensure the continuous flow of service
- guest areas are checked to ensure that dirty glasses, empty bottles and cans are removed

Potential problems

The following are potential problems that could be encountered and how best to address them.

Guests have not yet been served

- Determine the length of time that they have been waiting and serve these guests on a first come first serve basis.

Guests have ordered but have not received their drinks

- Determine how long they have been waiting.
- Investigate what the delay is and assist with the service.

Guests are ready to order again

- Bring to the attention of the service staff those guests who require service.

Guests do not appear to be enjoying themselves

- Investigate if there is a problem and if there is, resolve it to the guest's satisfaction.
- Should there be delays in service because of business pressure, apologise to guests as necessary.
- Ensure that you speak to individual groups of guests.

In the workplace

A supervisor or head waiter must have strong employee relations with the rest of the staff.
A supervisor or head waiter should be able to establish standards for hygiene, conduct, dress code, resignations, evaluations and harassment and offer ideas on proper ways to address each issue with employees.
A supervisor or head waiter should run a restaurant as if it were her or his own. She or he should be just as passionate about the restaurant as the manager and/or owner is.

Maintaining staff performance

The section or restaurant manager must visit tables two to three times during the meal, without becoming a nuisance.
- Inquire if guests are satisfied with the meal and the service.
- Keep an observant eye on the staff to detect if a staff member is being awkward with the guest.
- Observe if orders and requests are being handled promptly.

When monitoring, the manager needs to look at the table and at what stage of service it is at. Give consideration to the expression on the guests' faces and their body language to determine whether the staff member's performance is up to standard.

In the workplace

Always remember that the quality of the communication between staff member and guest can be determined by observing the expression on the face of the guest along with his or her body language.

Unit 2:

Legal requirements

This unit will describe the legal requirements for the operation of licensed premises.

Know the kind of liquor license

When you are starting work at a new establishment, it is of vital importance to ask what type of liquor license the establishment has. Ask how it will affect you in your work and what responsibilities you will have. Knowing how to deal with all types of situations in regard to the serving of wine and other alcohol is very important. It may affect your position and may possibly affect the establishment, too.

Legislation and licensing

The Liquor Act 59 of 2003 came into effect on 13 August 2004. Before proclamation, provincial Liquor Authorities were responsible for the regulation of all the categories of the Liquor Industry.

The Act provides for the manufacturing and distribution of liquor to be regulated at national level while micro manufacturing and retailing continue to be regulated at provincial level.

An important aspect of the new Act is social responsibility. Those wishing to register must set out their commitment to black economic empowerment, and their proposed contribution to combating alcohol abuse, as well as how they will promote job creation, diversity of ownership, exports, competition, new entrants to the industry and efficiency of operation. Failing to meet these commitments can result in a review of, or placing new conditions on, registration.

Liquor license registration

The National Liquor Act (NLA) will set up and maintain a national register of licenses, which will be published on the dti website.

The register will provide information about all liquor registrations, whether issued nationally or provincially, including:
- Name of registered person (including any alternative trade name) and date registration was granted
- Principal place of business and where registered activities may take place

Did you know?

The dti is The Department of Trade and Industry.

The address of its Consumer and Corporate Regulation Division is

Private Bag X 84 • Pretoria • 0001.

Tel: 0861 843 384 • Fax: +27 (0) 12 394 0555

E-mail: nationalliquorauthority@ thedti.gov.za

- Activities permitted and any conditions attached
- Dates and details of any complaints laid, notices of non-compliance, compliance certificates, suspensions, and prosecutions and convictions in terms of the Act or any law mentioned in section 19
- Dates and details of any transfer of registration, notice given, reports filed or cancellations.

As well as being published on the website, this register can also be viewed and copies made from it on request, during normal business hours and upon payment of a prescribed fee.

Likewise, copies of registration certificates issued may also be inspected or copied upon payment of the prescribed fee.

Complaints may be laid against people selling alcohol in cases of non-compliance to the Liquor Act. Members of the public may approach the Provincial Liquor Authority with representations on the granting, inspecting, withdrawal or suspension of registrations.

Inspectors

The Minister may designate persons as inspectors to exercise powers in terms of this Act, and will issue a certificate stating that such persons are inspectors. Inspectors may investigate complaints submitted to them in the prescribed manner and form. All inspectors must be designated peace officers in terms of the provision of Section 334 of the Criminal Procedure Act.

Inspectors will have the powers to:
- enter any premises
- ascertain compliance with the basic conditions stipulated in the Act
- instigate a procedure which could lead to the suspension or withdrawal of the registration of the business
- submit reports to the Provincial Liquor Authority.

Who is disqualified from getting a license?

- Minors (Persons under the age of 18years)
- Unrehabilitated insolvents
- Persons committed in terms of the Mental Health Act, 1973
- Persons who have contravened this Act or provincial liquor laws to the extent provided for in the Act.

Offences

It is an offence to do the following:
- Manufacture or distribute liquor if not permitted to do so in terms of the Act
- Manufacture or distribute methylated spirits if not permitted to do so in terms of the Act
- Manufacture, sell or supply any impotable substance or add an impotable substance to liquor
- Employ a person who is not yet 16 years old, unless such employment meets the provisions of the Skills Development Act

- Supply liquor or methylated spirits to an employee in lieu of payment (or deduct from employees' wages or remuneration any amount relating to the cost of liquor or methylated spirits supplied to or purchased by them or other persons on their behalf)
- Advertise liquor in a false or misleading way
- Advertise liquor in a way that intends to target or attract minors (under the age of 18)
- Fail to display a notice on the premises – or on a bottle label, in the case of manufacturers – that no liquor may be sold to any person under the age of 18 years or to intoxicated persons and that the consumption of alcohol by a pregnant or breast feeding woman is dangerous to her baby
- Supply and sell liquor to a minor
- Produce, supply or import liquor if a person is a minor
- Make a false claim about age to buy or obtain liquor, if a person is a minor (likewise, other persons may not make false claims about the minor's age in order to induce someone to sell or supply liquor to the minor).
- Sell liquor to intoxicated persons
- Be drunk, violent or disorderly in premises which have been licensed or in public places
- Consume liquor on a road, street, lane or thoroughfare
- Introduce or sell liquor on sports grounds; or sell liquor from a vehicle.

Legal requirements

Legal requirements as set out by the licensing board are as follows:
- Trade within the determined legal hours.
- Obtain a permit for extended hours of trading.
- Comply with age restriction laws (guests under the age of 18 may not be served).
- Maintain health and hygiene standards.
- Adhere to the standard intoxication limits; i.e. do not serve guests who are already intoxicated any further. If you suspect a person to be drunk, you must not serve them wine or any other alcohol. If there is a person at the door of your establishment who is checking for identification, then they will also be monitoring the entry of people into the establishment and will not allow intoxicated persons onto the premises.

Penalties

Appropriately harsh fines and imprisonment for the above offences will be imposed.

Possible avenues to appropriate the fines imposed, will be investigated by the Department of Trade and Industry.

Should it be possible the funds thus generated will be utilised for the rehabilitation of alcoholics and awareness campaigns relating to alcohol abuse.

Service times

These are established once the establishment acquires a license.

The days and hours that you are allowed to serve alcohol are outlined in the license.

There are restrictions that apply to public holidays, Sundays, and days like Christmas Day and Good Friday.

You must never serve wine or alcohol to anyone outside these times.

Your supervisor will advise you of the organisational requirements regarding times.

Communication to staff

Ensure that staff is kept aware of regulations obtained from legislation, and that their knowledge is updated accordingly:
- Legal hours of operation
- Permits that may be required for extended hours, and the possible consequences of trading illegally
- Age restrictions for sitting at the bar or in a certain area
- Level of intoxication beyond which guests may not be served any more drinks
- Consequences of short-totting or diluting spirits and liqueurs
- No guests under the age of 18 to be served any alcoholic beverage
- Health and hygiene requirements and the possible consequences of failing Health Department Inspection
- Occupational safety legislation as it applies to drink service staff.

Communicating licensing laws to customers

Ensure that guests are given appropriate information, should queries arise. They may particularly need to know about legislated age restrictions, hours of operation and alcohol limits.

When confronted with guests who are under the legal age of consumption, bring the legislative requirement to the guest's attention.

Should the guest insist that he/she is over the age, then politely ask to see documentation.

If the guest insists on being served drinks after closing time, address him or her in a courteous manner bringing his or her attention to the establishment's closing time.

Make the guest aware in a polite manner that there are certain laws which the establishment needs to abide by and that it cannot compromise.

Unit 3:

Selling alcohol to under-aged or intoxicated persons

This unit will explain the consequences of selling alcohol to under-aged or intoxicated persons.

Non compliance with the law

Non compliance could result in:
* The liquor license being revoked
* The company being fined
* The company being shut down
* Lawsuits.

Age limit

You must know what this limit is before you serve anyone alcohol. The age limit is 18 years of age in South Africa.

If you are unsure of a person's age, you must ask for identification. Your organisational requirements will tell you what forms of identification are acceptable.

Some establishments will have someone at the door checking ID (identification).

You should also check at the bar in case someone got in without being checked.

Checking ID

When you are checking ID, you must be aware of the following:
* Pay close attention to the customers physical features, such as the shape of the nose, presence of freckles and so on and check that the picture matches the person.
* Check the photo for bumps where a photo may have been inserted.
* Check the date of birth carefully to make sure that it has not been changed using liquid paper, scratching or letra-setting.
* Check carefully that the person on the ID is the one standing in front of you.
* You must also be aware of when and under what circumstances underage persons are permitted to be on your premises, for example, when they are having a meal or are accompanied by a parent, spouse of guardian.
* You must also be aware when underage people are permitted to consume alcohol on your premises, for example, with a parent or guardian and with a meal.

Did you know?

New liquor regulation entails two key aspects:
* a change in legislation which will facilitate easy entry into the liquor trade
* harsh penalties for those who contravene the legislation.

Think about it

New liquor laws recognise that liquor is a potentially harmful substance, and recognise that its abuse is widespread in our society; the government seeks to introduce laws which will regulate the sale and distribution of alcohol in the public interest.

The new liquor policy is therefore centrally concerned with making socio-economic interventions, particularly with regard to public health, welfare, transport, religion, gender and youth.

There is a significant increase in the consumption of alcohol amongst youth. This causes related problems into adulthood.

Intoxicated persons

If you suspect that a person is drunk, do not serve them wine or any other alcohol.

Staff at the door of the establishment should be checking for identification, and should also be monitoring the entry of people into the establishment.

Any intoxicated persons should not be allowed access to the premises.

Intoxicated persons can be recognised by:
- slurred speech
- staggering, swaying, falling, tripping, stumbling
- spilling drinks
- dropping money
- bumping into things
- becoming annoying
- loud speech, singing, swearing
- getting emotional
- getting overly friendly
- getting abusive
- bleary eyes
- smell of alcohol on the person
- falling asleep.

Unit 4:

Product knowledge and service standards

This unit will help you to understand why staff needs product knowledge and should comply with service standards.

The range of products sold in a bar include: soft drinks, draught, bottled, canned beers, wines, spirits, snacks, liqueurs, cocktails, snacks, sundries, new products and promotional products.

Staff should be given "product training" courses – they should be tested on the ins and outs of a specific product. Contests can be held to see who knows about the product intently and expertly.

Words & terms

Sundries: Snacks sold at the bar, such as popcorn or nuts.

Product knowledge

It is important to ensure that staff is trained in product knowledge so that they are sufficiently equipped to provide the necessary service required for customer satisfaction.

Service staff needs to be able to provide guests with relevant information about the products that are being served such as:
- the name and price of the product
- the taste of the product
- the alcohol content
- how the product may compliment what the guest will be eating.

Waiters should have a thorough knowledge of all items on the drink list.
- Know how drinks are made and how they taste. It is also important to know which country/area the drinks come from.
- Know the trends in consumption and what is in fashion.
- Know how to serve all drinks correctly.

Recommend drinks

If a customer ask for a recommendation, it is important to remember that each customer has different requirements and different tastes. You must identify these tastes by asking the customer questions, since what one person likes, another may not.

When you are telling customers about what drinks are available, be careful not to use high pressure selling techniques. These may not be welcome. Try to use suggestive selling techniques.

When you are asked for an opinion or recommendation about a drink, do not be vague. The customer obviously thinks you know more about the drinks on the list than they do, so have a few good cocktails, unusual beers or other drinks up your sleeve to recommend to customers. Never recommend the most expensive drink first off, since

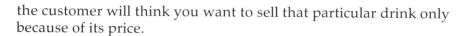

the customer will think you want to sell that particular drink only because of its price.

Answering questions

Always answer all questions promptly.

- Customers may ask you about the strength of certain drinks. This is always printed on the bottle, so if you do not know the exact strength, at least know where to find the information.
- If it states on the bottle that the drink contains, for example, 16% alcohol, it means that in every 100ml of the drink, 16ml will be pure alcohol.
- Customers may also want to know the amount of alcohol that goes into each drink. This is vital information that you must know.

Promoting drinks

Use every opportunity possible to promote any types of drinks.

The first opportunity to promote drinks is when customers arrive. This gives you the chance to tell them about the house specials, possibly the cocktail of the month.

Presenting the customers with the drink list is also a form of promotion.

When customers have finished a drink, recommend another.

If customers have not been drinking alcohol at all, then you should suggest a non-alcoholic cocktail or fruit juice, which may be freshly squeezed.

If customers appear to have had enough alcohol to drink, do not suggest more alcohol. You might suggest coffee, or some food or a non- alcoholic drink.

If you know that a customer has to drive, this gives you the opportunity to promote low alcohol drinks.

If the occasion appears to be a special one, you may wish to promote champagne to celebrate the occasion.

Promoting drinks to customers will increase the amount they are spending, so will increase the revenue for the business, and also, if customers tip a certain percentage, you may get a higher tip.

If promotional material, such as tent cards, drinks lists and posters, is used, it must be accurate and up to date.

Sometimes drinks are promoted by way of specials such as "two for the price of one", or prizes that can be won depending on how many drinks customers buy.

In the workplace

The key to effective staff training is to identify the principal duties of the staff members themselves, and to ensure that they are aware of their individual roles and responsibilities. Beyond that, a regular scheduled session should be put in place that not only addresses current responsibilities, but also acknowledges that all staff should be interested in developing their own skills and understanding the importance of their role in the business.

Staff training

It is essential that service staff receive regular training in service and selling skills. Follow the procedures below:
- Inform staff of the expected level of service to guests.
- Ensure that regular short training sessions are held.
- Inform staff what the organisational goals are.
- Assist staff in handling difficult situations and ensure that he/she learns from you.

Reasons for staff knowledge

Informative and pleasant staff will ensure repeat business.

If a customer talks to one of the staff members, he/she should not only talk to someone who sells the products but who also uses and enjoy the product. Unfortunately some staff members are not motivated; no matter how good the training programmes and sales management, if you aren't selecting salespeople with the right internal motives you're not taking advantage of the marketing money you've spent getting people in your bar. The resultant shoddy customer service will damage your reputation. The process for delivering that required level of motivation are called advanced sales coaching.

Reasons for staff to comply with service standards

To meet or exceed customer's expectations requirements, because:
- a customer is the most important person in our business
- a customer is not dependent on us … we are dependent on him
- a customer is not an interruption of our work … he is the purpose of it
- we are not doing a favour by serving him … he is doing us a favour by giving us an opportunity to do so
- a customer is a person who brings us his wants. It is our job to handle them profitably to him and ourselves.

Topic 4, Module 4

Unit 5:

Devise ways to motivate staff in increasing sales

Some might sum up the "art of listening" in two simple words: Be Quiet! While this is definitely a major part of listening, it is only part of the art when you are serving guests in a restaurant.
Servers must listen not only to what guests are saying, they must also listen to what guests are not saying. Servers have to know what questions to ask in order to find out how to best serve their guests.

Motivating staff

Motivating staff on a regular basis is absolutely necessary for the successful provision of a drinks service and customer satisfaction. Motivating staff to excel in their work will be a benefit to the company since this will ensure customer satisfaction, which will, in turn, ensure repeat business.

Increased sales of food and beverage have a positive impact on turnover and this increases profitability, which is the purpose of any business. For this reason it is important that the manager encourage and reward waiters to promote sales through the skill of up-sell, on-sell, specials and promotions.

Ways to motivate staff in increasing sales

- Keep staff informed of what the service objectives are. Motivate staff to meet organisational goals by having regular staff meetings
- Motivate staff to transform organisational goals to personal goals through delegation and accountability.
- Surveys done on successful people have shown that what they have in common is a set of written goals. Let staff members write their and the company's goals down and remind them of these often. They should also list their long-term goals and goals for the next 6 months.
- Recognise and reward individual and team success (with, for example, an incentive bonus or a day off). Do this consistently and publicly.
- Monitor individual and team/departmental performance and provide feedback to individuals and teams/departments.
- Implement the agreed recognition and reward processes consistently and publicly. This will motivate staff to improve performance.
- Serious performance problems must be handled away from the drink service area.
- Determine if there any obstacles and remove the obstacles where possible.
- Remind staff members of performance standards and counsel on areas where standards are not being met.

Staff training

Ensure that service staff members receive regular training in service skills.

Initial training may be off the job (although it does not have to be).
- Staff should attend regular, short training sessions in which you and the service staff participate and discuss relevant work situations.
- Make sure that staff is kept informed and that they have the information they need to provide the expected level of service to guests.
- When you provide support to a staff member in handling a situation that he or she feels unable to handle, have that staff member with you so that he or she can learn from you.

Staff morale is a very noticeable yardstick of an organisation's efficiency. Staff must be motivated and co-operative in order to be efficient. Each staff member relies on the co-operation and support of others to fulfill their role efficiently.

Every team member is an individual. They will all be different from each other in a number of ways. For example, some may be argumentative or dominant, and others may be quiet. How you handle your interactions with each member of your team will determine your success as a team leader.

Ensure repeat business

Motivate staff to ensure repeat business. Informative and pleasant staff will ensure repeat business.
- Always greet the client in a friendly and courteous manner.
- Make sure that the service provided is fast, efficient and accurate.
- Ensure that the prices are competitive.
- Resolve problems to the customer's satisfaction.

Improve internal communication

Open channels for feedback should be established.
- Management should encourage the use of suggestion boxes and letters and the establishment of social and sporting clubs so that the social distances can be bridged.
- Policy and procedure for communication should be laid down.
- Top management should communicate directly to all staff using the public address system or public notice board.

Do this activity in small groups.
1. Have a group discussion on the following question.
   What are the necessary guidelines as far as communicating with your staff is concerned when you are a supervisor or manager?
2. Take notes during your discussion.
Your lecturer will assess your discussions.

You will assess each other's ability to participate in a group discussion using the following assessment grid:

Student Name:				
Activity:				
Criteria	Outstanding 80-100%	Highly competent 70-79%	Competent 50-69%	Not yet competent 40-49%	Not achieved 0-39%
Confidence in speaking	Student spoke very confidently and with great authority.	Student spoke with some confidence some of the time.	Student occasionally spoke with confidence.	Student did not speak with confidence.	Student did not contribute to the discussion at all.
Expression of opinions	Student expressed opinions and has a strong factual base for opinion.	Student expressed strong and substantiated opinions.	Student expressed an opinion.	Student expressed very little opinion and had no factual base.	Student did not express any opinion.
Ordering of points made	Student presented well thought-out points made into a logical sequence.	Student made logically ordered points.	Student did organise points to be made but the logic was sometimes lacking.	Student made points in no logical order at all.	Student did not make any points at all.
Attention of the group	Student spoke in a way so as to keep the attention of the rest of the group.	Student usually managed to keep the interest of the group.	Student sometimes managed to keep the interest of the group.	Student seldom kept the interest of the group.	Student either did not speak at all or did not hold the interest of the group at all.
Group participation	Student always encouraged other students to participate in the discussion.	Student usually encouraged other students to participate in the discussion.	Student occasionally encouraged other students to participate in the discussion.	Student seldom encouraged other students to participate in the discussion.	Student never encouraged other students to participate in the discussion.
Listening skills	Student listened attentively and with interest when other students spoke.	Student listened with some interest when other students spoke.	Student listened with little interest when other students spoke.	Student fluctuated between listening to other students speak, and not listening at all.	Student did not listen to others students at all.

Keep the grid used to assess you.

Staff meetings

Meet with your subordinates and colleagues on a daily basis. Use these daily meeting to discuss any concerns that the staff may have regarding their work.
• Discuss any potential problem areas, conflicts, obstacles and so on.

- Reinforce the idea that customer service is their primary responsibility and objective and that this objective is most successfully achieved when they are all working toward this as a team.
- Disclose any new developments.
- Ask questions and encourage questions from staff to ensure that they understand their responsibilities.

Improve skills and knowledge

There are many factors which contribute to an individual's inability to fulfill certain areas of responsibility. The individual may be lacking training or the areas in which he or she is performing poorly may not be on the training agenda of the hospitality establishment in question. In all cases the staff member needs positive support in order to overcome difficulties and obstacles.

Staff development and training

The improvement of skills and knowledge through staff development and training is vitally important. This training can take different forms such as:
- mentoring
- attendance at courses and seminars
- re-training at a technikon or at a university.

Advice should be given by the staff member's mentor or manager.

Personal skills training should be provided by a counselor. Team building activities conducted by team members should be organised to encourage integration.

Unit 6:

Violent or disruptive customers

This unit will discuss ways to deal with violent or disruptive customers and identify the guidance that should be provided to staff in this area.

Violent and disruptive guests

In the event of guests becoming violent and disruptive it is recommended that staff do not get involved but that they call the manager immediately. They must continue with serving other guests. Staff getting involved could lead to the other guests feeling uncomfortable.

Offensive behaviour

Offensive behaviour includes sexual harassment, racist remarks and obscene behaviour. Refer to the table below for further details.

Sexual harassment	This action includes unwelcome touching, sexually suggestive remarks and attempts to persuade someone to provide sexual favours by threatening their jobs or their personal safety.
Racist remarks	These would include derogatory remarks directed towards staff members as well as towards guests who are of a different colour and/or creed. This is totally unacceptable behaviour.
Obscene behaviour	This would include loud, obscene language, which offends other guests. Exposing parts of the body, particularly the private parts, and making offensive and suggestive gestures to other guests or staff would also be considered obscene.

In the event of offensive customers being encountered the following procedures must be followed:
- Call your manager and explain the situation. He or she will choose to do one or more of the following:
- politely and firmly ask the offenders to stop the offensive behaviour, explaining that it is unacceptable to the company and to other guests
- ask the offenders to leave
- call security to remove the offenders from the premises
- blacklist the offenders
- call the police and lay a criminal charge.

Physical threat or damage to premises and property

Guests who are threatening to damage premises or property must be handled with caution since they could harm staff and other guests. Be aware of guests who are verbally threatening to damage premises or property by physical violence, fire or water.

Threatening to blow up the premises with a bomb is a criminal offence and you should take immediate action. These threats cause guests and staff to feel unsafe, which is damaging to the business.

- Physical damage to property occurs when an individual or a group of individuals begins causing damage to the premises, or to hotel or guests' property.
- Call Security immediately.
- Remove other guests and staff from the problem area to a safe area.
- Ensure that you have reliable witnesses. Keep a senior staff member with you but make sure that neither of you will be endangered.
- Do not expect guests to be witnesses since they may not be in the country should the case goes to court.
- Call the police immediately in the case of a bomb threat. Try to ascertain all the information that may be required by the police, such as:
- the names of people involved (if you know them)
- what the individuals are wearing and what each of them looks like
- any other information you may have.

Inability to pay

Should guests be unable to pay, handle the situation with sensitivity, since the guest is likely to be embarrassed.
- Contact the manager and explain the situation.
- Request permission to handle the bill as an account.
- Write down the client's personal details after you have received approval to handle the bill as an account. Include:
  - full name and address
  - identity number
  - residential address
  - home, work and cellular phone number.
- Enquire when the guest intends to pay.
- Advise the guest that an account will be opened.
- Obtain the managers signature on the bill or sign it yourself if you have the authority.
- Process the bill as a signed docket.

Refusal to pay

- Investigate why the guest refuses to pay.
- Determine after investigating the complaint if the guest is still liable for the bill.
- Inform the guest of your decision.

If the client is liable for the bill, and still refuses to pay,
- call the head security immediately
- inform security about the problem
- notify all security staff at the exits of the establishment that the guest must not be allowed to leave the premises.
Should the guest still refuse to pay, call the police.

Nuisance to the general public

This usually involves the rowdy behaviour that occurs outside the hotel in the street or car park after guests have left, such as shouting, hooting, revving of engines and racing vehicles.

Rowdy behaviour is disturbing to hotel guests, as well as to residents in the local area and this must be curbed immediately. The goodwill of local residents is extremely important to the hotel, so it is essential that you do not allow such behaviour to persist.

Call hotel security to handle the situation. If they are unable to resolve the situation, they may decide to call the police.

Recording customer behaviour

Write down the following:
- the date, time and location of the incident
- what happened
- the names and addresses, if you have this information, of the people involved
- the names and telephone numbers of witnesses who are willing to come forward if necessary
- what was done to resolve the situation
- recommended follow-up such as blacklisting the guest(s).

It may also be necessary to complete an Incident Report. If so, Security will inform you. Assist Security to complete the Incident Report by providing any information you have.

Make sure that all such incidents are brought to the attention of your Manager.

It is also important to discuss such incidents with your staff, especially if they were involved as victims of the incidents. They will need reassurance, support and advice about what to do in future, so make time to spend with them.

Learning Activity 4.2

Complete this activity in pairs.
1. Practise ways to deal with disruptive customers by role playing the following scenarios in groups:
   - a manager deals with violent and disruptive guests
   - a junior staff member deals with violent and disruptive guests
   - a manager deals with offensive behavior from two or three guests
   - a junior staff member deals with offensive behavior from two or three guests
   - a manager deals with threats of physical damage to premises and property
   - a junior staff member deals with a guest's inability to pay
   - a manager deals with a guest's refusal to pay
   - a junior staff member deals with guests who are being a nuisance to the general public
   - a manager deals with guests who are being a nuisance to the general public

Your lecturer will assess your role plays.

This rubric will be used to assess you in your role play. It is the same rubric as was used in Activity 1.4

Student Name:					
Activity:					
Criteria	Outstanding 80-100%	Highly competent 70-79%	Competent 50-69%	Not yet competent 40-49%	Not achieved 0-39%
Role	Student assumed both the role of being a waiter and the role of a customer accurately and appropriately.	Student was able to assume both roles required well.	Student was able to assume both roles.	Student was not able to assume both roles, but managed one of them.	Student was not able to assume either role on a believable way.
Responses	Student responded to their partner in a completely relevant way to both of the roles that they played.	Student responded to their partner in a partly relevant way to both of the roles that they played.	Student responded to their partner in a partly relevant way to one of the roles that they played.	Student responded to their partner with little or no relevance.	Student did not response to their partner.
Listening skills	Student showed active listening skills by reacting appropriately and timeously to what their partner said or did.	Student showed active listening skills by reacting to what their partner said or did.	Student listened to their partner some of the time and usually reacted to what they said.	Student listened to their partner some of the time and occasionally reacted to what they said.	Student did not seem to listen to their partner at all.
Use of language	Student used language extremely effectively to portray a point of view.	Student used language effectively strategies to portray a point of view.	Student usually used language effectively to portray a point of view.	Student occasionally used language effectively to portray a point of view.	Student did not use language skills at all.
Speech	Student spoke clearly, accurately and in character.	Student generally spoke clearly and accurately.	Student occasionally spoke clearly or accurately.	Student never spoke clearly or accurately.	Student did not speak.
Body language	Student used body language (eye contact, posture, gestures) appropriately and effectively to enhance and support speech.	Student used most aspects of body language to enhance and support speech.	Student used some aspects of body language to enhance and support speech.	Student used a little body language.	Student used no body language at all.

Compare this completed rubric with the one from Activity 1.4. Notice the areas in which you have improved as well as the areas which still need attention.

Unit 7:

Maintenance of equipment

This unit will make sure you understand why equipment should be maintained safely and hygienically.

Why equipment should be maintained safely and hygienically

There are different reasons for maintaining equipment safely and hygienically.

Maintaining equipment safely

As far as safety is concerned, these reasons include the necessary compliance with the law as well as making sure that precautionary prevention measures prevent illness of, and injury to, guests. In turn, this will ensure cost effectiveness.

The equipment provided is there to enable you to perform your work effectively and efficiently. When it is faulty, doing your work becomes potentially dangerous to you and to guests, more difficult, more time consuming and therefore more costly.

Compliance with the law

It is required by law to maintain a work environment that meets the requirements of the safety standards stipulated in the Occupation Health and Safety Act. Organisational standards must also be met. This means that all equipment and work areas are to be closely monitored and checked for safety, and also for potentially hazardous situations.

Precautionary prevention measures

The company is under a moral obligation to guests to do the very best to ensure their safety on the premises and to see to it that every precaution and preventative measure is taken to eliminate any risk of injury to them or damage to their property.

Preventing injuries to guests

Failure to take preventative measures can result in injury to guests and staff which have a huge impact on the costs of:
* repairs to damaged equipment and property
* down time because of broken equipment
* guest dissatisfaction
* guests getting sick because of unhygienic conditions
* possible legal action from injured and /or ill guests.

Preventive maintenance (PM) is defined as a program in which wear, tear, and change are anticipated and continual corrective actions are taken to ensure peak efficiency and minimise deterioration. PM involves a planned and controlled program of systematic inspection, adjustment, lubrication, and replacement of components, as well as performance testing and analysis. The result of a successful PM program extends the life of the facilities and equipment, and minimises unscheduled downtime that causes major problems. It ensures that equipment is operating properly, and will improve the image of an establishment, since unscheduled breakdowns are held to a minimum.
Source: Adapted from: http://www.plantops.umich.edu/utilities/operations-engineering/pm.html

Cost effectiveness

Prevention and Maintenance procedures are also cost effective measures. The implementation of preventative maintenance is less costly than having to repair and replace equipment promptly in the event of an accident or disaster.

All guests needs to feel safe when they are in a hospitality establishment. Create a sense of safety by taking proper care of the guests' environment.

Maintaining standards of hygiene

The reasons for maintaining equipment hygienically include complying with the law and ensuring the health and well-being of guests as well as staff. In addition, the cleanliness of the hospitality establishment will attract guests and ensure repeat business.

Compliance with the law

It is required by law to maintain a work environment that meets the requirements of the standards of hygiene and cleanliness as stipulated in the Occupation Health and Safety Act. Organisational standards must also be met. This means that all equipment and work areas are to be closely monitored and checked for correct hygiene practices and also for potentially hazardous situations.

Ensuring the health and well-being of guests

Meeting the standards of hygiene and cleanliness will ensure the health and well-being of your guests.
• Clear the bar counters of dirty glasses.
• Ensure that used ashtrays are correctly stacked in racks and removed as soon as possible: don't wait until they are full and overflowing.
• Remove empty bottles and cans from the counters and discard them appropriately.

- Maintain service stations and counters in a state of tidy cleanliness.
- Ensure that refrigerators and optics are cleaned regularly to maintain hygiene.

Check guest areas to ensure that:
- dirty glasses and empty bottles and cans are removed promptly
- arrange all chairs and tables neatly and keep all areas clean and tidy.

Maintain equipment hygienically

The objective of identifying and reporting any drop in the hygienic standards of any equipment is to ensure that the equipment is cleaned in time to avoid contamination of any food or service, and to avoid operational setbacks.

In the workplace

Almost 200,000 people get sick every year from Staphylococcus aureus food poisoning.
Nearly half the population carries this bacterium. It lives in the nose and throat of healthy people.
Preventative measures include:
- Not picking your nose anywhere near any food or drinks or food and drink service and/or preparation areas.
- Not coughing over food or drinks.
- Good hand washing practices and limiting bare hand contact with glasses and other containers served to guests.
- Cleaning and sanitising equipment and utensils after each use or after four hours of continuous use.

Unit 8:

Fault and maintenance reporting procedures

This unit explains how to implement the fault and maintenance reporting procedures and complete all the necessary paperwork.

Reporting faults and problems

Problems with any equipment must be reported immediately to either the Maintenance Manager or the Duty Manager for repairs. If equipment continues to go unattended to, despite your having reported it, inform the Head of Department.

Maintenance procedures

Once staff members have completed their maintenance inspection, compile a maintenance request and give this to the Maintenance Department. If the maintenance team is unable to sort the problem out, contact the suppliers immediately.

If an outside contractor or service agent is used, make arrangements for the equipment to be serviced and make sure that the paperwork is completed properly according to organisational requirements. Record your report in the Hand-over Book and make this available to your manager.

Inspect repaired equipment

- When equipment has been repaired and returned, inspect it to ensure that the faults reported have been rectified.
- Check that the equipment is working properly and that it is as clean and hygienic as is appropriate for that particular piece of equipment
- If you are not satisfied that the equipment has been properly repaired, return it to the Maintenance Department or contractor. Do not accept it until you are satisfied with the repairs.
- If equipment is returned to the Maintenance Department or contractor, make a note of this in the Hand-over Book and inform the manager.

Recording equipment faults

Once you have completed your maintenance inspection, compile a maintenance request and give this to the Maintenance Department. Record your report in the Hand-over Book and make this available to your manager.

The supplier of the equipment would have given the company some idea of its projected life expectancy given the work load it carries within the company. Review the purchase or hiring documentation regularly to keep up to date with equipment that is nearing this projected date.

Ensure that the log book is kept up to date and audit it on a regular basis. The log book is where all servicing documentation and reports of incidents are recorded regarding the history of a specific piece of equipment. This information also gives an indication of the condition of the equipment and whether or not it will continue to function optimally and for how long.

Equipment does not last indefinitely and will, at some point, require replacement. Report poor functional operating of equipment to the Maintenance Manager and record it in the log book.

The Maintenance Manager is responsible for evaluating the risks involved in keeping the machine and, for example, replacing a part, against the cost of replacing the entire piece of equipment.

Unit 9:

Complete all set-up procedures

Set-up procedures

All set-up procedures required prior to service delivery should be completed for all the different types of service: normal service, events, functions and special promotions.

This includes cleaning; clearing and restocking the drinks service area and preparing all equipment ready for service.

Normal bar service is discussed in this unit.

Clearing and cleaning of drinks service areas

It is important to supervise the clearing and cleaning of the drink service area in a logical and orderly fashion so that the drinks service begins on time.
* Allocate staff to the cleaning areas. Check that all staff members responsible for preparing the drink service area are working together as a team and that the workload is fairly distributed.
* Communicate cleaning requirements in terms of the expected standard, the cleaning agents to be used and the time frame in which the cleaning must be completed.
* Check the cleaning of the following
* counters
* shelves
* floors
* brass work
* displays and bottles
* glassware and glassware storage areas
* glass surfaces and mirrors
* glasses and drinks service equipment
* utensils
* dispensers

The vacuuming, dusting and polishing in guest areas must also be checked.

Ensure that staff members have the following resources required to carry out the cleaning functions:
* chemicals for the glass washing machine
* glass cloths, counter cloths, bar runners and other linen.

Customer service areas must be kept clean and maintained tidily at all times. These areas must be clean at the beginning of the shift, maintained during the service period, and properly cleaned at the end of the shift. Customers like the look of a busy establishment, but, at the same time, it must be clean and tidy.

Ensure that the cleaning standards have been met. If standards have not been met discuss the situation with the responsible staff member.

Table 1: Bar preparation checklist

The bar	Preparation
Counter tops	Clean, and remove all residues
Beer taps	Clean, and remove all residues
Display shelves	Clean, and remove all residues
Garnishes and accompaniments	Prepare garnishes and accompaniments and store hygienically
Bar stock	Check all stock and requisition stock as necessary
Storage shelves	Clean, and remove all residues
Refrigerator	Clean, and remove all residues from shelves, rotate stock and check 'use by dates'
Glasses	Wash and polish, where appropriate
Small equipment	Disassemble, clean, remove all residues, and reassemble
Bottle skips	Empty and wipe out
Point of sale	Obtain float
Staff	Check personal appearance, health and hygiene
Menus	If available, clean if necessary
Promotional displays	Clean, and remove all residues and set up where appropriate
Entrances	Clean, check equipment
Exterior	Clean, check equipment

Restocking the drinks service area

Stocks and accompaniments for drink service must be maintained at organisationally determined levels.

Stocks include the following:
- bottled/canned beers
- draught beers
- wines
- spirits
- liqueurs
- ingredients for cocktails
- promotional products
- cold drinks and soft drinks
- hot drinks – tea, coffee, hot chocolate
- sundry items – coasters, straws and napkins.

Accompaniments include the following:
- ice and water
- cordials and juices
- food garnishes for drinks such as cocktails and mixed drinks
- decorative items for drinks
- nuts, chips or other snacks served with drinks.

Restocking and preparing the bar

- Refer to the bar stock list. Check what stock is required and order replenishments and collect these from the stores.
- Ensure that all the optics are stocked, and that all bottles on display are adequately stocked.
- Ensure that there is an adequate supply of kitchen stocks. If you are aware of a delivery problem contact the stores-person to establish when the items will be delivered.
- Ensure that perishable items such as lemons, apples and fresh fruit juices are fresh.
- Return drinks products and items that do not meet the required standards of quality and ensure their replacement.
- Ensure that bar runners are clean and there are replacements immediately available.
- Check that sufficient stocks of clean glasses are in place and that glasses needed are stored on the service counters.
- Store extra glasses in racks on the shelves in the glass washing area to prevent breakages.

Maintaining stocks and accompaniments at appropriate levels

Stock is kept behind the bar, on the shelves, and in the drink cabinets to ensure that orders can be served quickly and efficiently. If the stock and accompaniments are kept in cabinets with glass doors and displayed so the customers can see what is available, it is extremely important to keep stocks at appropriate levels according to organisational requirements.

Stocks and accompaniments are kept in storerooms according to organisationally determined levels and collected when needed in the bar. If any stocks or accompaniments are running low, you must report this to your supervisor so that more can be ordered.

In the bar you will also have a level that must be maintained. When this is low it must be stocked up from the main storeroom. Stocking up of stocks and accompaniments is usually done at the beginning or end of a shift.

You must avoid running out of necessary items during service, since fetching more wastes time when you should be serving customers. The only time that you should have to get more stock or accompaniments during service is when you are very busy and you do not have enough storage space in the bar. In this case, you must be prepared to go and collect these things but they should be ready for collection in a convenient place in the store room.

Remember that having too little stock on hand is not good, but having too much stock is not good either, since you may waste unused stock or even trip over it if the bar is too crowded.

Storing, arranging and rotating stocks and accompaniments

The storage, arranging and rotation of stocks and accompaniments is extremely important in order to be cost effective and because this can have an impact on the quality of the drinks.

When an order arrives, it must be checked in according to organisational requirements and then be arranged in the allocated area. Each item that is delivered will have a particular area assigned to it. This is to make it easier for everyone to locate stuff as and when it is needed. This will also allow for easy re-ordering, since it is possible to see how much is still available.

It is very important to put the new stock behind the old stock always. This is so that the older stock is used first. This is called stock rotation or FIFO (first in first out). The same must happen in the bar when you are stocking it up. Never just put the new stock in front of the older stock.

All stock should be packed away neatly so that you and the customers can see what is available. This will make counting easier as well so you will know how much stock you are going to need for re-stocking.

All food accompaniments, such as garnishes, sugar, nuts and other snacks, as well as biscuits and chocolates that may be served with coffee or tea, must be stored in the refrigerator if necessary or in their appropriate places. The stock levels on these must be carefully monitored, since they perish a lot faster that bottled drinks do. Never over-order these types of items.

Checking facilities in customer areas

Customer areas are areas that are used by your guests. Most people judge an establishment from their first impressions. In a hospitality establishment, a guest's first impression is often linked to what he or she sees and experiences on arrival.

In order to maintain a professional image, these areas must be kept clean and maintained at all times.

When you are walking amongst the guests, make sure that all is going well.

Always be sensitive to signs of trouble among the customers, such as a possible fight, under-age drinking and, even drug dealing.

You as the supervisor or head waiter should be observant and monitor the work of the other waiters. They should:
* Ensure that the restrooms are well stocked, and notify housekeeping if there are shortages.
* See that the bar sideboards are well stocked and tidy.
* Wipe down the counter top with a warm damp cloth to keep it clean and to remove the sticky residue that can be left by drinks.
* Ensure that the smoking lounge and bar area have enough clean ashtrays. Ashtrays must be emptied regularly and thoroughly washed. For reasons of hygiene, ashtrays must be washed separately from other dirty equipment.

- Discard any dead floral arrangements or unsatisfactory table decorations.
- Remove outdated or dirty promotional material.
- Ensure that ice buckets are kept full.
- Make sure any water jugs kept on the bar for customers to help themselves, are kept full.
- Remove empty glasses left on the bar.
- Place coasters and drip mats placed neatly on the counter. Replace dirty and/or torn ones.
- Keep bowls of nuts, chips and snacks kept on the bar for customers to help themselves, topped up.
- Make each journey worthwhile so keep collecting glasses, emptying ashtrays, picking up rubbish.
- Work as a team in the bar with their colleagues, so one person does not always have the worst jobs to do.

Table 2: Daily cleaning schedule for a bar

Item	When	How	Name of cleaning person	Signature
bathroom mirrors	each shift	spot clean		
service hand sink/handles	every 4 hours	wash, rinse and sterilise		
bar equipment and utensils (food contact)	every 4 hours	wash, rinse and sterilise		
bar counters and non-food contact surfaces	end of shift	wash, rinse and sterilise		
waiter station shelves and utensil containers	end of day	wash, rinse and sterilise		
cleaning room	end of day	organise, sweep and mop		
coffee machines	end of day	wash, rinse and sterilise urns clean steamer and spout wipe and buff exterior		
coffee pots	end of day	wash, rinse and sterilise		
counters	throughout shift and end of day	wipe clean and buff dry		
dining area tables	throughout shift and end of day	wipe clean and buff dry wash, rinse and sterilise where appropriate		
dining area chairs and railings	throughout shift and end of day	wipe clean		
cold drink machine	throughout shift and end of day	wipe clean and buff dry		
cold drink machine nozzles	end of day	soak diffusers in steriliser solution scrub interiors		

Date: _____

Stocking the pay point area

To avoid delays and to ensure fast efficient service when customers want to pay, it is important to ensure that the pay point area is well stocked with the following:
- enough bar dockets
- easily accessible order books
- an adequate float
- enough credit card rolls and vouchers
- pens and till rolls
- cash-up sheets and cash-up envelopes.

Set-up procedures for events and functions

Before proceeding with preparing, servicing and clearing function rooms, pay particular attention to the Function Sheet. This documents all the details and information for the function. It is crucial to follow instructions on the Function sheet because all the customer's requests are specified on it.

A bar set-up will depend on the following:
- Customer's requirements
- Type of function
- Size and shape of function room
- Number of people to serve
- Whether it is a cash bar/or 'on the house' bar

Set-up procedures for special promotions

Make sure all waiters know exactly how the promotion works.

There should be enough stock available of the products on promotion and enough stock of equipment needed to serve the products on promotion.

If Bar tokens are given which can redeemed later that same day or on a future date, make sure there is sufficient stock.

Keep the cash collection in one place and the serving in another as a theft protection method. This works especially well for establishments using casual staff for one-time events where bringing in outside untested help is necessary.

If souvenir t-shirts, shot glasses, and beer mugs are given as a promotion, make sure there is enough stock for the expected number of customers.

Unit 10:

Communicate with customers in a polite and friendly way

Being polite and friendly to customers

Good customer relations are vital to a good licensed premise. If the staff members are grumpy or rude, or if they ignore the customers the latter will not return

Staff must be well trained and extremely knowledgeable about the drinks they are selling and what is available in their establishment. They must be able to impart this knowledge politely.

Staff must be able to correctly and politely describe how drinks are prepared and what is in them.

Staff must be friendly at all times, even if they are having a 'bad day' since personal problems should influence your work.

Always speak to customers in a clear voice and a calm manner, neither too loudly nor too softly, but always with energy and enthusiasm.

All customers should be treated equally, but at the same time remember that each one of them is special. Even apparently small things should be dealt with. You may not think these important, but to the customer they may be very important.

It is vital to 'read' your customers in relation to their mood and possible requirements. If they arrive with a small child, get them a highchair immediately. If they walk in with a packet of cigarettes, get them an ashtray.

In order to deal correctly with customers, staff must also be honest, loyal to their establishment and trustworthy: if you say you will do something, follow it through.

As soon as customers walk in the door, they must be acknowledged.

Greet customers immediately as they enter. If possible, open the door for them and assist with prams, wheelchairs, children, and elderly people.

Take coats and excess bags and luggage if applicable.

If you are busy and unable to meet the customers at the door, make sure you acknowledge them by smiling, nodding or greeting them. This is very important otherwise the customer will think that you are not interested in them and will not feel welcome.

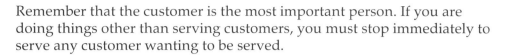

Remember that the customer is the most important person. If you are doing things other than serving customers, you must stop immediately to serve any customer wanting to be served.

Never spend too much time talking to one customer. If the customer engages you in conversation, you should excuse yourself politely at the appropriate time in order to carry out other duties.

Customers must be dealt with promptly at all times. Never assume that customers have all the time in the world, they may be in a hurry, so do not delay in attending to them

Customer queries on drinks served

If staff members do not know enough about the drinks served to make suggestions and answer guests' questions, the head waiter or supervisor should be available to assist. If possible, allow the staff member concerned to listen to your handling of the situation so that they can learn.

Examples:

Guest A: What liqueur coffees can you suggest?

Waiter: Would you prefer a liqueur or a spirit? Depending on this, I can offer you an Irish coffee, or a Kahlua, Drambuie, Benedictine or Tia Maria coffee.

Guest B: Can you make a Dom Pedro with Kahlua or Malibu?

Waiter: Yes, a Dom Pedro can be made with any spirit or liqueur.

Guest C: What good whiskies do you have?

Waiter: Do you prefers Scotch, Irish or American whisky?

Guest C: Scotch, thanks.

Waiter: Would you care for single malt or a blend?

If a guest asks about which liqueurs, cognacs, brandies and so on are available, give them this information. In answer to a query about brandies, mention that you have Calvados or Armagnac as well, if these are in stock.

Unit 11:

Be able to handle unexpected operational situations

Unexpected operational situations

These can include a number of problems such as the non delivery of goods, power failures, equipment failure, problems with the supply of bar and other items and being short-staffed.

Non-delivery of goods

Should goods not be delivered on schedule, contact the store-person and enquire when the goods will be delivered. If the explanation is unacceptable contact the supplier to complain. Ascertain when delivery is expected.

Follow up on this information and check that the delivery has been made.

Power failure

In the event of a power failure, ensure that you have an alternative power supply available. Large hospitality establishments will have a generator but smaller ones may not. Make sure that you have candles and matches as well as oil lamps and a supply of oil for them.

Equipment failure

In the event of equipment failure, call a technician immediately and improvise if you can until the equipment is repaired.

Guests should never be discomforted or inconvenienced because of problems with equipment. This will give a very bad impression and your hospitality establishment will be seen to be unprofessionally run.

Unacceptable drinks items

If these items are found to be stale or in any other way unacceptable, return them to the supplier and ensure that they are replaced as soon as possible. Remember to record this in the Ullage book and keep proof of the defective drinks or other items according to organisational requirements. If you are out of stock, apologise to the guest and suggest something similar.

Being short-staffed

Running any section of a hospitality establishment with too few staff members can be very challenging. If possible, bring in staff from other areas to assist.

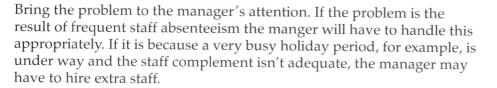

Bring the problem to the manager's attention. If the problem is the result of frequent staff absenteeism the manger will have to handle this appropriately. If it is because a very busy holiday period, for example, is under way and the staff complement isn't adequate, the manager may have to hire extra staff.

Assessment Activity 4.1

Assignment

1. Describe five legal requirements to providing a drinks service. (10)
2. Discuss the procedure you would follow if you know of a person or an establishment that is violating the requirements of the licensing law. (5)
3. "New liquor laws recognise that liquor is a potentially harmful substance, and they recognise that its abuse is widespread in our society; we seek to introduce laws which will regulate the sale and distribution of alcohol in the public interest."
   Discuss why you think the new liquor laws are an improvement on the previous laws. (5)
4. Describe six steps that you will follow in dealing with offensive and disruptive customer behaviour. (6)
5. Describe two ways of dealing with a customer whom you suspect of being drunk. (4)

Assessment Activity 4.2

Simulation

Complete this activity in groups of three.

1. Decide who will be the customer and who will be the drinks server and the food server.
2. The servers must both take an order from the customer.
3. The drinks waiter must then explain in detail how the drink would be mixed, what glass the drink will be served in and any appropriate garnishing.
4. The food waiter must describe the ingredients and cooking methods of the dishes.
5. Each member of the group must take a turn being all three of the roles.
6. Each group member must explain all of the roles and tasks they would be responsible for as the drinks waiter and the food waiter. You may use the provided checklist to guide you with regards what needs to be considered.

You will decide, together with the lecturer decide which of the following TWO events are going to be used for simulation and which TWO are going to be used for assessment.

Possible themes:

- Grade 12 and/or level 4 College farewell.
- Twenty first birthday party.
- Small, formal wedding reception.(30-50 guests)
- A company's year-end party.

Each function should include the service of wine, cocktails and a silver service option.

The checklist which follows should be used to assess your simulated event. Assess each other using it. The lecturer will use the same checklist during Assessment Activity 3.

PRACTICAL CHECKLIST – Topic 4: Maintain a drinks service

Provision of a food service event – the role of the Drinks Service team

Student's name: _____

Assessor name: _____

Date: _____

	Yes	No	Comments
1. Planning			
1.1 Composition of drinks and wine list (based on menu)			
1.2 Creation of drinks (if cocktails or new drinks will be used, the recipes and presentation, etc)			
1.3 Suitable method of taking orders that is to be used.			
1.4 Decision on uniforms. (Neat and professional appropriate for theme)			
1.5 Correct and complete equipment requirements. (Equipment ordered from store room)			
1.6 Stock requirements (Requisition form to store room for drinks to be served complete)			
1.7 Allocation of roles (sommelier, drinks waiter, barman, quality checker, etc.)			
1.8 Work schedule and checklist complete up to and including day of service.			
2. Hygiene on day of function			
2.1 Dressed correctly and neatly, according to organisational requirements.			
2.2 Personal hygiene up to standard: Hair, nails, appropriate jewellery and no odour e.g. smoke and sweat.			
3. Mise en Place			
3.1 All service equipment e.g. glassware, waiters cloth, salver with napkin, pen and note pad/docket book is clean and free from damage.			
3.2 No equipment missing needed for service.			
4. Service of drinks			
4.1 Take orders for alcoholic drinks only from those people whom you are permitted to serve by law.			
4.2 Take down customer's orders clearly and repeat it to guests accurately.			
4.3 Deal with customers in a prompt, polite and helpful way.			
4.4 Promote certain drinks to customers at the appropriate times.			
4.5 Give customers accurate information about drinks offered by the establishment.			
4.6 Serve wine correctly (According to checklist for Topic 1)			
4.7 Serve cocktails correctly (According to checklist for Topic 2)			
4.8 Deal effectively with unexpected situations and inform the appropriate people where necessary.			
4.9 Carry out duties in an organised and efficient manner.			
4.10 Offer to replenish the guests' wine once the glass is 2/3 empty/ ask what else if cocktail is finished.			

PRACTICAL CHECKLIST – Topic 4: Maintain a drinks service

Provision of a food service event – the role of the Food Service Team

Student's name: _____

Assessor's name: _____

Date: _____

		Yes	No	Comments
1.	Planning			
1.1	Selection of table settings based on menu (linen, crockery, cutlery, condiments).			
1.2	Method of taking orders.			
1.3	Creation of menus according to theme.			
1.4	Decision on uniforms according to theme.			
1.5	Choice of music.			
1.6	Room decorations according to theme.			
1.7	Table decorations.			
1.8	Equipment requirements.			
1.9	Consumable requirements.			
1.10	Allocation of roles (host/ess, waiter, runner, quality checker).			
1.11	Work schedule and checklist up to and including day of service.			
2.	Hygiene on day of function			
2.1	Dressed correctly and neatly, according to organisational requirements.			
2.2	Personal hygiene up to standard: Hair, nails, appropriate jewellery and no odour e.g. smoke and sweat.			
2.3	Hygiene during service of food – don't touch hair, pick nose.			
3.	Set-up of function room			
3.1	All flooring is vacuumed or swept.			
3.2	Furniture clean and undamaged. Tables and chairs evenly spaced, all chairs are positioned correctly.			
3.3	Table linen, glassware, decorative items, sweets or mints etc is placed in the correct order.			
3.4	Lay tables according to requirements. The type of menu will influence the way the tables are set. For functions table d'hote menus are mostly used.			
4.	Interacting with customers			
4.1	Meet and greet guests, welcoming them to the establishment and introducing yourself.			
4.2	Escort customers to an appropriate table and help seating customers.			
4.3	Hand over menus; assist and explain.			
4.4	Take down the food order, repeating it back to the guest.			

5.	Silver service of food			
5.1	Prepare the table for food service by e.g. adjusting covers.			
5.2	Serve the lady to the host's left first; move to the right around the table.			
5.3	Present dish to the table of customers before serving, so that all the customers can admire the dish.			
5.4	Silver serve from the left of the guest. The main item is served first and placed closest to the customer, on the lower centre of the plate (main item is meat, fish, poultry or a vegetarian item).			
5.5	Potatoes are served next to the top right of the plate vegetables are then served at the top left. Gravy or sauce is served last.			
5.6	Correct portions served.			
5.7	Service cloth and underflat placed/used correctly.			
5.8	Service spoon and fork held and used correctly.			
5.9	Platter with food just overlaps the customer's plate, but do not touch the plate.			
6.	Clearing the table.			
6.1	Remove plates and cutlery after each course when the whole table has finished eating and crumb down.			
6.2	Start clearing with the person on the host's left, moving around the table to the right, finishing with the host.			
6.3	Stand to the guest's right, lean forward and pick up the plate with your right hand.			
6.4	Follow correct method for stacking plates in left hand.			
6.5	Offer menus for desert order and take the order.			
6.6	Serve and clear desert.			
6.7	Offer tea/coffee/liqueur/cocktail.			

Assessment Activity 4.3

Assessed practical

Complete this assessment activity in groups. Each group will complete the activity as a food service team and as a drinks service team.

1. As each college has its own available venues, budgets and the time of day that may be used for functions, your lecturer will provide you with the following information:
   - The venue to be used
   - The timing of the event
   - Any budget requirements for each team
   - Any constraints that apply (e.g. maximum covers or tables that can be accommodated, licensing regulations, safety precautions).
   - The role of the team leaders and other team members.

2. As a team the Food Service Team should decide on the following:
   – Selection of team leader(s)
   – Selection of table settings based on menu (linen, crockery, cutlery, condiments)
   – Method of taking orders
   • Creation of menus
   • Decision on uniforms
   • Choice of music
   • Room decorations
   • Table decorations, etc.
   • Equipment requirements
   • Consumable requirements
   • Allocation of roles (host/ess, waiter, runner, quality checker, etc)
   • Work schedule and checklist up to and including day of service

3. As a team the Drink Service Team should decide on the following:
   • Selection of team leader(s)
   • Composition of drinks and wine list (based on menu) and creation of such (if cocktails or new drinks used, the recipes and presentation, etc)
   • Method of taking orders
   • Decision on uniforms
   • Equipment requirements
   • Consumable requirements
   • Stock requirements
   • Allocation of roles (sommelier, drinks waiter, barman, quality checker, etc.)
   • Work schedule and checklist up to and including day of service

4. The two events NOT used in Assessment Activity 4.2 will be used for this activity.

The lecturer will use the same checklists that were used during Assessment Activity 2 to assess each student on drinks service and on food service.

Topic Summary

This topic focuses on how to maintain a drinks service.

Unit 1 explained how to implement the procedures for the maintenance of a drinks service. Unit 2 described the legal requirements for the operation of any licensed establishment. Unit 3 then looked at the consequences of selling alcohol to under-aged or intoxicated persons.

Unit 4 helped you to understand the reasons why staff need product training as well as why they should always comply with service standards. Unit 5 looked at ways to motivate staff in increasing sales.

Unit 6 was the first to look at specifically at customers; it looked at how to deal with violent or disruptive customers. It also identified the guidance that should be offered to staff in this regard. Unit 7 looked at why equipment should be maintained safely and hygienically and Unit 8 explained how to implement the fault and maintenance reporting procedures. Included in this unit is also how to complete all the necessary paperwork.

Different procedures are required prior to service delivery. Unit 9 looks at how to complete all set-up procedures. Unit 10 looks at how to communicate with customers in a polite and friendly way. The topic ends with Unit 11 which looks at how to handle unexpected operational situations.

The following are important things to remember:
- There are many different types of establishment that serve drinks, basically divided into licensed and unlicensed premises. Licensed premises are permitted to serve and sell alcohol and unlicensed premises are only permitted to sell non-alcoholic beverages.
- When serving drinks in a licensed premise, we must be aware of a number of issues including customer requirements, complying with licensing legislation, correct service of all drinks and adhering to organisational requirements. It is extremely important to have a very good understanding of all these different things, especially the licensing legislation.
- Wines and spirits can either be free poured with a measure or an optic can be used. Each establishment will have its own organisational requirements regarding the correct procedure for pouring wine and spirits and this must be adhered to carefully.
- All relevant health and safety principles and food hygiene principles must be adhered to.

Assess yourself

Assess your understanding of the information covered in this Module by completing the following table:

	Yes	Partly	No
I am able to implement the procedures for the maintenance of a drinks service			
I can describe the legal requirements for the operation of a licensed premise			
I have the knowledge to explain the consequences of selling alcohol to under-aged or intoxicated persons			
I understand why staff needs product knowledge and should comply with service standards			
I am able to devise ways to motivate staff in increasing sales			
I can discuss ways to deal with violent or disruptive customers and identify the guidance that should be provided to staff in this area			
I understand why equipment should be maintained safely and hygienically			
I am able to implement the fault and maintenance reporting procedures and complete all the necessary paperwork			
I can complete all set-up procedures required prior to service delivery including cleaning; clearing and restocking the drinks service area and preparing all equipment ready for service			
I am able to communicate with customers in a polite and friendly way			
I am able to handle unexpected operational situations			

If you answered no or partly, then you need to revise that section again, or ask your lecturer for help.

Topic 5:
Maintain the cleaning programme in a specified area

Module 5

An effective cleaning programme

Develop and consistently maintain an effective cleaning programme in the area of responsibility. This includes safety checks and hazard identification and on-the-job training.

In this module you will…

- understand why it is important to implement a cleaning programme
- be able to communicate the requirements of a cleaning programme to staff
- minimise hazards occurring through the misuse or mishandling of chemicals
- conduct cleaning inspections
- take appropriate actions when service quality is reduced through operational problems
- record, file and make available all information as required
- adapt cleaning programmes to different situations.

Unit 1:

The importance of a cleaning programme

This unit will help you to understand why it is important to implement a cleaning programme.

Importance of a cleaning programme

Without the implementation of a cleaning programme no organised and well controlled cleaning will take place. This will mean failure to comply with legislation and will result in poor hygiene, low levels of guest satisfaction, low staff morale and lowered cost effectiveness.

Failure to comply with legislation

To ensure a healthy and organised work environment that complies with current legislation, according to the Occupational Health and Safety (OHS) Act, a cleaning programme must be implemented. This ultimately ensures that anything produced in, and served from, the kitchen, dining area and bar are of a sufficiently high standard.

Health Inspectors conduct random inspection to see whether or not cleaning programmes for work areas successfully meet the high standards required by current legislation. Non compliance with standards could result in financial penalties or even closure of the business.

Key aspects of the OHS Act should at all times be available for staff to consult.

Standards of hygiene

The observance of standards of hygiene is the most important way of ensuring that food and drink will not be **detrimental** to anyone's health. In order to maintain an environment where food and drink is handled in a clean and safe manner, provision should be made for:
* a clean and tidy food service unit
* neatly dressed staff members who display a high standard of personal hygiene
* staff members who are concerned about the way food and drink is handled
* appropriate, clean equipment and utensils
* the purchasing of clean and safe food items
* clean toilets and changing facilities
* the prevention of disease.

Words & terms

Detrimental: Causing harm or damage.

Guest satisfaction

In order to maintain a professional image, customer areas must be kept clean and maintained at all times since most people judge an establishment in terms of the cleanliness and tidiness of such areas.

A bad experience will result in low levels of guest satisfaction. This will, in turn, result in the loss of repeat business.

The dining experience for the guest will be greatly improved if the dining area and bar are well set-up, clean and hygienically maintained. Staff members who are clearly organised in relation to clearing and cleaning will create a professional image. It is important that a continual process of clearing and cleaning must take place during the service of food and drink to ensure the comfort of the guests. A healthy, sanitised work environment results in excellent customer service.

It is essential to have a work plan including a cleaning schedule in order to work efficiently and thus ensure customer satisfaction at all times.

Staff morale

The effective planning of tasks and allocation of people to these tasks will ensure that activities are completed competently, and that staff members are motivated and productive. Working according to a schedule contributes to a positive, less stressful, and more enthusiastic work force with high staff morale.

An organised work environment affects staff turnover as well as morale and these factors have a positive impact on production.

Cost effectiveness

The failure to maintain an organised work environment results in serious costs to the company.

Providing customers with a clean, hygienic establishment that is second to none will ensure repeat business but dirty and unhygienic conditions will lead to the loss of such repeat business.

The cleaning equipment provided is there to enable you to perform your work effectively and efficiently. Cleaning equipment which is well maintained will last far longer. When equipment is faulty, it becomes more difficult, more time consuming and, therefore, more costly for work to be performed.

Resources for developing a cleaning programme

If the cleaning team is expected to comply with the cleaning schedule, it is essential that they are given the means to complete the job properly. These resources include information and equipment.

Information

Staff must be given information in the following areas:
* conditions necessary for bacterial growth
* the importance of good hygiene practices

- cleaning procedures
- the use of the correct equipment and cleaning agents.

Cleaning equipment

Cleaning equipment includes brooms, brushes, buckets, cloths, drain rods, dusters, mops, sponges, squeegees, scrubbing and polishing machines, vacuum cleaners, wet and dry suction cleaners, scouring pads, detergents, disinfectants, dustbin powder, washing-up liquids, fly sprays, detergents, scourers, steel wool and soap.

All re-usable cleaning equipment such as cloths, mops, brooms and brushes should be washed, disinfected and left to dry after use.

The cleaning and sterilising of cleaning and washing-up equipment such as, for example, dishwashers, mops, buckets and squeegees should also be included in the cleaning programme.

Cleaning agents

Cleaning agents may be divided into three groups: detergents, disinfectants and sanitisers.

Detergents

These are chemicals used to remove dirt, grease and debris from a surface before disinfection takes place.

Disinfectants

These are chemicals which reduce harmful bacteria to a safe level.

Sanitisers

These substances combine detergents with disinfectants.

Protective clothing

All food handlers should wear protective clothing that is:
- clean
- washable
- light coloured to show up any dirt.

This clothing should be without pockets since these they may catch in machinery and may be used to keep unhygienic objects such as used tissues, for example, in them.

It should have fasteners which cannot come undone and fall into the food.

If protective clothing is worn over outdoor clothing which, under normal circumstances is not good practice, it should completely cover all outdoor clothing, including sleeves, cuffs, collars and so on.

Unit 2:

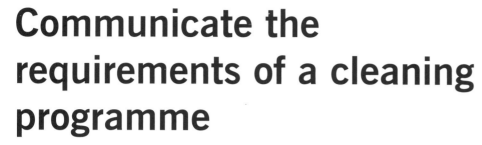

Communicate the requirements of a cleaning programme

This unit will equip you with the skills to be able to communicate the requirements of a cleaning programme to staff.

Communication with staff

Meet with your subordinates and colleagues every day to reinforce the importance of implementing the cleaning programme. Use these daily meeting to discuss any concerns that the staff may have regarding their work schedules.

Ask questions and encourage questions from staff to ensure that they understand their responsibilities.

If there is clear communication this will help ensure that tasks will be performed correctly and that no time and personpower is wasted. Avoid unnecessary information, difficult words and long explanations.

To ensure that the work objectives and activities have been received and understood, you can ask for staff to repeat the information back to you. This allows you to make sure that the message has been understood.

You can ask questions relating to the assignment to determine whether the instructions were received correctly. You must avoid any potential misunderstandings by saying that you want only to ensure that you gave the assignment clearly and didn't leave anything out. Staff must know that they can approach you at any time if they have problems or are looking for any information and advice. This contributes to the successful completion of the task.

Use the following communication methods to communicate information: writing, speaking and diagrammatic communication.

Writing

Formulate the instructions carefully and simply, keeping the desired outcome in mind. Avoid using slang or technical terms unless you know that the employee understands them. Type the instruction so that they are legible. Write the instruction in one or more of the most commonly spoken local languages.

Speaking

Speak clearly and audibly. Check that the receiver of the message understands the instructions.

Diagrammatic communication

Use diagrams and symbols or characters which will be easily understood by all. Avoid symbols which are patronising or insulting to staff. Ensure that the instructions are visible to all.

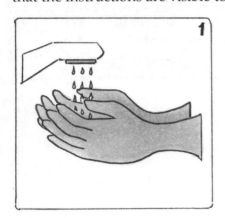
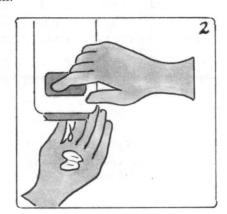
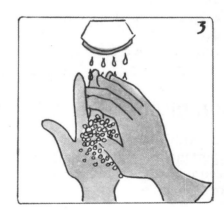
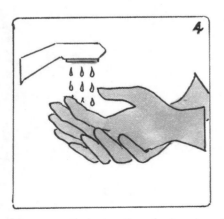
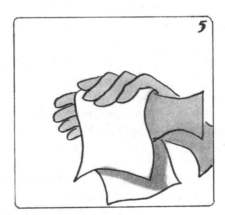

Diagrammatic instructions for hand washing

Requirements of tasks

Any task to be performed must meet certain predetermined requirements. The supervisor must clearly explain to staff what quality and quantity of work will be expected of them. The time frame in which the cleaning must be completed is very important and should be emphasised to staff. State the work objectives and standards of performance clearly.

Do this activity in groups.
1. Hold a class discussion on how to instruct staff on cleaning procedures in food storage areas. 2. Following this discussion, each group should use one of the following communication methods, as allocated by your lecturer:
   - written
   - verbal
   - diagrammatic
3. Create a role play in which the selected method of communication is illustrated.
4. Perform your role play for the rest of the class.

Your role play will be assessed using the same rubric as was used for Activity 1.4. Refer back to that activity to check the criteria before you create your role play.

Training

It is essential that service staff receive regular training in the requirements of a cleaning programme and related cleaning skills. Follow the procedures below:
- Ensure that regular short training sessions are held.
- Inform staff of the expected level of cleaning.
- Inform staff what the organisational goals are.
- Motivate staff to meet organisational goals.
- Assist staff in handling difficult cleaning procedures and ensure that they learn from you.

As part of their induction into the department, all new employees should be informed of the requirements of the cleaning programme.

This induction should include information on:
- required standards of personal hygiene
- expectations regarding uniforms
- hygienic work methods
- the specific cleaning programme relating to the area of responsibility.

All employees in the department must be trained in the use of the various chemicals and equipment to be used in the cleaning tasks for which they are responsible. If there is a change in products, it is necessary to train employees on the use of the new products.

Consulting with staff

Hold regular one-on-one discussions with each individual staff member to establish performance issues and objectives. Every person needs to feel involved and worthwhile, and will perform better if consulted regularly.

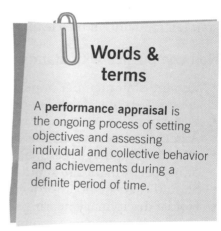

Words & terms

A **performance appraisal** is the ongoing process of setting objectives and assessing individual and collective behavior and achievements during a definite period of time.

Schedule regular performance appraisals and discussions for each staff member.

Agree on and record appraisal discussions and targets.

Be open to new ideas and suggestions and try, wherever possible, to implement these. This will encourage staff to communicate ideas on possible improvements.

In the workplace

Performance appraisals are primarily about counseling and feedback on ways to improve performance at an individual and team level, and the quality of work relationships. It is a system of determining how well an individual employee has performed during a period of time, and is frequently used as a basis for determining merit.

Disciplinary Measures

Communicate disciplinary measures that must be complied with should staff fail to maintain the cleaning requirements.

Non-compliance with standards

- Remind staff member of performance standards and counsel them on areas where standards are not being met.
- Determine the reasons for non-compliance with standards.
- Agree on corrective actions to be taken, and by when.
- Give the employee reasonable opportunity to improve and review her or his performance to standard and as agreed.
- Should there be no improvement, issue a written warning.
- Hold a disciplinary hearing if there is further non-compliance with standards and no improvement in performance.

Depending on the outcome of the hearing, terminate the services of the employee and advise him or her. Ensure that all details from the start of the counseling are carefully documented and filed accordingly.

Think about it

When workers feel that they are actively participating in the setting of their own goals, they are much more motivated to perform with distinction than when they feel that they are merely being told what to do. Workers like goals that inspire quality performance, but the goals should be attainable and realistic.

Unit 3:

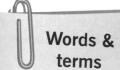

Minimise hazards associated with chemicals

This unit will look at how to minimise hazards occurring through the misuse or mishandling of chemicals.

Minimising the misuse of cleaning chemicals

The following precautions should be followed to ensure the prevention of accidents:

- Store chemicals separately from food, and according to type.
- Rotate stock so that no expired products are stored.
- Check for leakages.
- Store chemicals on labelled shelves and not on the floor where they could be kicked over.
- Sealed chemicals that are not in use must remain in storage areas.
- All chemicals in the storage area should be clearly labeled with their content and should have product-specific precautionary measures clearly outlined on the container.
- Only authorised persons may handle the chemicals.
- Personnel responsible for distributing the chemicals must know the chemical properties, so as to minimise risks like, for example, storing a highly flammable chemical near a stove.
- Open chemicals should be poured into specific dispensing equipment for use when cleaning. (For example, a plastic tank can be connected to the washing-up sink with tubing to dispense ready mixed soapy, washing-up water into the sink. This can be set to fill the sink with exactly the right amount.)
- The dispensing equipment should be laid out strategically to suit each task and set to dispense correct quantities to accommodate each task. This way, the dispensing equipment ensures that only the correct measure or mixture of the chemical is used and it also helps to ensure that it is used only for the appropriate task.

In the workplace

Always take note of and report any incident or anything that may pose a danger to guests, colleagues and visitors.

In the workplace

When you start working at a new hotel or restaurant, you should immediately ask for a written copy of the organisation's operational procedures. You will find answers to questions like:
To whom should faulty equipment be reported to in the establishment?

- Ensure that the suppliers of the cleaning agent provide training on the use of it, both at the beginning of their contract, and also when there are new staff members. (This training is included in the price you pay for these chemicals.)
- If you change products, it is necessary to train employees on the use of the new products.
- Check that subordinates are competent in the use of the cleaning chemicals before delegating cleaning tasks to them.
- Ensure that the required protective clothing (uniform and gum-boots) is available and in good condition. This protective clothing is subject to wear and tear and must be replaced regularly.
- Be consistent in taking action when cleaning materials are not being used properly.
- Make sure that you set the example – always use them properly, and always use the required protective clothing.

Taking corrective action

If cleaning areas do not meet the expectations of organisational standards, it is important to take immediate and consistent action.
- Bring the problems to the attention of the person responsible for carrying out the cleaning.
- If it is a new employee, or a new skill, provide coaching and allow the employee to practise using the chemicals properly.
- If it is a performance problem, take disciplinary action.
- Ensure that all cleaning materials and equipment are available, and that equipment is in good working order.
- If a pest problem is evident, ensure that the Pest Control Contractor is called to correct the problem.
- When you become aware of problems with the supply of chemicals from the supplier contact the supplier and address the problem immediately. The contract agreement with the supplier requires that stock levels and delivery times be adhered to.

Safety measures

Put the following in writing, hand copies out to staff and discuss at staff meetings and/or training sessions.

- Always wear the correct safety gear when you are working with powered equipment and chemicals. This gear includes gloves, face masks, goggles, safety shoes and a protective apron. This not only protects your clothes against damage, but also protects you against injuries and burns.
- Always replace worn or damaged protective gear immediately.
- An employee with an open wound, cut, sore or any similar injury who works where a chemical substance is used or handled, shall immediately report such injury to his or her employer. The employee may not continue to work until the injury has been cleaned with soap and water or with a diluted disinfectant, and dressed.
- The manufacturer's cleaning chart and data sheets for the cleaning materials must be visibly displayed in your unit. This will guide you in what should be used for specific cleaning and how materials must be diluted, if applicable.
- Chemicals should never be mixed! Some chemicals can become volatile when mixed and can cause chemical reactions, explosions, toxic fumes and so on.
- If materials need to be diluted, follow the manufacturer's instructions. Incorrect dilution can cause damage and/or make the chemical ineffective.
- All chemicals should be clearly labeled. Bottles used to store already diluted chemicals should be colour coded so that staff will know that, for example, pink bottles are toilet cleaner, blue bottles are all purpose cleaners and so on.
- Never use empty bottles that contained, for example, vinegar or tomato sauce to store chemicals. If bleach is stored in an empty vinegar bottle, for example, someone might think it is vinegar and use it in food.
- Correct dilution will save money for the company and will avoid excessive build-up on surfaces
- Store chemicals away from heat and sunlight and away from food items.

Learning Activity 5.2

Do this activity in pairs.
1. Bring empty containers of different chemicals, used in the establishment where you do your in-service training, to class.
2. Read the labels on the containers and discuss this information with your partner. Write down the following:
   - the name of the chemical
   - the directions for usage
   - the dilution ratios
   - the equipment required to use it correctly
   - the potential hazards of the product
   - how to prevent accidents and misuse
3. Create a poster which could be used to warn users of any one of the products you have analysed.

You will assess each other's posters using the following rubric:

Student Name:					
Activity:					
Criteria	Outstanding 80-100%	Highly competent 70-79%	Competent 50 – 69%	Not yet competent 40-49%	Not achieved 0-39%
Information included	Student included enough relevant points to make the poster valuable.	Student included a large number of relevant points.	Student did not include enough relevant points.	Student included almost no relevant points.	Student did not include a single relevant point.
Labeling	Student clearly and accurately labeled all aspects of the poster.	Student labeled most of the items of the poster or used mostly accurate labels	Student labeled some of the items of the poster or used some accurate labels	Student labeled few of the aspects of the poster or the labels were inaccurate.	Student did not use any labels on the poster.
Graphics	All graphics used were relevant.	Most graphics used were relevant.	Some of the graphics used were relevant.	Few of the graphics used were relevant.	None of the graphics used were relevant.
Visual appeal	Poster is visually appealing and pleasing.	Poster has many aspects which are appealing and pleasing.	Poster has some aspects which are appealing and pleasing.	Poster has very few aspects which are appealing and pleasing.	Poster has no visually appealing aspects.
Language including legibility, grammar and spelling.	All language on poster is appropriate.	Most of the language on poster is appropriate	Some of the language on poster is appropriate	Little of the language on poster is appropriate.	There is no language on the poster.
Balance	Student has achieved a remarkable balance between graphics and written information.	Student has achieved a balance between graphics and written information.	Student has achieved very little balance between graphics and written information.	Student has included either only written information or only graphics.	Student has included neither graphics nor language on the poster.

Keep your completed rubric somewhere safe.

Faulty cleaning equipment

- Faults in the operational equipment should be reported directly to the duty Manager, who in turn will report the fault to Maintenance.
- Maintenance is responsible for ensuring that the fault is documented and recorded and signed off once the fault is fixed.
- If the in-house maintenance team cannot fix the fault, then they are responsible for contacting the supplier to come in and sort it out.
- All documentation will remain within the Maintenance Department.

The Maintenance Department is conveniently on site and may be able to fix the problem without any extra expense to the company. Before resorting to calling in the supplier or service provider, which is time consuming and potentially costly, check whether the Maintenance Department can fix the problem.

Faulty cleaning agents

Should a problem arise with the chemicals, the kitchen staff is to report directly to the Duty Manager. The Duty Manager will contact the chemical suppliers

Not all staff is sufficiently aware of the properties, precautions and potential hazards of the chemicals in the work area to be able to handle a problematic situation authoritatively and competently. The Duty Manager will therefore take responsibility in such circumstances.

Faulty protective clothing

Even comparatively minor faults in the uniforms or protective gear, such as incorrect company labels inside chef hats, for example, will not be accepted.

The Divisional Manager must send the clothes back straight away.

The clothes are sent away immediately to ensure that the company resolves the issue immediately and is able to get a refund or replacement item.

Injury

If a staff member has been injured on duty, report the incident to the Duty Manager and the First Aid representative immediately.

The injury incident is to be documented in fullest detail and appropriate action taken by the First Aider and the Duty Manager.

In cases of injury attention to the patient is important and it requires the correct authorities present to make decisions and to take corrective action. It is important to document the incident extremely carefully so that you have an exact record of the incident, should circumstances require investigation or have legal implications.

Conduct cleaning inspections

Types of inspections

Inspections include ongoing inspections, regular inspections and spot checks. Frequent check-ups by the divisional manager and supervisor should be conducted rigorously to ensure that all staff is working as a team to maintain excellent standards in their work area and to ensure that the cleaning programme is efficiently carried out and that it complies with regulations.

Ongoing inspections

This is part of an ongoing awareness of daily cleaning and hygiene work practices.

For example, food preparation areas are constantly busy so a clean-as you-go method should be applied during shifts as well as a final clean at the end of the day.

Conducting ongoing inspections is important because it demonstrates the seriousness of the cleaning programme.

Regular inspections

Regular, scheduled inspections must be carried out to ensure that the cleaning schedule is being carried out. These must be done using checklists, and a note must be made of any problems that have been noted.

Regular daily inspections are carried out for a number of reasons
- to monitor staff activities and cleaning methods
- to ensure that work is completed in the required time
- to ensure that areas have been cleaned and replenished according to company procedures
- to ensure that establishment standards are maintained
- to identify problems or faults before the guest does
- to ensure that problems and faults are followed up
- to check that health, safety and hygiene procedures are followed
- to monitor areas as well as equipment, supplies and machinery.

Spot checks

These are **ad hoc** inspections that are useful in ensuring that the cleaning programme is being carried out at all times.

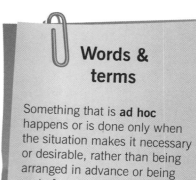

Words & terms

Something that is **ad hoc** happens or is done only when the situation makes it necessary or desirable, rather than being arranged in advance or being part of a general plan.

Example of a checklist: Public Area Cleaning Checklist

Date: _____

Time: _____

Name: _____

Public area	Yes	No	Comments
Floors			
Furniture			
Walls			
Windows			
Window coverings			
Lighting			
Temperature			
Ventilation			
Fireplaces			
Entertainment equipment			
Restrooms			
Waste bins			
Gardens			
Entrances			
Exterior			

Signed: _____

How to conduct cleaning inspections

- Provide an inspection schedule for the supervisor of each area, to ensure that they are checked routinely and regularly. For example, toilets in public areas need to be checked many times during a shift.
- Provide inspection checklists for all areas including public areas, offices, toilets, corridors and passages, store rooms and so on. This will ensure that areas or items are not forgotten or left out.
- Allocate trained and responsible people or supervisors to check specific areas.
- Ensure that inspections are recorded and signed on a daily basis so that it is easy to follow up in the event of non-compliance, problems or complaints.
- During busy periods, enlist the help of Duty Managers to help inspect areas.
- Record the results of the inspections and draw up a report and give feedback to staff; show them the report as proof.

This is effective in gaining their co-operation as a team and it also provides an opportunity to discuss and delegate responsibilities in taking immediate actions to rectify any problems.

To ensure consistent quality it is important to do the following:
- Double check cleaning sequences/methods and update the check list to suit new procedures.
- Supply constant on-the-job training, especially where new procedures are implemented. It is also advisable to schedule time for group training sessions.

Staff should do continual checks on their own area of responsibility. This demonstrates that they are serious about the cleaning programme.

Example of a checklist used by kitchen cleaning staff

	Yes	No
Cleaning		
Do you work according to a set cleaning schedule?		
Do you keep all your work surfaces clean and tidy?		
Do your cleaning procedures all include the following steps:		
wash		
rinse		
sanitise		
Are your dishwasher temperatures as follows:		
wash cycle 60°C		
rinse cycle above 70°		
Are your manual washing temperatures as follows:		
pre-wash 40°C		
wash 49 – 60°C		
rinse and sanitise above 70°C		
Do you have enough cleaning materials and equipment and do they work?		
Do you keep your cleaning equipment clean and in good repair?		
General Cleaning		
Do you ensure that your floors and drains are clean?		
Are your extractor fans and canopies clean?		
Is all your large equipment clean?		
Are all your small kitchen utensils clean?		
Do you avoid using wooden utensils?		
Do you avoid using steel or wire wool for scouring?		
Staff changing facilities and toilets		
Are they clean?		

Are bactericidal soap, disposable towels and nail brushes available?		
Do you store your personal clothes away from the kitchen?		
Do you wash your hands after visiting the toilet and other areas outside the kitchen?		

Learning Activity 5.3

Do this activity on your own.
1. Obtain completed checklists used by your establishment to show how inspections are carried out and recorded.
2. If no written checklists are available, draw up your own checklist to use when you are checking areas that you are responsible for.
3. File these in your portfolio of evidence.

Unit 5:

Reduction in service quality through operational problems

This unit will equip you to take appropriate actions when service quality is reduced through operational problems.

In the workplace

Planning and organising are very important management functions.

Take appropriate action

It is important to resolve a problem before the guest is negatively affected. Carry out all activities with consideration for the comfort and well being of customers and residents in the vicinity.

You may have to plan and organise thing differently to cope with operational problems that threaten to reduce service levels. For example, you might need to adapt the cleaning programme.

Adaptation of the cleaning programme

You might need to do this under certain circumstances. For example you could have a bigger workload than usual if you have to cater for more functions than usual. Equipment failure, interrupted electricity supply, staff shortage and absenteeism could also affect service levels.

It is critical that appropriate changes to the cleaning programme are implemented to ensure that organisational standards are always met regardless of any operational challenges that occur.

To be effective and efficient in this process, it is critical that:
- all kitchen staff be cross-trained to handle other jobs
- the team operates as a unit to complete the daily projects.

If one member of the team is absent or has not performed satisfactorily, it is still up to the rest of the team, even though it is reduced in number, to efficiently tackle the project together and complete it successfully as a unit

Managers and/or supervisors should have a hands-on approach and should get involved with the team and be prepared to help out wherever it is needed.

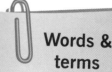

Words & terms

To **plan** is to outline a course of action to achieve an intended result.

Organising can be defined as that function of management that involves the arrangement of the actions and resources of the organisation through the allocation of duties, responsibilities and power to persons and sections in order to promote co-operation and to accomplish the objectives of the organisation as effectively as possible.

Source: www.theta.co.za

Unit 6:

Record, file and make available all information as required

Maintaining and updating records

The cleaning operation cannot be controlled unless records are maintained and updated daily. All activities in the department must be reported and recorded.

The types of records will vary according to the size and procedures of the operation. Records that will need to be maintained and updated on daily, weekly or monthly may include:
* Inspection Reports and Certifications
* Staff attendance registers
* Staff rosters (schedules)
* Staff leave forms
* Staff training and assessment
* Staff appraisals
* Completed checklists
* Recruitment, interviewing and selection records
* Disciplinary records
* Orders and purchases
* Deliveries
* Requisitions and issues
* Maintenance requests and reports
* Stock takes
* Damaged or condemned items
* Costs and budgets
* Minimum and maximum stock levels (par levels)
* Accidents/injuries on duty

Record and file the cleaning programme details

Put the cleaning programme in writing and have it displayed where all employees can see it, to avoid misunderstanding of expectations.

A cleaning programme should include:
* After use cleaning – these are items or areas that must be cleaned immediately after each use, and before using them for another task
* Daily cleaning – items or areas that are cleaned once a day at a specific time of day
* Pre-shift cleaning – items or areas that must be cleaned at the beginning of the shift
* Post-shift cleaning – items or areas that must be cleaned at the end of shift
* Weekly cleaning – items or areas that must be cleaned once a week
* Periodic cleaning – items or areas that are cleaned either more often than once a week but not daily, or items that are cleaned less regularly than once a week.

The cleaning programme must identify the following:
- the item or area to be cleaned
- how often it is to be cleaned (frequency)
- who is responsible for carrying out the cleaning (responsibility)
- what chemicals and equipment are to be used.

Checklists

- Keep completed checklists of inspections on file and make them available to management and the Health and Safety Committee as required.
- Give feedback to your team on the results of inspections – including positive feedback. (They need to be recognised when performing as required.)
- Keep records of training attended by each staff member, their achievements, planned development and so on.
- All documentation in terms of Inspection Reports and Certifications issued by the Health and Safety Department, Local Council Inspectors and Biochemist needs to be filed for record purposes and compliance with the law.

Stock documentation

Each Department is responsible for controlling a large and varied number of items ranging from uniforms and cleaning agents to equipment and machinery.

Strict control should be kept of all items in use and storage, to ensure that adequate stock is in hand for the routine cleaning operations of the organisation.

This will ensure that
- supplies do not run out
- there are minimal losses
- costs do not exceed budget
- the products and services are consistent and to the satisfaction of the guest.

Machinery and equipment should be recorded according to procedures (stock counts and control sheets, issues, records of repairs etc).

Accurate records will help prevent the loss and theft of items.

Learning Activity 5.4

Do this activity on your own.
1. Obtain examples of the following:
   - Fault Report Book
   - Incident Report Form
   - IOD (Injury on Duty Form)
2. Examine the documents taking notice of the information each requires.

Unit 7:

Adapt cleaning programmes to different situations

Adapt cleaning programmes

Procedures for maintaining an efficient cleaning programme will depend on a number of variables: the size, style and type of the hospitality establishment, and the service levels of the operation. This is why cleaning programmes need to be adapted for different situations. One kind of cleaning progamme may have been adequate at one stage but this is no longer the case.

The scope of responsibility and the cleaning activities will depend on the size and number of guest rooms, the size and range of public areas, offices and other departments, conference facilities, restaurant areas, additional facilities such as entertainment or games rooms and exercise rooms, storage areas, laundry facilities and so on.

All members of the cleaning programme must work closely and effectively with all other departments in the hotel to achieve the following objectives:
* organisational standards
* service levels
* financial targets
* guest satisfaction.

Adapt a cleaning schedule

In order to adapt a cleaning schedule effectively all factors that may have an influence on the implementation of the plan should be taken into consideration:
* Is there a time limit?
* How long will it take to execute the plan?
* Is enough time available?
* Can I save time?
* How much will it cost to execute the plan?
* Has provision been made in the budget?
* What can be done to economize?
* How many people should be involved in the execution of the plan?
* Are the available persons able and/or have they been trained to execute the plan?
* How can personpower be saved?
* How can available personpower be optimally utilized?
* Will the situation change in the near future? And if so, to what extent?
* How will this affect the execution of my plans?
* What alternative goals must I determine?
* Does my supervisor agree with the plans?
* Do the plans fit in with current policy and legal requirements and restrictions?
* Are the plans to the benefit of all concerned?

Follow the following steps if you have to adapt cleaning programmes
- Obtain the necessary information. Find out exactly what the altered situation is.
- Gather any other information necessary to do the organising as effectively as possible.
- Take note of the contents of any plans already made and anything facilitating them, such as, for example programmes, schedules, budgets and standards.

In this way a clear reflection of the activities to be organised can be obtained.

Identify and analyse the activities to be carried out

Determine the activities to be undertaken so as to implement the plans involved and accomplish the set objectives. These activities have to be analysed in detail in order to determine their precise nature and extent.

Assessment Activity 5.1

Training exercise

1. Develop a short training programme to train staff in the use of a new chemical.
2. Enact the training event with a Level 2 learner.

Use the table below as a guideline to develop a short training programme to train staff in the use of a new chemical.

Stage	Trainer activties	Trainee activities
Introduction	Explain the purpose of the task. Ask questions that enable you to assess how much the trainee already knows.	Answers questions from the trainer.
Demonstration	Demonstrate the task Explain what you are doing, how it should be done and why it should be done that way. Ask questions to involve the trainee. Ask if the trainee has any questions.	Observes. Answers questions. Asks questions.
3. Practice	Ask the trainee to do the task and explain what he or she is doing and why. Ask questions when the trainee does not explain. Correct the trainee if a mistake is made. Allow the trainee to practice until he or she gets the task right.	Trainee practises the task and explains what is being done and why. Trainee answers questions from the trainer.
4. Summary	Summarise the task and what was learned. Ask questions to check that the trainee understands the task completely. Ask if the trainee has any questions. Tell the trainee what will be learned in the next training session.	Trainee answers questions and asks any final questions he or she may have.

Assessment Activity 5.2

Assignment

1. Develop a Bar inspection schedule and Bar Preparation Checklist to use before evening service starts.

Class test

Complete this activity on your own.
Answer the following questions:

Question 1

Name FOUR records that should be kept concerning staff management.

Next to the name of each record, write down the reason why it should be kept. (8)

Question 2

Why do you have to keep filled in checklists on record? (2)

Question 3

Name FOUR stock control documentation records that should be kept. (4)

Question 4

Name THREE reasons why it is important to keep records of matters concerning the stock in your department. (3)

Question 5

How will you adapt the cleaning programme for a dining room during peak season e.g. December? (2)

Question 6

Name THREE factors that may have an influence on the implementation of a cleaning programme. (3)

Question 7

Name TWO steps you have to follow if you have to adapt a cleaning programme. (2)

Question 8

Why is it important to inform staff about the reasons for adapting a Cleaning programme? (1)

Total: 25

Topic Summary

This topic focused on maintaining a cleaning programme in a specified area. Unit 1 covered the importance of a cleaning programme and the results of failing to comply relevant legislation. Unit 2 looked at how to communicate the requirements of a cleaning programme to staff. Various forms of communication are examined. Unit 3 looks at the very important aspect of minimising the hazards which occur though the misuse or mishandling of chemicals. Included in this unit are corrective actions and safety measures. Unit 4 explains how to conduct cleaning inspections and includes possible checklists.

Unit 5 will equip you will the skills to take appropriate actions when service quality is reduced through operational problems. Unit 6 discusses the recording and filing of information as well as how important it is to have the information available when required. The topic ends with unit 7 which looks at how to adapt cleaning programmes to different situations.

The following are important things to remember:
- An effective cleaning programme for each area of an establishment should consistently be maintained to ensure the safety of staff and customers.
- Supervisors have to co-ordinate the relatively scarce production means like staff, cleaning equipment, cleaning agents, protective clothing, in such a way that the aims of the organisation are effectively reached.
- Test the understanding of your staff by encouraging team members to ask questions about their cleaning responsibilities, cleaning procedures and inspections.
- Get to know each member of staff personally. In this way you will find out their individual strengths and weaknesses, likes and dislikes.
- Conduct regular training needs analyses with staff to establish what training should be scheduled or provided.
- Allocate tasks according to staff capabilities. For example, a staff member who lacks confidence or finds it difficult to communicate with guests should not be allocated duties in busy public areas.
- Regular performance appraisals or assessments will enable you and the staff member to identify strengths and weakness and performance objectives or development targets.
- Discuss and agree to objectives with each employee, either formally or informally.
- All employees in your department must be trained in the use of the various chemicals and equipment to be used in the cleaning tasks for which they are responsible. If you change products, it is necessary to train employees on the use of the new products.
- Care needs to be taken that the cleaning agent used is suitable, since an incorrect cleaning agent may not only permanently damage equipment, but also be hazardous to people using it.
- Always follow the manufacturer and supplier's guidelines when using cleaning equipment and chemicals.
- It is important to ensure that all work is prioritised, delegated and completed on time. Good time management has an impact on profit.

Assess yourself

Assess your understanding of the information covered in this Module by completing the following table:

	Yes	Partly	No
I understand why it is important to implement a cleaning programme			
I have the skills to be able to communicate the requirements of a cleaning programme to staff			
I know how to minimise hazards occurring through the misuse or mishandling of chemicals			
I can conduct cleaning inspections			
I am able to take appropriate actions when service quality is reduced through operational problems			
I have the skills to record, file and make available all information as required			

If you answered no or partly, then you need to revise that section again, or ask your lecturer for help.

Topic 6:
Plan and conduct meetings

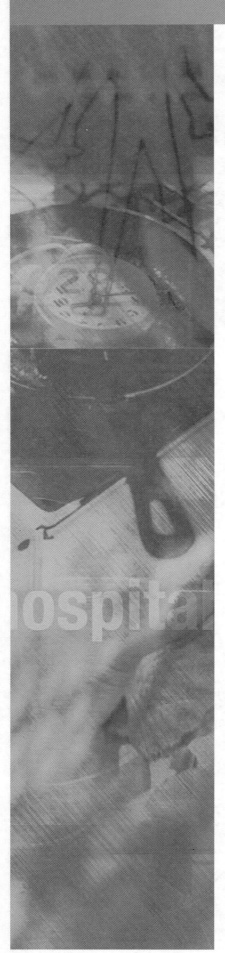

Module 6

Plan and organise meetings of various types

To plan and organise meetings of various types including the preparation of agendas, minutes and other documentation as required

In this module you will ...

- describe standard meeting protocols and the importance of using them
- describe ways to determine the need and objectives of a meeting
- understand the importance of reaching decisions in meetings
- explain ways of managing discussions and problem solving
- describe ways to determine the appropriate delegates for a meeting

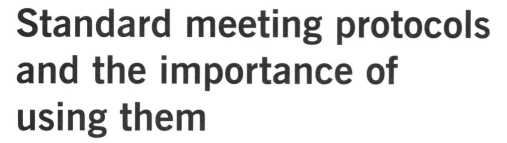

Unit 1:

Standard meeting protocols and the importance of using them

This unit will describe standard meeting protocols and explain the importance of using them.

Different types of meetings held within organisations

People organise different kinds of meetings for different groups of people, depending on what needs to be discussed. Examples of different types of meetings are:

- informal meetings: these are meetings between colleagues and are less structured.
- formal meetings: these are held within an organisation and often include managers or people from outside the company. Examples are shareholder meetings, board meetings, meetings involving managers or supervisors and suppliers to discuss contracts, and so on.
- once-off meetings: these are held to discuss specific issues that arise.
- regular meetings: these are meetings that are held at regular intervals or after regular events, such as safety meetings, departmental meetings, and so on.

Words & terms

In this context a **meeting** refers to a group of people (two or more) gathering to discuss a pre-planned list of items. These discussions are intended to achieve a particular purpose.

Protocol refers to the rules and procedures that people should follow to ensure, in this particular context, functional message exchange between two or more communicating persons. **Protocol** can also refer to the order in which people may speak.

The purpose of meetings

Meetings are about communication. They are also about learning and potentially about team building. Some of the main reasons that people call for meetings are as follows:

- To solve problems: Complex issues in organisations may involve a number of departments and require input from a variety of experts and disciplines in order to address or solve these issues.
- For decision-making: These meetings allow authorised people to come together to summarise options and make a decision about an issue or event.
- For post-mortems: These meetings are used to analyse the success, difficulty or failure of a project or activity in detail so that future successes can be designed and developed.
- For creating ideas: Meetings are a good forum for creative people to present their views and ideas. These ideas can be examined and discussed in a constructively critical light. Usually these meetings are very informal in order to encourage interaction and will involve brainstorming ideas and suggestions.
- For giving out information or briefing people: Some meetings are less about interaction and more a place where one person can share information with others. These meetings do not allow for feedback or

discussion so they can sometimes be ineffective and boring for those attending them.

- For progress reporting: These meetings are usually held to update various teams or team members on the progress of a particular project or work activity.
- Meetings that comply with legal or company requirements: These meetings are compulsory and are forums where important information is shared with others, such as health and safety meetings where important health and safety information is shared with a department in a company, or the Annual General Meeting that is open to share-holders and staff to inform them about how the company performed over the last year.

Learning activity 6.1

Do this activity in pairs.
1. Create a list of meetings held within your department and organisation, such as your college.
2. Indicate the following about each meeting:
    - the type (informal, formal, once-off or regular)
    - the purpose (problem-solving, decision making, post mortems, creating ideas, giving information, progress reports, legal)
Place this list in your portfolio of evidence.

Good meeting etiquette

Certain meetings are more formal than others, for example a Board Meeting, a Trade Union Meeting, and a disciplinary meeting will each be more formal and have stricter meeting procedures and processes than a creative brainstorming meeting.

There are certain things that you must do for most meetings, and more specifically for formal meetings. This behaviour is called etiquette and the following meeting etiquette should be encouraged in organisations:
- always arrive on time.
- if you are unable to attend the meeting send your apologies well before the meeting to let whoever is organising it know that you will not be attending it. Also, if you know you'll be late, also let them know beforehand; it is very rude to just not arrive or to arrive late.
- during the meeting listen to other people's points of view.
- participate and actively involve yourself in the process and discussions.
- do not speak over others or interrupt others while they are speaking.
- concentrate on what is going on during the meeting and do not do other work while you are in a meeting.
- do not have side conversations with others while the meeting is in progress.
- speak through the chairperson; this means that if you want to say something you need to ask the chairperson if you may do so and then wait for her or him to acknowledge you before you proceed. This is very important in large meetings, and the larger the meeting the more important this process becomes.

Learning activity 6.2

Do this activity in small groups.
1. Use the list of meetings in your department, organisation or college and draw up meeting protocol guidelines for these meetings. Use the SMART approach for conducting effective meetings. (See the 'Think about it' on this page)
2. Ask for permission to sit in on at least one of these meetings to get a better idea of the proceedings and how the meetings work. Some meetings may be confidential so you won't be able to sit in on them, but there should be some general meetings that you can attend.
File these guidelines in your portfolio as evidence.

A good method to follow when you conduct a meeting is the SMART approach. When you organise a meeting you want to achieve a specific outcome, such as sharing information, identifying alternatives, reaching a decision, or developing an action plan. One way to measure how practical your goals or aims are for the meeting, and how well you think you'll achieve them is to see if they are SMART goals, in other words are your goals:
- S – specific
- M – measurable
- A – attainable
- R – relevant
- T – time and resource based

This is a good method to see if you can achieve what you want to achieve in your meeting and then to see, after the meeting, if you did achieve this goal.

Unit 2:

The need and objectives of a meeting

This unit will describe ways to determine the need and objectives of a meeting.

How to determine the need for a meeting

It is important to know when you need to organise a meeting and when not to. Meetings take up a lot of time and involve many people. Because of this you must be sure before you call a meeting that it is more effective to call the relevant people together and discus or share information then to send the information out via email or letters.

- The items of information that need to be discussed and the formality needed for the discussion can determine whether or not to call a meeting.
- Meeting face-to-face is more effective than sending communication back and forth when you are dealing with colleagues, customers and suppliers and you want to get feedback form the sender right way or clear up any misunderstandings.
- Meeting face-to-face is also preferable if you need to share or communicate negative information. Written criticism often provokes stronger emotional reactions than oral discussions, so meeting to discuss bad news can often soften the impact of the news and it allows people to respond and to be heard.

Guidelines to help you decide on whether a meeting is the best way of addressing an issue or situation or not

DON'T have a meeting:	DO have a meeting:
• to share uncontroversial information that can be described in a memo, email or voice mail	• when the expertise or committee of several people is needed in order to make a decision or a plan
• to give the impression of involving people in a decision that has already been made without them	• when it will save time for many people in the long run
• when you should hold a performance discussion with one or two individuals	• if creativity is needed in order to solve a problem

Source: Personal Productivity: Tips and Tools for Daily Success

Alternatives to meetings

The following are alternatives to meetings that you might consider, especially when you need to share information that is uncontroversial and unlikely to lead to discussion:
- memos
- email memos
- corridor meetings
- phoning people
- having a telephone conference (this is similar to a meeting but it saves people having to leave their offices or travel to the meeting)

Did you know?

The skill of setting objectives is something you will get better at with experience. Part of setting objectives is to give those attending your meeting as much information as possible on why you have called the meeting and what you expect to accomplish. You will also want to set a clear timeline. This will help you to meet the objectives of the meeting more effectively since everyone will be prepared for it.

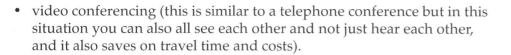

- video conferencing (this is similar to a telephone conference but in this situation you can also all see each other and not just hear each other, and it also saves on travel time and costs).

The purpose or objectives of meetings

The protocol for formal meetings is to have a written agenda that is sent out beforehand to all those attending so that they know what will be discussed in the meeting. The problem with agendas is they don't always state or make clear what the main objective of the meeting is. What is important to realise is that there are differences between meeting objectives and the meeting agenda, and these are:
- objectives define the desired outcome of the meeting; agendas define only the topics to be covered
- objectives give teams and groups something to strive for; agendas give them something to follow
- objectives call for active participation; agendas permit passivity.

How to determine the objectives of a meeting

The main thing is for you, or the person who called the meeting, to know what their main objectives are. You can then include these in the agenda if you wish, or else just make sure that as the meeting progresses, you are getting the information or outcome that you need to effectively achieve your objectives.
- If you have called a meeting then you must know what you want to achieve in that time.
- It is a good idea to write your objectives down and to clarify with attendees what they believe the purpose of the meeting is, and what your objectives are.
- You can communicate the main objective of your meeting when you send out the agenda or separately via e-mail or telephone.

Establishing the purpose of a meeting

In order to establish the purpose of a meeting the following are useful questions to consider and answer this question: Why are we meeting?
- Are we meeting to impart and receive information or facilitate learning? This is called an inform meeting; the focus is on content.

- Are we meeting to make a decision, resolve conflict or solve a problem? This is known as a form meeting. The focus is on identifying concerns and the resolution of conflict and problems.
- Are we meeting to complete a task? This is called a perform meeting. The focus is on working as a team to complete tasks.
- Are we meeting to maintain a routine or a standard image? This is called a conform meeting and the focus is on the status quo and allowing people to develop a sense of identity and unity.

In the workplace

Do the following to make meetings matter:
- eliminate unnecessary meetings
- use an agenda
- prepare
- set a time limit
- restrict the meeting to those whose participation is necessary
- before closing, summarise.

Ways to write out the objectives of a meeting

Writing out the objectives for a meeting helps everyone to understand its purpose. A meeting objective should have three parts: an action, an outcome, and qualifiers (if necessary).
- Actions: these are what groups can accomplish in a meeting and are described using words such as plan, develop, decide, determine, generate, identify, recommend, list, prioritise, solve, resolve, and so on.

When you write out the objective, start with an action word that describes what the group will do during the meeting. It must be something that can be observed.
- The outcome: this is what the product or result of that action will be. For example, in "Decide how to improve the use of our new telephone system", the action is: to decide, and the outcome is: to improve the use of our new telephone system.
- Qualifiers: objectives need additional words to clarify the focus of the meeting. These words are called qualifiers, and they describe the objective further and set important parameters, such as time frames. For example, if your objective is "Generate a list of ideas that will improve customer service and select the top two or three for immediate implementation", then the qualifiers are the words that specify that the ideas have to improve customer service, that the group has to select the top two or three ideas (not just one and not all of them), and that the two or three ideas that are selected have to be implemented immediately.

Source: Fran Rees: How To Lead Work Teams: Facilitation Skills

Guidelines for stating the objectives of meetings

There are guidelines that will help you state an objective in such a way that it is clear and so more likely to be met. These are:

- Be specific and concrete: state what needs to be done by when and where

- Be positive and optimistic: expect success and avoid using negatives like not and never.

- Be realistic and practical: set an objective that is attainable and measurable (use the SMART method to help you do this).

- Pose the objective of the meeting as a question rather than a command: the chairperson of the meeting can do this at the beginning of the meeting, and by doing this it encourages people to buy into it. Most people prefer to give answers than to follow orders.

- Confirm the objective of the meeting at the start: by confirming the objective of the meeting as the meeting starts you will ensure that all participants are clear in terms of what is required of them. If people stray off the topic the chairperson can remind people of the agreed upon objective.

Unit 3:

Reaching decisions in meetings

This unit will ensure that you understand the importance of reaching decisions in meetings.

Decision-making meetings

These are important meetings and it must be clear at the start of the meeting what is to be decided on. The following are good points to remember about these kinds of meetings:

- Before a decision is made, the Chairperson should ensure that everyone understands what the outcome will mean. For example, if a decision is made to hold a fundraising event it means that people will be responsible for organising the event and each of them must be clear on what their role in this is. When a decision is made, there are consequences and people must understand what they are making a decision on and what these consequences are.
- When participants reach decisions, the chairperson or facilitator will need to devote time to how they will implement those decisions. Thinking they are done, euphoria sets in, and participants fail to convert the decision to an action plan. Before participants leave the meeting, the facilitator should pin down action steps: Who is responsible for taking what action and by when? The decision-makers are responsible for putting what they have said into action and to commit to a time-line and a due-date that they will follow to make sure the changes are implemented.
- Good decision-making helps make good meetings, which in turn helps your organisation run more effectively. They can also save time.
- At the end of the meeting summarise the decisions that have been made, confirm with each person what their responsibility is from this point onwards to put the decision into action and clarify what the time lines are for all the work or changes to happen. This can take 5 or 10 minutes, but it is very important because it ties everything together and clarifies the objective, the solution and how it will be met.

Ways of reaching decisions in meetings

In some instances, if members don't attend a meeting, or don't submit their opinion in writing, they give up their voice in the decision making process and do not need to be consulted about the matter any further. In other instances, members who are absent must still be contacted to find out what their opinion or decision is before the final decision can be made. How decisions are made with or without members must be established before any decision-making meetings are held, and preferably when the group first comes about. You must:

- make an agreement about how to handle participation from people who do not attend a meeting. It can be very frustrating to delay a decision because one or more people missed the meeting.

Think about it

"The main thing people hate about meetings is that they are poorly run or don't accomplish anything. The purpose of a meeting is to make a decision, for example solving a problem or answering a query."

Source: Meeting Excellence: 33 Tools to Lead Meetings that Get Results by Glenn Parker.

Did you know?

The quorum is the minimum number of people required to be present at a meeting to make valid decisions. This is usually set out in the constitution of the company or organisation. An example can be that at least 50% of the total committee must be present for a decision that is made to be accepted. A meeting can be declared invalid if incorrect notice is given or if a quorum is not present.

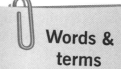

- decide how many people must be present to constitute a quorum. Establish this in your bylaws or other written agreements.
- Communicate all decisions made. Regardless of how decisions are taken, all delegates should be clear about exactly what has been decided and the decisions should be clearly formulated.
- encourage all members to participate. If everyone plays a role in determining the solution, each team member is more likely to be motivated to follow the project through to completion.
- make clear that each member shares a portion of the responsibility. No matter who came up with the final solution, the project is the property of the group. Everyone is accountable for the project's result. If anyone fails, everyone fails. This attitude creates a supportive system and encourages communication and responsibility.

There are two main ways that groups can make a final decision: either by votes (the majority decision is implemented), or by consensus, (all members must agree before a decision is made).

Decision-making by vote (the majority rule)

In this case, whatever the greatest number of people choose to do can be implemented, even if a few people don't agree. And this process makes sense when:
- many people are involved in the decision-making process.
- the group of members, or population, is very diverse.
- it is important that a decision is made and not delayed.
- the issues can be discussed thoroughly before the members cast their votes.
- the discussions consider a wide range of options and do not limit what people can vote for.

The disadvantages of this process are that:
- it leads to an all or nothing outcome.
- those whose votes were outnumbered may not support the final decision or outcome and may not be fully committed to implementing the changes.
- the concerns that were raised by those who were outvoted can now be disregarded, but this can lead to future problems if these concerns become a reality. Who is then accountable?
- if there is to much discussion around the issues then this can negatively affect the voting process. People might not be able to make a decision at all.
- this system is not good when a small group of people is meeting. In this instance it is better to work towards a consensus because then all the members will be committed to the final outcome.

Decision-making by consensus

Consensus happens when everyone agrees on something. It is the joint development of a decision that all group members accept and support. In a consensus each person involved in decision-making has veto power, which means that if one person does not agree then you do not have a consensus and no decision can be made. During this process:

- responsible team members should use their power only to achieve the best results for the group's purpose, and not for their own personal gain. In other words, if a team member objects, it is necessary for the others to find out why and give considerable thought to the concerns expressed by the disagreeing member. When you make a decision you have to think of what is best for the group and not for yourself.
- a common and remarkable result of giving individuals veto power is that they seldom use it! If participants are reassured that nothing can go forward without their approval, they tend to relax, and contribute more to the content and worry less about procedural matters.

Consensus does not mean there is an absence of conflict; it means that there is a commitment of time and energy to work through the conflict. Consensus requires taking all concerns into consideration and attempting to find the most universal decision possible that satisfies all members.

Factors working against consensus include: competition, individualism, passivity and solution-orientation.

Unit 4:

Managing discussions and problem solving

This unit will explain ways of managing discussions and problem solving.

Managing meetings

From the time that a meeting starts to when it ends it has to be managed, directed and controlled so that problems do not arise and that the objectives of the meeting are met, and that you keep to the scheduled running time of the meeting. There are certain things to take into account while you are managing a meeting and these are listed here.

- The role of the chairperson is to ensure that everyone stays on track with the process and to set an open, non-judgmental tone for the meeting. He or she is not there to force communication in any direction.
- When people come into a meeting they must not do so with an idea in mind and then try to win people over to their way of thinking. If this starts happening the leader or chairperson must manage this and allow each person to contribute equally to the discussion.
- The leader must make it clear that no one will be criticised for his or her ideas. The goal is to get as much input, ideas and data out of the group as possible.
- Remove insecurity and make sure all participants have the same key information and have the opportunity to discuss that information together in the meeting.
- If the direction of the meeting starts to wander, frame the dilemma so that participants see the big picture and recognise their interdependence. You could ask, "What decision do we need to make and why do we need to make it?" You can refer to the mission and purpose of the group for guidance: "If we do this, are we in line with what we are all about?"
- Build little agreements along the way:
- "So we agree that this is a good way to state the problem we are trying to solve."
- "Do we at least all agree that something has to be done, and that things are unacceptable as they are now?"
- Motivate creativity by asking, "Is there anything else you can suggest?" and then allow for a long pause to give others the chance to reply.
- Summarise and fractionate as the meeting goes along,
- "This is what we agree on, and this is still in question. What are the specific causes for concern?"
- "How can we get the benefit from doing this, but not the detriment?"

Solving problems that arise during meetings

Any number of problems can arise during meetings, and as the meeting leader you have to be able to manage these. Some possible problems are discussed here as well as possible solutions to these problems.

Exceeding time limits

Each meeting should run within an allocated amount of time.
- To help manage the time properly, allocate sections of the meeting time to discuss the various items on the agenda. If each issue has no clear discussion time, people tend to ramble on while they discuss the first few items and by the time the meeting ends the full agenda has not been worked through.
- It is very important to stay on schedule; to do this you can time individual presentations.
- Make sure all the speakers know in advance that someone will time each presentation and signal them when their time runs out.

Dealing with very complex issues

Sometimes you will be faced with very complex problems or situations to deal with. When this happens you must use your common sense, your experience, and your knowledge of everyone in the meeting to decide what to do.
- You might decide it is best to postpone the rest of the meeting until the issue has been looked into and dealt with.
- You might decide it is best to carry on with the meeting, and make a note of the issue and then resolve it outside of the meeting in the most appropriate way possible.

Whatever you choose to do, remember that it is better to delay something than to go ahead knowing that there is potential conflict, cost or problem that will arise because of the decision that was made.

Deviating from the topic

If discussions in meetings do not cover the topic then none of the objectives will be met. To stop this you must:
- keep conversations focused on the topic.
- feel free to ask for only constructive and non- repetitive comments.
- tactfully end discussions if they are getting nowhere or becoming destructive or unproductive.

Managing conflict

During meetings, members should never get into an argument, or even a direct discussion, with each other. If a confrontation begins between two members, the chairperson should remind everyone to address all remarks to the chairperson and not to each other. Sometimes tempers flare and people are emotional so, as a chairperson, it is expected that in these situations you consider the following:
- use humour to diffuse the situation,
- find a way to agree even if it is only partially,
- use 'and' instead of 'but'. The use of 'but' creates an either/or situation and discounts others' positions and views.
- focus on the behaviour and the issue and not on the person.

- use an "I message", for example "I can see that you feel passionate/ angry/upset. I just want to check that I am getting the correct facts. Could you please list the main facts for me again so I can make sure I am following you?"
- focus on the here and now. We cannot change the past but we can change how we respond to the present and the future.
- use the FOCUS model outlined in "Making Meetings Work" by Karen Anderson, namely:
  - What are the **f**eelings about the situation?
  - What are the **o**bjections or concerns?
  - What are the **c**onsequences?
  - What would **u**topia be?
  - What **s**atisfaction are you looking for?

Dealing with one person dominating the meeting

The purpose of most meetings is to encourage discussion and interaction and to work as a team. It can be a problem if one person dominates the discussion and has undue influence over the outcome.
- At the start of a meeting make the process you want to follow clear and ask for everyone's support.
- Propose ground rules for the meeting, such as "Everyone will have a chance to speak, no one must repeat what he or she has already said, and everyone's opinion should be heard."
- Some people need to be encouraged to share their views. You'll accomplish better results with the whole team pulling the discussion than with one dominant person trying to push everyone else to speak.
- State up front the "non-purposes" of the meeting, or what participants are not there to discuss or decide.
- If you have an idea that one person might dominate the meeting, talk to him or her before the meeting starts. You can say, for example, "I know you're eager to share your opinions, but I'm not sure everyone else will be as comfortable, especially when they hear you speak with so much passion. Can you help get others to talk more?"
- Discourage inappropriate behaviour from others. For example, cut off those who interrupt. You could say "I understand that you disagree but let Sheila finish what she was saying before we discuss it."

Handling an unfocused meeting

A good way to prevent an unfocused meeting is to involve participants in creating the agenda in advance so they will agree that the topics are important. Also, make sure that the topics in the agenda are not too broad. Once the meeting begins, keep a copy of the agenda in front of you as well as a watch so that you can keep track of the schedule , the time, and make sure that the topics are discussed and the meeting does not lose focus. It is the job of the meeting leader or chairperson to keep the meeting focused.

Handling inaccurate minutes

Prevent inaccurate minutes by sending out draft minutes as soon after the meeting as possible and ask those who attended the meeting for their input. Once the input has been incorporated, send out the final version of the minutes. For both these steps, set a timeframe that makes sense for the complexity of what was discussed and decided at the meeting. If it takes to long to finalise the minutes they can become inaccurate.

Dealing with bad manners

There is never a good reason for anyone to behave badly during a meeting. To prevent people from behaving in an inappropriate way you can do the following:
- have the meeting off-site to minimise distractions.
- set and post ground rules about meeting behaviour.
- include breaks so participants can make phone calls, get coffee, use the rest room, and so on.
- hold the meeting at a time suitable to everyone.

Words & terms

Minutes are an instant written record of a meeting. They often give an overview of the structure of the meeting, starting with a list of those present, a statement of the various issues before the participants, and each of their responses thereto. The minutes of certain entities, such as a corporate board of directors, must be kept and are important legal documents.

Learning activity 6.3

Do this activity on your own.
As a chairperson you are required to encourage and promote discussion and participation.
1. Rephrase the following responses so that they will be less likely to inhibit discussion:
   - That idea will never work!
   - You have talked too much already. Give someone else a chance!
   - Forget it! We tried it before and failed.
   - Management will never agree to that!
   - You are so caught up in the details you forget about the big picture!
   - Let's stop beating about the bush and come up with some real solutions.
2. Select one of the phrases and draw two scenarios – one in which the new phrase is used and one in which the old one is used. Use your drawing to show how the reaction to the phrase would differ.

Unit 5:

Determine delegates

This unit will describe ways to determine the appropriate delegates for a meeting.

Who should attend meetings?

Deciding who should attend a meeting depends on what you want to accomplish in the meeting. This may seem obvious to you, but it's surprising how many meetings occur without the right people there. Don't only depend on your own opinion about who should come, ask several other people involved in the decision or project who they feel should attend; this way you are less likely to leave anyone out. Here is a list of things to keep in mind when you are thinking about who should attend a meeting.

- If someone who has important information or strong feelings does not know about the meeting and cannot attend he or she may feel left out.
- Those invited to attend the meeting should be those who need to be informed about the topics, who are affected by the issues, who will be able to contribute to the required outcomes, and are who authorised to make decisions or speak for those who are.
- There is no need to waste the time of people who will not get any noticeable benefits or give any relevant help in a particular meeting.
- On the other hand, you could invite an additional person or people who could provide some helpful expertise, insights, or first hand facts relevant to the meeting's objectives.

It is important that the decisions taken during a meeting are within the authority of participants otherwise the meeting has been a waste of time for all concerned and it is de-moralising for participants. This is why it is important to know from the outset what the objectives of the meeting are since this governs who will be invited to attend the meeting. For example, there is no point inviting the Sales Team to a meeting about the long-term financial viability of a venture if they do not have the authority to make financial decisions concerning the organisation as a whole.

Criteria of those invited to a meeting

According to a book called "*How to hold successful meetings*" people invited to a meeting must meet the following criteria:
- They must have some expertise about the issue or project to be discussed.
- They must have some involvement or invested interest in the outcome of the discussion.
- They must be skilled in the group decision-making process and appreciate diversity of opinions.
- They should share the overall values of the organisation. It makes no sense to include people in decision-making that affects these goals.

Tips to help you choose who to invite to a meeting

You can ask yourself the following questions to help you make sure you have invited the right people to attend the meeting:

- What is the purpose of the meeting? Is the purpose to brainstorm new ideas, make an important decision, or to gather information and provide feedback to managers, and so on?
- Who has the authority to make decisions?
- Is certain expertise required about the issue or project being discussed? If so, have I invited these people?
- Who will be affected by the outcome of the meeting? Have I invited these people?

How many people should attend a meeting?

It is important to match the number of attendees to the objectives of the meeting, and to make sure that you have enough people to achieve the outcome of the meeting, such as a quorum, or all the relevant authorities to make a decision.

A useful guide of how many people to include in different kinds of meetings includes:

- for decision-making meetings – invite a maximum of 15 people.
- for a brain-storming meeting – invite a maximum of 30 people, unless attendees are broken up into smaller groups.
- for skill building meetings – invite a maximum of 20 people.

Remember that the larger the group, the longer the meeting will probably last.

Conduct a meeting

Conduct a meeting in a structured and effective manner.

In this module you will ...

- arrange a meeting and compile an agenda
- inform the delegates about the meeting
- structure a meeting in accordance with the protocols (select a chairperson, minute taker, etc.)
- run a meeting to achieve the objectives within the timeframe

Unit 6:

Arrange a meeting and compile an agenda

The best way to ensure a productive meeting is to plan, plan, plan!

Planning a meeting

To ensure the success of a meeting you must plan it well and well in advance. The following guidelines will help you with your meeting planning.

- Schedule the meeting as far in advance as possible.
- Announce in advance the time, date, and place of the meeting.
- Hand out a copy of the agenda to those attending the meeting and any other materials they might need at least 48 hours before the meeting.
- Avoid having the meeting during peak productivity times, such as Tuesday through to Thursday mornings. Karen Anderson, the author of "Making Meetings Work" suggests that the hours before lunch or quitting time are the best times to have meetings because people are more likely to work through the agenda without wasting time, since they lose out on their own time if they delay things.
- Make sure that the venue you have chosen is set up before the meeting starts. If possible, book a room that is slightly bigger than you need, and has comfortable chairs, and so that the room does not get cramped or stuffy during the meeting. Make sure you have all that you and the others need for the meeting ready, such as notepads, pens and pencils.
- Arrange all equipment that you might need, such as an overhead projector, and test it before the meeting,
- Make extra copies of the agenda and all handouts and have them with you before the meeting starts. Don't assume that people will remember to bring this material.
- Decide how to handle meeting processes (such as brainstorming, tracking decisions and action items, voting, and so on) so that the time can be spent productively.
- No part of the meeting should last longer than two hours.
- Breaks must be taken away from the room so that people get a good break.
- Arrange refreshments to be served or to be available during the breaks.
- Arrange that there be no interruptions during the meeting and ensure that there is quiet outside the room where the meeting is being held. You can put a sign on the door asking for people to be quiet if necessary.

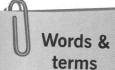

Words & terms

An **agenda** is an order of events at a formal meeting or a list of items to be discussed or acted upon. Items on an agenda are often listed in an order that facilitates the flow of the discussion or flow of work that must be done.

Setting up the venue

The seating arrangement and room set-up is very important to plan. Different seating arrangements work best for different types of meetings and the style of seating has an impact on the levels of participation.

- If possible, arrange the room so that members face each other. For example, put the chairs and tables in a circular or semi-circular shape. For large groups, try U-shaped rows.
- You can use the guidelines for recommended seating arrangements in the table below to help you plan your seating:

Table 1: Setting up a venue

Style of seating	Room Size	Group Size	Primary function
Conference	Small	Small	Inform/Perform
U-Shape	Small/Medium	Small	Inform/Form
Circle	Small/Medium	Small/Medium	Inform/Form/Conform
Pod	Medium	Medium +	Form/Perform
Classroom	Medium	Large	Inform/Conform
Chevron	Medium	Large	Inform/Conform
Theatre	Medium	Large	Inform/Conform

For a good overview of seating arrangements revise what you learnt in Topic 4 of Level 2, "Prepare, service and clean function rooms."

Learning activity 6.4

Do this activity on your own.
You are required to arrange a meeting. Decide what the objective of the meeting would be.
1. Write down the objective of the meeting.
2. Use the list provided to create a checklist to help you with the logistics of the meeting.
3. Identify and tick off all the items that you will need for the meeting, according to what you have planned in the agenda and to meet the objectives of the meeting.
Attach the checklist to the agenda and file them in your portfolio of evidence.

Items for possible inclusion in a meeting checklist

Room/Amenities

chalkboard/white board/eraser	camera/film
table(s), chairs	paper/pencils/pens/markers
room arrangements	bulletin board
electrical outlets	thumbtacks, tape, prestik
temperature regulation	note cards
lighting	phone availability
try out equipment	rest rooms

Refreshments

stairs/elevators

access to building/room

smoking area

parking facilities

wastepaper bin

food/beverages

cups/dishes/utensils/napkins

coffee/tea/hot water dispenser

water jugs & glasses

Materials/Directions for participants
Equipment/Tools

handouts/agenda copies

video monitor and player

flip chart(s)

tape recorder

overhead projector

computer

network connection

pre-work created/distributed

name tags

directions to meeting place

confirmation of attendance

previous minutes/decisions/reports

how to get phone messages

slide projector/screen

Get myself prepared

extension cords

podium

microphone

check out PA system

preview materials

post flip charts/material

Source: Adapted from "Personal Productivity: Tips and Tools for Daily Success"

The Agenda

As you have learnt, an agenda is a very important meeting tool that must be well written, well planned out and sent out to inform all those who are to attend the meeting what they will be discussing or doing during the meeting.

The aim of a written agenda

The aim of an agenda is to:
- confirm the time, duration, date and place of the forthcoming meeting.
- give members prior warning of what will be discussed at the meeting.
- guide members through the meeting, indicating subjects that will be discussed and the order in which they will be discussed.
- state clearly who will be leading discussion on specific issues.
- present a manageable list of items that can be adequately discussed in the time available.

Writing an agenda in advance, when you are planning your meeting helps you to make sure that you have a realistic amount to work to get through in the time given, and that the discussion will be focused.

Also, by asking different people who will attend the meeting to lead the discussion around that issue it helps to ensure that these people will be prepared and so lead to a more efficient discussion of each issue. Also, it will encourage more conversation and involvement on the part of others.

How to compile an agenda

An agenda can and should be drawn up with the involvement of other key participants who will be at the meeting. That way you will be sure to include all the relevant issues and state them clearly.

- Agendas have a standard format that you must follow, and this format depends on the type of meeting that it is for.
- An agenda should start off covering the easier items first so that a good rapport can be established and then you can move on to discuss the more difficult items.
- Develop a standard process and format for creating the agenda for regular meetings so that the attendees won't have to repeatedly discuss how to do it or how to read it. You can do this is various ways, such as:
  - through voice mail, e-mail, or a team bulletin board: the leader or assigned team member should urgently request agenda items before each meeting.
  - by asking people to submit an item for the agenda item in advance: they must include a brief description of what they want discussed, the amount of time needed to cover it, and the name of the person who will lead that part of the discussion.
  - having the first item on the agenda: "Changes or Additions to the Agenda": this allows attendees to re-prioritise items if they need to and it prevents the group from running short of time since time will be allocated for this to be discussed if it needs to be .

The format of an agenda

The format for the agenda for different kinds of meetings will change slightly but there is a basic format and order that you must follow whenever you draw up an agenda. It is as follows:

- State the name of the meeting, for example Sales Meeting, Annual General Board Meeting, Safety Meeting.
- State the time, date, and place for the meeting: it is a good idea to include the starting and ending time of the meeting, since this allows people to plan the rest of their day and allows those who are planning the meeting a timeframe in which to work.
- State who must be present at the meeting: this is a list of the core group of people who must attend the meeting as well as any other people who have been specially invited to attend to participate in discussion or decision-making. These people can be given time slots during which they can attend. That way you won't waste their time talking about issues that do not involve them. The core people must be present for the full meeting.
- State that those who will be absent from the meeting must send you their apologies letting you know they won't be there. This is important because some items on the agenda may need particular people to be present and if they are unable to attend then you might have to remove certain items for discussion from the agenda.
- Include the minutes of the last meeting: people attending the meeting must read the minutes of the previous meeting before the forthcoming meeting so that the previous meeting's minutes can be confirmed.

- State the matters arising: these are usually matters from previous meetings. These are not included to discuss or debate these matters further, but to allow the group to follow up on the actions that should have been taken in the interim.
- Include a list of routine business: a certain number of routine items arise in every meeting and it is a good idea to have these typed up and circulated with the agenda.
- State the non-routine items: these are items that have arisen in the interim that require discussion and / or decision-making during the meeting. These are included so that people know what is expected of them during the meeting.
- State any other business (AOB): there may be one or two items for discussion that will arise after the preparation of the agenda and before the meeting. This is the where these items can be included in the agenda.
- State the date, time and place of the next meeting.

An example of an agenda

Agenda

Meeting of the Funny Fruity Caterers

Date: Friday, April 11, 2008.
Time: from 9:30 to 13:30.
Venue: Orange Conference Room, Funny Fruity Caterers.

To be present:
D. Langa (Chair)
B. Whitherspoon (Secretary)
S.J. Quinn
U. Figgo
A. Barnaby
B.S. Naidoo (from 12:15 to 12:40)
R. Khumalo (from 11:00 to 11:30)

• Apologies for absence	
• Minutes of the last meeting	10 mins
• Matters arising	20 mins
• Report of finance committee (routine)	30 mins
• Report of the catering sub-committee (routine)	30 mins
• Report re Fruit and Veg, Ltd. Takeover (non-routine) (Descriptive paragraph detailing the purpose of discussion and desired outcome, decision, recommendations, and so on. The information in this paragraph is to brief all attendees and make clear what is expected of them).	110 mins
• Report re company stationery (non-routine) (Descriptive paragraph detailing the purpose of the discussion, the desired outcome, decision, recommendations, and so on. The information in this paragraph is to brief all attendees and make clear what is expected of them).	25 mins
• Any other business (AOB)	10 mins
• Date, time and place of next meeting	5 mins

Distributing the agenda

The agenda and its attachments should ideally be sent out a week before the meeting is to be held, but you can send it out 48 hours ahead of the meeting if that's all the time you have. This gives people enough time to read the attached reports, the briefing papers and minutes from previous meetings before the meeting. By sending the agenda out in advance you allow enough time for attendees to contact you with any queries they may have and to incorporate any additional issues or points that need to be brought up at the meeting on the agenda.

It is also a good idea to send out an e-mail reminder, or to phone people to remind them about the meeting closer to the time and make sure that they are prepared.

Learning Activity 6.5

Do this activity in pairs.
1. Source copies of agendas for various meetings held within your organisation, department or college. These could be, for example, safety meetings, departmental meetings, Board meetings, and so on.
2. Familiarise yourself with the format of each of the agendas and write a short description explaining what you think the objective of each meeting was.
File what you have written and the agendas in your portfolio.

Learning activity 6.6

Do this activity on your own.
1. Draw up a sample agenda for a forthcoming staff departmental meeting using the following items as a guideline:
   • Incidents or accidents and customer complaints (routine)
   • Induction of new staff (non-routine)
   • Briefing staff on takeover bid by competitor (non-routine)
   • Work schedule and overtime roster (routine)

Inform the delegates about the meeting

Informing delegates

To organise a successful meeting you must make sure that all your delegates are well informed.

- Notify members well enough in advance so that they can plan their work schedules around the meeting.
- If possible, phone each person to tell them about the meeting, what the purpose of the meeting is and why it is important that they attend the meeting.
- Follow up your call with a meeting notice that clearly explains the purpose of the meeting, where it will be held and when, who will be attending the meeting and who they can contact if they have any questions. Send out a copy of the proposed agenda and other documents along with the meeting notice.
- Make sure that you have informed all the participants who have to attend the meeting and check that they can all make it. If some critical staff members can't attend the meeting you might have to postpone it, and the sooner you know to do this the better.
- If a crucial decision maker or person of authority cannot attend, and another delegate attends in their place, make sure you know who this person is and verify that he or she has the authority to make decisions. If not, you will have to postpone the meeting.
- Always confirm appointments the day before. Leave nothing to chance.

Whoever takes the minutes of previous meetings must also be kept informed so that they can prepare the previous minutes in time to be sent out with the agenda for the next meeting.

Meeting notices

A good way of keeping all the delegates informed is to send out a meeting notice before the next meeting

Reasons for sending out a meeting notice

Meeting notices:
- let all attendees know in advance what is expected of them before the meeting so they are more likely to come prepared for the meeting.
- let all attendees know what they need to bring to the meeting so they are more likely to have what they need at the meeting.
- prevent time being wasted because they ensure that inadequate information is provided to all delegates before the meeting.

What must be included in a meeting notice?

The following must be included in a meeting notice:
- a full list of attendees
- the name of who called the meeting
- the date and time (beginning and ending) of the meeting
- the meeting venue; remember to include directions to the venue if necessary
- the meeting objective
- who to confirm attendance to
- the agenda
- a list of what information or material to take to the meeting
- what material to read before the meeting
- any necessary attachments
- the name of who will be taking the minutes so that he or she knows to come prepared with pen and paper or computer
- the name of who will be keeping time during the meeting so that he or she will come prepared with a watch or timer.

Distributing meeting notices

Meeting notices must be distributed in sufficient time before the meeting to be effective. There is no point going to all the work putting together the meeting notice if you send it out the day before because no-one will have time to go through it. The meeting notice must be distributed in sufficient time for attendees to:
- fit the meeting into their schedules.
- do the preparatory work.
- inform you if they can't make it and then give you enough time to reschedule the meeting.
- ask questions in advance of meeting.

Unit 8:

Structure a meeting

This unit will enable you to structure a meeting in accordance with the protocols.

Choosing a Chairperson

A chairperson is usually chosen according to the type of meeting. For example there is little point asking the receptionist to chair a meeting of the Board of Directors – she probably does not have the skills or sufficient knowledge to accomplish this task.

It is therefore important to consider the following when you are choosing a chairperson:
*   Does the person have the required level of skills to chair this level of meeting?
*   Is the person a good facilitator, harmoniser, listener and leader for this group of people?
*   Does the person have the required knowledge to chair the meeting?
*   Is the person aware of, and clearly able to, state the objectives of the meeting?

The qualities of a Chairperson

In order to choose the correct chairperson for a meeting, you must know what you are looking for in a chairperson. The following are qualities of an effective chairperson, meeting leader or facilitator:
*   objectiveness: he or she must be able to see things from a number of perspectives
*   knowledgeable, but not an expert
*   a good co-ordinator
*   a firm decision maker
*   a good and aware listener: they must be aware of those who are not speaking as well as those who are
*   be able to clarify meeting objectives
*   be responsive to the needs of the meeting and the attendees
*   be able to draw information of out people by asking questions or encouraging people to talk
*   be a harmoniser
*   be a leader.

The responsibilities of a Chairperson

Being a chairperson means being responsible and accountable for the following:
*   keeping the meeting focused on the subject at hand whilst being responsive to the needs of the people at the meeting
*   ensuring the objectives of the meeting are met within the allocated time
*   ensuring that people understand what is being said by paraphrasing and summarising information

- reminding the attendees of their obligations and the level of confidentiality of what is being discussed if necessary
- managing the discussion and encouraging involvement
- fostering an environment that is conducive to promoting discussion and open communication between participants
- encouraging involvement in meetings by doing the following:
- invite participants to provide options rather than advice. For example, "Have you thought of …" works better than "I think you should …".
- building in reflection time or quiet time that allows participants to think
- recognising emotions and body language. For example during discussion you see Miranda shaking her head so you say: "Miranda, you are shaking your head. Would you like to share with us what you are thinking?" or "I see that a number of people are shaking their heads in disagreement, would someone like to share what they are thinking with the group?"
- interpreting silences: silence does not always mean consent
- asking whether the group has any questions, concerns or suggestions
- asking the group to determine the best action plan, including specific tasks; the people responsible for these tasks and the time frame in which these must be completed
- focusing on mutual gain, let people know that they all have an interest in the outcome of the meeting
- dividing the meeting into smaller groups to discuss issues
- asking members of the team to prepare in advance for specific items on the agenda.

The benefits of rotating the role of chairperson

For regular team meetings, it is a good idea to rotate leadership duties because this:
- builds leadership skills throughout the team
- increases awareness of the how demanding chairing a meeting can be
- avoids overburdening one member of the team with these duties.

The person responsible for taking minutes

Meetings would be ineffective without well-taken minutes because there would be no record of what was said and what decisions were made. The minute taker is a very important person in any meeting and he or she is responsible for keeping accurate records of all the interactions, discussions and decisions made during meetings.
- In partnership with the meeting's Chairperson, the minute taker holds the key to transforming what could otherwise be general discussions into precise action plans, by producing short, sharp minutes that accurately record and clarify the meeting's objectives, decisions and "to do" lists.
- These everlasting and unchangeable records help organisations learn from past successes and challenges, and are vital to prevent arguments and who people avoiding accountability.
- As a general rule the more formal and larger the size of the meeting, the less likely participants will be responsible for minute taking. For

example during a disciplinary inquiry the person responsible for the minutes will not be anyone involved in the case. In this situating there will be a designated minute taker to record the proceedings.

- If an informal meeting is taking place between colleagues, one of the participants can be responsible for recording the discussion, the decisions taken and the actions to be taken and who is responsible for these.

To help you work out if you need a designated minute taker in a meeting or if one of the attendees can take the minutes, look at this able:

	Question	Answer	Action
1	Are verbatim minutes required?	Yes	It is recommended that an outsider who does not participate in the process to take minutes.
2	Are narrative minutes required?	Yes	Minutes can be taken either by the chairperson, a member of the meeting or third party.
3	Are resolution or decision minutes required?	Yes	Either the chairperson or a member of the meeting can note decisions taken.
4	Are action minutes required?	Yes	Either the chairperson or a member of the meeting can note actions and who has volunteered to fulfil these actions.
5	Is the meeting small and short?	Yes	The chairperson or a member of the meeting can probably manage to take minutes.
6	Will taking minutes distract the person from participating in the meeting?	Yes	It is preferable to get a third party who is not a decision-maker to take minutes.

Source: www.theta.co.za

Other meeting roles

There are some other roles that people must perform in a meeting in order to ensure that it runs smoothly and is efficient.

- A role is a specific job, such as Chairperson or minute taker.
- When you create process roles you must write down the duties that this person must fulfil and explain what your expectations are of the person taking on this role.
- Most groups use a combination of roles during a meeting, for example:
- the vibes watcher: looks for feelings such as anger or frustration and monitors how people in the group are treating one another
- the turn keeper: keeps track of the order in which people indicated they want to participate
- the time keeper:
- keeps track of how much time has been spent on an issue
- advises the group when time allotted for an agenda item is up
- notifies the group when the agreed upon discussion, action, or announcement portions of the meeting are about to expire
- notifies the group of beginning and ending times of the meeting
- and if necessary, indicates to a speaker that their allotted time is about to expire.
- the door keeper: sits near the door and informs late comers what the current status of the meeting is and what has been discussed so far.

Unit 9:

Run a meeting

This unit will cover the skills required to run a meeting to achieve the objectives within the timeframe.

How to meet meeting objectives

One of the most difficult tasks in a meeting is managing time. Too often time seems to run out before tasks are completed. In time management the biggest challenges are keeping momentum up and keeping the process moving, and achieving the set objectives within the available timeframe. The following list shows you ways to organise or facilitate meetings so that they meet objectives.

- Choose an appropriate meeting time. Set a time limit and stick to it, as much as possible. Remember, members have other commitments and they will be more likely to attend meetings if they know they will be productive, predictable and as short as possible.
- Always make meetings that you organise or facilitate worthwhile. This will ensure better quality decisions are made and those attending will be more motivated
- Don't overload the agenda and set a duration for each item in the agenda. Together these short periods should total the overall meeting timeframe.
- Start all meetings on time. Don't wait for latecomers and don't go back and review what has already been covered for latecomers. This prioritises the late comers and wastes the time of those people who arrived on time
- Ask attendees to help you keep track of the time. It's amazing how often people will complain about a meeting being a complete waste of time, but they only say so after the meeting. Get their feedback during the meeting when you can improve the meeting process right away.

Keep evaluating meetings as they progress. If you evaluate a meeting only at the end it is then too late to do anything about participants' feedback. To do this you can have 5 to 10 minutes of "satisfaction checks" every hour or two hours have to see how the meeting is going and if each participant feels that progress is being made.

Remember that the chairperson plays a very important role in managing meetings and making sure that the meeting objectives are met within the allocated time.

The role of the chairperson to achieve the objectives in the given time

As a chairperson:
- Make sure that the most important issues are given the most amount of discussion time and make time for opening and closing comments. Participants will appreciate that you've set such a clear structure and

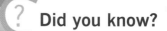

> **? Did you know? ?**
>
> The four most important factors that help ensure effective meetings are:
> - open communication
> - task focus
> - a systematic approach
> - timeliness.

that you have are in control of the time schedule. This will reassure them that the meeting will progress at a suitable pace.
- If something comes up that needs to go beyond the preset timeframe, simply eliminate one of the other topics of discussion or agree to meet at another time to continue the discussion.

If there are smaller group discussions or tasks during a meeting, it is a good idea is to ask members of the small groups to stand up when they are done. This gives members a chance to stretch their legs, it encourages slower groups to finish quickly and let's you know when you can continue with the rest of the meeting.

Think about it

It's amazing how often meetings are set with a start time, but no end time. Setting up a meeting without establishing an end time is asking for a time management disaster. These meetings can end up taking the most of the day.

Learning activity 6.7

Do this part of the activity in 5 groups.
1. Each group takes on one of the provided scenarios and creates a role play.
2. Before starting the role plays, discuss what will be used to assess the management of the meeting. As a group decide which aspects of the management of the meeting are more important than others
3. In each group one person will manage the meeting and the other group members will be attending the meeting. The 'attendees' will evaluate how well they think their meeting was managed.
   - A performance appraisal where you are raising points of concern with staff around performance
   - An informal meeting with colleagues
   - A departmental meeting
   - A meeting with an external supplier to discuss quality and service issues
   - A safety meeting

If there is time, groups can swap scenarios and another student in each group can take on the role of meeting leader.

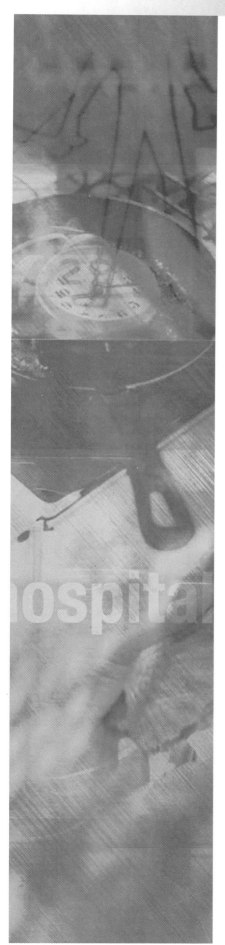

Module 8

Completion of actions

Complete and/or monitor the completion of actions arising from the meetings conducted.

In this module you will ...

* ensure that all documentation is complete and circulated after the meeting (for example, minutes, attendance, etc.)
* suggest ways to make meetings more effective.

Unit 10:

Documentation

This unit will ensure that all documentation is complete and circulated after the meeting.

Types of minutes

There are different types of minutes taken depending on how much information needs to be recorded.

- Verbatim minutes are a word-for-word recording of everything said in a meeting. These are used in inquiries, such as a taking a statement in an accident inquiry or during a disciplinary hearing.
- Narrative minutes give a fuller account of the meeting in that they include the discussions leading up to a decision.
- Resolution or decision minutes record the decisions taken at the meeting only.
- Action minutes are used to ensure that members of the meeting are reminded of actions that they have volunteered to take or that have been delegated to them. They often include the timeframe in which the required task needs to be carried out.

Source: www.theta.co.za

How to take minutes

Minutes can be taken or recorded in any way that ensures an accurate record of the meeting. Then they are typed up so that they can be distributed to all the meeting participants as soon after the meeting as possible.

- Minutes are usually taken during a meeting by a typist or they are handwritten using shorthand, and typed up after the meeting before being distributed. Alternatively, the meeting may be recorded and the minutes typed later.
- Minutes serve as a record of the discussion that has taken place, the decisions taken and the actions implemented for future reference. It is therefore the responsibility of the person taking minutes to ensure that they have accurately captured and recorded the meeting.
- Minutes must be typed and sent out soon after the meeting. A delay in distributing the minutes can affect the accuracy of the information as well as delay the outcomes of the meetings because many people wait for the minutes to arrive before they begin to tackle their commitments.
- Studying the agenda before the meeting will help the minute-taker know what to expect in the meeting and what kinds of minutes are required. He or she can then focus on the job at hand rather and know what important items to listen out for. This will help improve the accuracy of the minutes.
- The following practical suggestions should assist you in taking minutes:
- For each heading in the agenda have a corresponding heading in the minutes.

- Write a summary of the agenda item in one to two paragraphs, taking note of discussion, actions and the responsible person. It must be clear in the minutes what was decided, what must be done, and, most importantly, who must do the job or task.

Ensuring the accuracy of minutes

To ensure that you, or the minute-taker, takes accurate minutes do the following:
- note what is said each time the chairperson summarises each item on the agenda during the meeting.
- type up and distribute the minutes within 48 hours of the meeting. The participants can then read through the minutes and give you feedback while the information is still fresh in everyone's minds. This is the best way to ensure that any inaccuracies are brought to your attention, or to the attention of the minute-taker.
- Make sure that accuracy of the minutes is verified at the next meeting and any changes are agreed to and implemented.

Guidelines for writing up minutes

There are certain guidelines to follow when you write up minutes, such as:
- Separate each paragraph by a one-line space.
- In decision minutes clearly identify the decision by being starting the phrase with "It was decided..."
- Actions points are identified by the word action, and having a blank right hand column, known as the action column. In this column you can fill in the surname and initials of the person who has volunteered or been volunteered to do the task.

The advantages of using a clear method are:
- that a reader can effectively scan the minutes in 30 seconds since the clear format makes the minutes easier to read.
- that no matter how long the minutes are, the person can quickly follow discussion, see the actions required and what decisions were taken.
- that a reader can flip through the pages, checking in the following order:
- any occurrence of his or her name in the action column
- every other name in the action column
- all the decisions taken at the meeting.

Distributing minutes

As you have already learnt, minutes should ideally be distributed within 48 hours of the meeting. This allows people to distinguish between a discussion that happened in the meeting and discussion that arose after the meeting. Minutes should be distributed to all attendees and those who sent their apologies. The following can be appended (attached) to minutes at the time of distribution if necessary:
- reports
- diagrams and statistical charts
- photographs.

An example of meeting minutes

Place of meeting: [place]
Date and time: [day, month, year] at [time].
Directors Present: [Name, Name, Name]:
Others present: [other Names, e.g. company secretary]
Absent: [Mention if there is a reason for absence]

Follow-up action	Person	Date
Next meeting	All	Date, time, place (if it changes)
A description of any action that someone committed to work on or complete before the next meeting	The person or group who committed to the action	Date and time for completion or ASAP, soon, or next week.

Agenda
- Xxxx xxxxx xxxxxxx xxxx
- Xxxxxxx xxxxxxxxx xxxx xxxx

Discussion, decisions, assignments
First agenda item. Xxxxxxxxxxxxxxxxxxxxxxxxxxxxxxxxxxxxxxxxxxxxxxxxxxxx
Xxxxxxxxxxxxxxxxxxxxxxxxxxxxxxxxxxxxxxx. Xxxxxxxxxxxxxxxxxxxxxxxxxxxxxx. Xx xxxxxxxx
xxxxxxxxxxxxxxxxxxxxxxxxxxxxxxxxxxxxxxxx.

Second agenda item. Xxxxxxxxxxxxxxxxxxxxxxxxxxxxxxxxxxxxxxx. Xxxxxxxxxxxxxx
xxxxxxxxxxxxxxxxxxxxxxxxxxxxxxxxxxxxxxx. Xxxxxxxxxxxxxxxxxxxxxxxxxxxxxxxxxxxx
xxxxxxxxxxxxxxxxxx.

Additional items. Xxxxxxxxxxxxxxxxxxxxxxxxxxxxxxx. Xxxxxxxxxxxxxxxxxxxxxxxxxxxxx
xxxxxxxxxxxxxxxxxxxxxxxxxxxxxxxxxxxxxxxxxxxxxxxx. Xxxxxxxxxxxxxxxxxxxxxxxxxxx.

Tentative agenda for the next meeting
- Xxxxxxxxxxxxxxx Xxxxx Xxxxxxxxxxx
- Xxxxxxxxxx Xxxxxxxxxxxx

The meeting ended at [------].

Call (insert minute taker's name and number) with additions or corrections to these minutes.

_____
(Signature Chairperson)

Learning activity 6.8

Do this activity on your own and then with a partner.
1. Find a time to take minutes of a discussion, such as during the next staff meeting using the format suggested.
2. If you cannot sit in on a staff meeting then, in groups, role-play a meeting and each group member can have a chance to take the minutes.
3. Once you have the minutes, share these with another student who was not at the same meeting.
4. Allow them to read the minutes while you read theirs.
5. Discuss if the minutes provided gave enough information for the person not at the meeting to understand what had happened and what decisions were reached. Take notes of what is said about your minutes.

Insert both your minutes and any comments from your partner as evidence in your portfolio.

Unit 11:

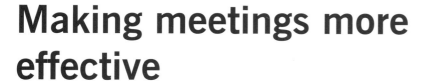

Making meetings more effective

This unit will help you to be able to suggest ways to make meetings more effective.

Meeting preparation and pre-work

You can make meetings more productive and ensure results by doing all the necessary preparation well before the actual meeting.

Documentation that will help you achieve the meeting goals

Part of meeting preparation is to have all the documents you need sorted out, copied and ready for each of the participants.

- Providing pre-work, charts, graphs, and reading material 48 hours before a meeting affects how successful it will be. The more preparation time you provide for, the better prepared people will be for your meeting.
- Distributing minutes, notes and follow-ups from earlier or related meetings and projects.
- Distributing reports, data and charts on all relevant information, such as information about competitors, month-to-date sales figures and production plans.
- Preparing Microsoft PowerPoint slides to illustrate key discussion points if necessary.

If you distribute this pre-work in a timely manner, you can fully expect that the attendees will read the pre-work before the meeting. Any and all preparation ensures a greater degree of meeting success.

Accomplish a commitment from the participants and do follow-up

Before the meeting is adjourned, identify the tasks and assign responsibility to each of the participants. This includes assigning someone the responsibility of notifying individuals or departments of decisions taken and actions required. To ensure that each of the participants is committed to their assigned task you can do the following:

- Arrange follow-up with the participants so that they can update the group on what they have or have not done and whether or not they have fulfilled the commitments they made. Follow up typically includes:
  - informing people of the new action
  - training people on how to implement it
  - creating forms or written instructions to help implementation
  - communicating with key people regarding the implementation and timing of actions

- discussing any problems that occurred during the meeting with other members of management; they may come up with ways improvements can be made.
- Establish the norm or custom of accountability for results early in your meeting cycle. Respecting and observing deadlines and follow-up sessions will help you achieve results from your meetings.
- Establish all deadlines during the meeting. Following the meeting, each person with an action item should make a plan how they personally plan to accomplish their task of fulfil their commitment. They write steps in their planner, delegate the tasks to another staff person, or complete the task themselves; whichever way it is done they still remain responsible for it and must attend the follow-up.
- The facilitator can do on the spot follow-up between meetings to keep participants motivated, and to renew the groups' commitment to succeed.
- Report on progress and outcomes at the next meeting and expect that all will have been accomplished, as planned. Alternatively, check progress at the next meeting and if there is a real roadblock to progress, determine how to proceed.

Debrief the meeting process for continuous improvement

Doing a meeting debriefing is similar to evaluating your meeting. You always want to make sure that both the meeting objectives and the staff expectations are met during each meeting.

The practice of debriefing each meeting is a powerful tool for continual improvement. During the debriefing process, participants take turns discussing what was effective or ineffective about the current meeting process. They can also discuss the progress they feel the group is making on the topic of the meeting.

One way to do effective debriefing and to get measurable feedback is to ask staff to fill out a questionnaire. The information that you collect from the questionnaires can help you identify areas that need to be improved within your department or organisation in terms of how meetings are organised and run. Below is an example of a questionnaire that you could use.

The meetings I attend at work ...	Strongly Agree	Agree	Neutral	Disagree	Strongly Disagree
1. result in high-quality decisions.					
2. take up more time than they are worth.					
3. result in participants' feeling good about the group's decisions.					
4. seldom result in creative solutions or ideas.					
5. often fail to reach a sense of completion.					
6. seem to be substitutes for more meaningful work.					

7. produce better solutions than would be produced by one person working alone.					
8. usually result in decisions that could be produced by one person working alone.					
9. promote a commitment toward the organisation by involving members in decisions.					
10. permit group members to freely participate and share ideas openly.					
11. move through the decision phase efficiently.					
12. are called only when necessary.					
13. begin and end on time.					
14. deal with agenda items that are not relevant to all participants in the group.					
15. allow offbeat or unusual ideas to be heard.					
16. follow an agenda rather than wandering off topic.					
17. are scheduled too frequently.					
18. are often dominated by a few members.					
19. give participants a feeling of organisational unity.					
20. seem to eat up to much of my workday.					

Source: Extracted from "How to hold successful meetings" by Paul R. Timm, p. 12 – 13

Think about it

Why do people within many organisations experience meetings as having no purpose and a waste of time?

Assessment Activity 6.1

Case study assignment

You are to complete all the preparation and documentation for a meeting as per the following:

Points for discussion in the meeting

- Whether we can introduce "Escapes & Entertainment", a new promotion, by the end of the month. (Note for delegates: this will depend on whether we can get Waterworld and the Aquarium on board).
- To co-ordinate overtime schedules for the workforce during the December/January period.
- To co-ordinate new overtime rates with the union representative.
- The maintenance schedules on the air conditioners in block A & B.
- To confirm the implementation of the new customer care programme.
- Routine report of the Finance department
- Routine report of the Banqueting department

You must produce an agenda and other documentation for the meeting described above. You can be creative; if information you need is missing, use your imagination.

Simulation

Working in groups of 4 or 5, convene a meeting on a topic of your choice. Run the meeting and complete all the necessary correspondence and documentation.

Topic Summary

This topic focused on the planning and conducting of meetings. It consisted of 3 Modules. The first module looked and the skills and knowledge required to plan and organise a variety of meetings including the preparation of agendas, minutes and other documentation.

Unit 1 described the standard meeting protocols and why it is important to use them. Unit 2 covered the ways to determine the needs and objectives of a meeting and included guidelines to help you decide if a meeting is the best option in a circumstance. Unit 3 looked at decision making in meetings and specifically at ways of reaching decisions. Unit 4 explained ways of managing meetings and problem solving. The module ended with unit 5 which described ways in which to determine the appropriate delegates for a meeting.

The second module of this topic, Module 7, looked at how to conduct a meeting in a structured and effective manner.

The module began with Unit 6 which explained how to arrange a meeting and compile and agenda. Unit 7 looks at methods of informing delegates about a planned meeting and Unit 8 equipped you with the skills to structure a meeting. The Module ended with Unit 9 which covered the skills required to run a meeting.

Module 8 discussed the completion of actions arising from meetings conducted and the monitoring of this completion. Unit 10 looked at the completion of documentation after a meeting and the circulation thereof. Unit 11 covered ways in which to make meetings more effective both during the meeting and afterwards.

The following are important things to remember:

Ask the following questions when you are planning a meeting:
- Is this the only means of fulfilling my objective?
- What are the alternatives?
- How effective are the alternatives?
- Will a meeting use my time and my colleagues to our best advantage?
- What do I want to achieve during the meeting?
- Are the right people invited?

Meeting protocol
- Prepare a written agenda and distribute it well before the meeting. The agenda must include:
- the objectives – (decision, information, brainstorming)

- the issues to be discussed
- the time frame for the meeting (the start and end time)
- the venue
- a list of the participants
- the preparation that must be done before the meeting.
- Distribute all data and information necessary for decision making before the meeting.
- Start meetings on time.
- Appoint a good facilitator or leader and timekeeper.
- Review the objectives and ground-rules for the meeting and have these ready to explain to the participants.
- Keep to the agenda.
- Discuss one issue at a time.
- Record action items.
- Once the objective(s) has/have been accomplished, end the meeting.
- Conduct a meeting evaluation by asking:
- Did we achieve the meeting objective(s)? If not, why?
- What three positive things can we do to improve the next meeting?
- What are three things we did that we should not do at the next meeting?
- How can the leader improve?
- How can the participants improve?
- Could we have done without this meeting? If so, how?
- Results of the meeting should be documented and distributed to participants within two business days of the meeting.

Rules for meeting participants

People attending a meeting also have an obligation to make the meeting worthwhile and not a waste of time and money:
- Participants must come prepared to participate.
- Question constructively, and be sure of, your value to the meeting before the meeting.
- Help keep the meeting on track by challenging the participants and leader if the meeting strays from the stated objective.

Conduct during a meeting
- Treat fellow participants with respect.
- Allow people to finish making their point.
- Allow for differing opinions or views.
- Avoid storytelling, digressions, and interruptions.

Tasks of the chairperson
- Greeting: Welcoming participants when they arrive.
- Opening: This includes introducing people (if required), stating the objective of the meeting, and introducing the agenda.
- Delivery: This is how you present the content or concern, or how you organise the task.
- Closing: This involves summarising decisions, listing recommendations, creating actions, assigning tasks and setting deadlines.
- Feedback: This is how the meeting is recorded and an evaluation of the progress of the items identified in the closing.

Assess yourself

Assess your understanding of the information covered in these Modules by completing the following table:

	Yes	Partly	No
I am able to describe standard meeting protocols and the importance of using them			
I am able to describe ways to determine the need and objectives of a meeting			
I understand the importance of reaching decisions in meetings			
I can explain ways of managing discussions and problem solving			
I am able to describe ways to determine the appropriate delegates for a meeting			
I have the skills to arrange a meeting and compile an agenda			
I know how to inform the delegates about the meeting			
I can structure a meeting in accordance with the protocols (select a chairperson, minute taker)			
I am able to run a meeting to achieve the objectives within the timeframe			
I have the ability to ensure that all documentation is complete and circulated after the meeting (for example, minutes, attendance)			
I can suggest ways to make meetings more effective.			

If you answered no or partly, then you need to revise that section again, or ask your lecturer for help.

Topic 7:
Maintain the receipt, storage and issue of goods

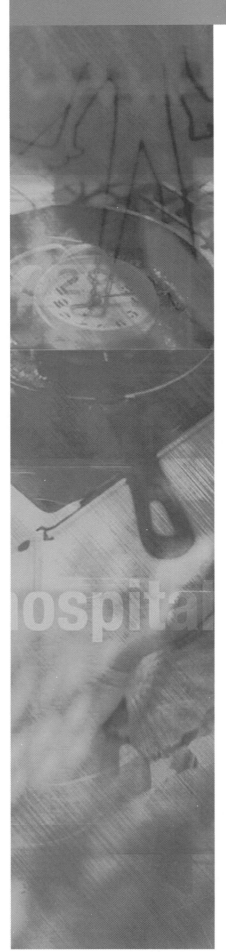

Module 9

Security and hygiene procedures

Maintain the security and hygiene procedures in the receipt, storage and issue of goods

In this module you will ...

- describe the relevant legislation and practises regarding, hygiene, quality and security of goods and the possible consequences of non-compliance
- prepare the receiving area in terms of hygiene, equipment and staff
- receive various types of goods and explain the quality checks required
- handle and store all goods in accordance with organisational requirements
- issue goods in accordance with organisational requirements

Unit 1:

Legislation and practises

This unit will describe the relevant legislation and practises regarding hygiene, quality and security of goods and the possible consequences of non-compliance.

Keeping storage areas clean and tidy

It is very important to ensure that all goods supplied to your establishment comply with health, hygiene and security regulations as stipulated in the Occupational Health and Safety Act.

Hygiene is very important and must be maintained at all times. Follow these guidelines:

- To ensure that your storerooms function optimally and that you don't lose valuable stock to poor hygiene practices, always keep your storage area clean and make sure your storage process meets the hygiene requirements.
- Stocktaking will be much quicker if your storage area is tidy and well organised.
- Make sure that the area allocated to storage is clear of foreign matter and has been thoroughly washed and cleaned and dried appropriately before you receive any stock.
- The person responsible for the cleaning the floors must make sure that signs warning people if floors are wet or slippery are clearly visible.
- Use an all-purpose chemical to clean the storerooms as well as a mutton cloth to clean shelves, etc. Do not use towelling cloths.
- Ensure that there are no insect or pest infestations before you put new stock on the floor or shelves.
- Make sure that all items that are to be stored are well packaged and that all the packaging is in good condition. All items should be sealed and nothing must be leaking.
- The temperature of all the fridges must be at a constant 4 degrees Celsius. Check this before you store any items in the fridges.
- In general, ensure that the standards you maintain in the storerooms comply with the Occupational Health and Safety Act, and remember that your premises should be inspected at least every 3 months.

In the workplace

Stock is an investment and should be treated as such. Limit access to storerooms by allowing only authorised people to enter the storerooms and fridges. Anyone who enters the storerooms or fridges must sign their name in a book provided when they collect the keys and they must write down what items they take out. This way you can keep a record of all your stock and be able to account for it when you are doing stock takes.

Security

Security is an important part of managing your stock.
* The person responsible for receiving goods must be honest and reliable. He or she must also be capable of working accurately.
* Only the supervisor or the person responsible for each store should have the keys to the goods receiving area and to the storage areas.
* Never leave delivery people unattended in your goods receiving area for security reasons and always ensure that a member of your security team is there during your absence.

Security checks

To keep your stock and your storage safe you must do regular security checks and make sure that your security procedures are being followed.
* Keep storage areas locked at all times when they are not in use.
* When storage areas are unlocked, make sure there is responsible member of staff in attendance.
* Do not give the keys to the storage area to anyone else.
* Keys should be correctly labelled and locked away when they are not needed.
* Report any security breaches in the storage areas for which you are responsible to your manager immediately and record the incident in the Report Book.

Quality control

An important part of managing your stock and your storage areas is to make sure that you perform and follow the necessary quality control measures.
* Ensure that all the goods deliveries are documented in the goods-receiving book and have the driver sign as proof of delivery. As the responsible staff member, you should sign the invoice. Keep a copy for your records.
* When goods are delivered it is important to check that the products have no broken seals and that the expiry dates are valid so that you don't receive old stock.
* If the stock is fresh produce, ensure that it is firm, neatly packed and clean. It should be ripe and well coloured.
* The amount and type of stock received should correspond with the invoice and the order, in both quantity and quality.
* Security must endorse the goods on arrival.
* The supervisor, or the responsible staff member, must tick off each item and sign if he or she is satisfied that the goods received are in order.
* If you are unsatisfied with the stock you have received then report this to your supervisor immediately. He or she will then be responsible for reporting any defects.

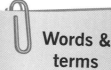

Words & terms

Quality refers to the degree of excellence or the distinguishing feature or characteristic of goods.

Quantity refers to the number or amount of goods which can be ascertained by measuring or counting.

Disposing of unsuitable stock

Unsuitable stock is stock that has passed its "sell-by date" or is no longer fit for consumption. Regulations in the Health and Safety Act require that when stock is disposed of it must be completely destroyed to make sure that no one can take the items for private consumption without proper authorisation. This is to prevent someone from eating the food and exposing themselves to food poisoning and as a result possibly taking legal action against your company. These rules are there to protect your company from unnecessary cost and to protect individuals from health hazards.

The regulations on how to deal with expired stock or stock that must be written off are as follows:
- All stock that has passed its given expiry date or is spoiled, becomes useless to the company and may not be used.
- The Head of Department authorises the disposal of stock. No documentation is necessary, provided the items are not put into someone's hands. As soon as this stock is given to someone, this procedure must be authorised by completing a Transfer note or Pass out note.

Important legislation

In the workplace

Goods supplied are used to supply guests with a quality product and quality service. To ensure the quality of your products, it is critical to adhere to the quality standards in the Occupational Health and Safety Act. Always insist that the stock supplied to you meets with these same standards.

General hygiene requirements for food premises and the transport of food

The Regulations Governing the General Hygiene Requirements for Food Premises and the Transport of Food (R. 918) were published by the Department of Health on 30 July 1999.

These regulations are applicable to all food handling situations, including restaurants, café's, shebeens, taverns, caterers and their suppliers at special events and so on. They cover the following important aspects related to how food should be handled:
- prohibition on the handling and transport of food
- standards and requirements for food premises
- standards and requirements for facilities on food premises
- standards and requirements for food containers
- standards and requirements for the display, storage and temperatures of food
- standards and requirements for protective clothing
- duties of a person in charge of food premises
- duties of a food handler

- standards and requirements for the handling of meat
- standards and requirements for the transport of food
- provisions concerning unprocessed products.

A certificate of acceptability, issued by the relevant local authority, is required before any person, including those involved in food handling at special events, can handle food.

The owners or persons in charge of such premises are advised to contact the Environmental Health Services at their respective local authorities for assistance and further information regarding this certificate, as well as on any other health requirements for the handling of food included in the above-mentioned legislation.

Application of the hazard analysis and critical control point system (HACCP)

On the 27 June 2003, the Regulation Relating to the Application of the Hazard Analysis and Critical Control Point System (HACCP) was put into action in terms of the Foodstuffs, Cosmetics and Disinfectants Act (Act 54 of 1972). This regulation states that once a specified sector and food handling enterprise has been listed, that sector and food handling enterprise may not handle food without a fully implemented HACCP system.

HACCP was originally developed as a microbiological safety system (to help establish the risk of *Salmonella* infection in food) during the 1960s and is a system focused on prevention to help ensure and maintain high levels of food safety. It is a system that:
- requires a certain level of expertise to be carried out, such as a thorough understanding of products, raw materials and processes and other factors, that, if not managed, can cause a health risk to the consumer.
- legislates the production, processing, use, handling, storage or transport of, and the exposure of employees and other persons to, hazardous articles, substances or organisms or potentially hazardous articles, substances or organisms.
- identifies, evaluates and controls hazards which are significant for food safety.
- has a written plan called the "HACCP plan", which outlines how to prevent and control food safety hazards within the segment of the food chain under consideration.

Possible consequences of non-compliance

As mentioned earlier, your establishment will be inspected regularly to make sure that you are complying with the laws that govern food safety and hygiene.
- If you don't comply with the food safety rules and someone gets ill or hurt because of this, your establishment will be investigated by the authorities.
- An inspector may investigate any incident that happens, or can be traced back to, a workplace, that has resulted in the injury, illness or

death of any person. The inspector will check whether it is necessary to hold a formal investigation to determine the cause of the incident and to look into the circumstances around it.

- After completing the investigation the inspector will submit a written report, together with all relevant statements, documents and information gathered by him or her, to the attorney-general within whose area of jurisdiction this incident occurred and he or she shall at the same time submit a copy of the report, statements and documents to the chief inspector.
- Depending on the findings you could be fined and/or imprisoned and your business could be shut down.
- If you do not comply with the health regulations you could lose money since stock kept in unhygienic conditions will deteriorate faster.

Unit 2:

Prepare the receiving area

This unit will describe how to prepare the receiving area in terms of hygiene, equipment and staff.

Safety in the receiving area

The receiving area must be located close to the delivery bay so that the receiving process is efficient. It must be a fairly large area, and must have a floor that is easy to clean.

- The best and easiest way to clean the floors in this kind of area is to hose them down. To help you do this there must be drains in or around the floor. Receiving area floors get very dirty.
- Always be on the look out for signs of a pest infestation in the receiving area. Because they have outside access and there are large amount of food moving in and out of these areas they tend to attract pests, especially if they are not cleaned properly. Report any signs of an infestation immediately.
- Make sure that the goods receiving area is clear of any obstructions, such as boxes.
- To make things easier and to work more smoothly, deal only with one delivery at a time and move all the received goods to the appropriate storage area as soon as you have completed the receiving process. This helps to prevent goods being lost or stolen in the process. This can easily happen if there are too many different deliveries being checked and counted by different people. Checking and storing goods quickly also makes sure that goods are stored properly and not left out for too long and then spoiling.

In the same way that receiving areas must be close to delivery areas, so too must storage areas be close to the goods receiving area. This makes the move from the delivery vehicle to the receiving area and then to the storage area a smooth and efficient process that is safe and does not involve carrying goods long distances and through other work areas.

Equipment in the receiving area

In your goods receiving area you should have the following equipment:
- a table and a chair; the surface of the table must be cleaned and sanitised after each use
- a pen that works
- an accurate scale that can measure quantities from 10 g upwards
- a duplicate Credit Note book with carbon paper; you must always have a copy for record purposes and this way you know here to find it if you need it
- hand trucks and trolleys to move goods around easily.

Staff who work in the receiving area

It is important that there should be enough assistants to help move goods from the receiving area to the storage areas as quickly as possible. If it becomes apparent that additional assistance is needed, for example for larger deliveries or deliveries of cold or frozen goods, let the manager know so that a plan can be made well before the delivery arrives.

Maintain storage facilities

The Occupational Health and Safety Act and company Operating Standards Manuals guide storage practices.
- All storage areas should be located close to the delivery area since this eliminates the problem of theft and food deterioration along the way
- All storage areas must be well ventilated.
- Refrigerators and freezers must not be overloaded; overloading prevents the air from circulating, which means that the food in the centre of the fridge or freezer will not freeze completely, and will therefore spoil.

Unit 3:

Receive various types of goods and explain the quality checks required

Words & terms

Specification refers to a document used mostly for purchasing since it describes the essential technical requirements for items. It can also prescribe, in a complete, precise, verifiable manner, the requirements, design, behaviour, or characteristics of the product purchased, or it could be a description of what the purchaser requires.

Receiving goods

When any goods are received they must be checked and processed according to organisational requirements.

- You must check the stock specifications, in other words aspects such as their size, weight, quality, quantity and type against the order form and against measuring charts if available, to ensure that the company is not paying for more than it is getting in terms of quality and quantity. For example, the weight of frozen chickens supplied must match the specifications on your order form.
- When purchases are delivered locate the relevant Purchase Order. Tick off each item on the Invoice as it is checked and make a note of any damaged or missing stock as you go along. Do not rely on memory to do this task at a later stage.
- Count and weigh to ensure that the correct quantity has been delivered.

- When food is delivered, the Executive Chef needs to do a quality check before he or she signs the documentation to accept the delivery. So you must always let the Executive Chef know as soon as a delivery arrives. The other receiving staff will do a quality check of the rest of the General Store items.
- If there are any discrepancies with the order (quantity, quality, price), contact the manager who signed the Purchase Order and tell her or him what the problem is. He or she will tell you if the goods should be accepted or not.
- When you are satisfied that the delivery is correct, stamp one copy of the Delivery Note and send this with the goods to the storekeeper. Then stamp the second copy of the Delivery Note and the Invoice and attach them to the Purchase Order. These will be sent to the Creditors Clerk.

An example of a delivery note

Name of supplier:				
Delivery note				
Name of Company: (This will be your company name)				
Description		Quantity	Unit Price	Amount
(Of the product)				
Requested by		Delivered by		
Signature		Signature		
Order Date		Delivery Date		

Accepting deliveries

Before accepting the goods you must complete the following checks:
- Check that the reference number on the delivery corresponds with the reference number on the Purchase Order.
- Check that the items delivered agree with the Purchase Order Agreement in terms of quality, specifications and quantity.
- Check that that price charged agrees with the quoted price on the Purchase Order.

Open and unpack all containers and check:
- that the packaging is in good condition – there must be no damage to packaging, especially not to the bottom layer.
- if there are any signs of pest infestations in the packaging or crates.
- that the temperature of perishables such as meat, fish, poultry, fruit and vegetables has been maintained. These must always be transported in a refrigerated truck.
- that all fresh produce is of the correct quality.

Quality checks for different products

Different quality checks relate to different products:

For perishable food check:
- the freshness
- the condition of the packaging
- the correct temperature
- the quantity
- the specifications, for example 10 × 200 g rump steaks, not 1 × 2 kg rump
- that the price charged agrees with the quoted price on the Purchase Order
- for any signs of pest infestation
- the Sell-by-dates and Use-by-dates
- any refills, for example, for syrup beverages check to see that you have received a full tin.

For non-perishable foods check:
- the condition of the packaging
- the quantity
- the specifications, for example 5 × 2 kg cans of tomatoes, not 20 × 500 g cans
- that the price charged agrees with the quoted price on the Purchase Order
- for any signs of pest infestation in the packaging
- for blown, swollen or rusted cans that must be rejected
- the Sell-by-dates and Use-by-dates.

For non-foodstuffs check:
- the condition of the packaging
- the quantity
- the specifications, for example 200 × 100g soap, not 400 x 50g soap
- that the price charged agrees with the quoted price on the Purchase Order
- for any signs of pest infestation in the packaging
- the condition of the goods, there must be no breakages
- the Sell-by-dates and Use-by-dates.

Learning activity 7.1

Work alone
1. Make a record to find out which suppliers are the most inconsistent deliverers for the establishment you are employed by. If you are not employed, then do research at a chosen establishment.
2. Make suggestions regarding how the problem can be solved.
3. Make a list of corrective actions you would take in the event of the following:
   - incorrect quality or quantity of delivery
   - late deliveries.

Unit 4:

Handle and store all goods in accordance with organisational requirements

Transferring goods to storage containers

All goods received must be transferred from the goods receiving area to the storage area either as they are or in storage containers.

- If goods need to be transferred to storage containers before being stored they must be packed in the goods receiving area, before they are moved to the storage areas. This prevents possible hygiene problems that can arise if items are spilled while being transferred.
- The following items may be transferred to large covered storage containers before being stored:
  - flour
  - sugar
  - rice
  - maize meal
  - salt.
- By transferring goods to their storage containers while in the receiving area, you prevent the risk of pest infestation in the storage areas – pests are often introduced via product packaging. To avoid pest infestations you must make sure that you dispose of all the packaging correctly.

Transferring goods to storage areas

Those goods that do not need to be transferred to storage containers can be checked and stored relatively quickly.

- As soon as each delivery has been signed off, remove the delivered goods to the appropriate storage area.
- Do not begin to process another delivery until this has been done.
- Occupational Health and Safety legislation requires employers to provide a safe working environment and to implement safe work practices and procedures for employees and these must be adhered to for the safety of all staff and customers.
- Proper handling equipment must be used to move heavy or bulk stock.
- Remove as much packaging as possible before transferring goods to the storage areas, to prevent the risk of pest infestation.
- Frozen items must be transferred to the freezers before you transfer any other items to prevent them from defrosting. Then you may transfer refrigerated items to the fridges, and, finally, transfer room temperature items and dry goods.

Did you know?

The Health Act Regulation says that food must not be displayed or stored in direct contact with the floor or on dirty surfaces and must be free from dust or any other impurity.

Do this activity in groups.

Your lecturer will divide your class into groups.

1. Each group must see how many reasons they can get as answers to the following question:
   - Why are quality control procedures necessary when receiving and storing goods?
   - What are the possible results of not adhering to the quality control procedures?
   - How may these results affect a business?
2. Compare your answers with those of another group.

Hazardous goods

It is important to know what all hazardous goods are and how to handle them. Hazardous goods include the following items:
- chemicals
- flammable items
- gas bottles.

Procedures for handling hazardous goods

These are the procedures to follow when you are handling dangerous goods.
- Check gas bottles to ensure that they are full, and the valves properly closed before they are moved from the Goods Receiving areas and stored in the appropriate kitchen and bar storage areas. The Executive Chef or Store Keeper must supervise the storage of gas bottles.
- Each type of gas bottle must be stored separately from each other type. Always be careful when you handle gas bottles because gas is flammable and the gas bottles can explode. Always store gas bottles away from open flames.
- Flammable items must be stored in cool conditions, and away from anything that could ignite them, to prevent fires.
- Store chemicals separately from all other goods. The kitchen, housekeeping and maintenance departments will all have their own chemical storage areas. If they do not, chemicals must be stored in a central chemical storeroom.
- Outer packaging on all chemical products must be removed in the Receiving area before transferring chemicals to the storeroom to prevent pest infestations.
- Make sure that chemical containers are tightly sealed, and in good condition. Store them the right way up with the labels facing forward so that each chemical can be easily identified.
- Store chemicals according to type so that they are easy to find and easy to count. Label the shelves so that items are always stored in the same place. This will make it quicker to pack deliveries away and easier to check stock levels.
- Store dry chemicals away from liquid chemicals to avoid any dangerous combinations if items are spilled. Such combinations could cause an explosion or fire.

- Store items on shelves to make the best possible use of the space available.
- Chemical stores must be thoroughly cleaned at least once a week, and any spills must be cleaned up immediately.
- Wear protective clothing, such as gloves, gumboots, etc. when handling open chemicals or spillages.

Procedures for handling non-hazardous goods

Non-hazardous goods are all non-food items such as:
- food and beverage operating equipment
- beverages
- housekeeping stock and so on.

Food and Beverage (F&B) Operating equipment is often stored in its original packaging so do not remove the outer packaging from these items. The F&B Controller must supervise the storage of these items. Kitchen, Maintenance and Housekeeping Operating Equipment should be transferred to the relevant department for storage.

Items are stored on shelves according to type. Shelves should be labelled to help with quick storage and counting of stock. Storerooms must be thoroughly cleaned at least once a week, and any spills must be cleaned up immediately.

Procedures for handling perishable goods

The Executive Chef or Store Keeper must supervise the storage of all perishable food items.
- Frozen items must be stored in the freezer and must be transferred from the receiving area as quickly as possible to prevent them from defrosting.
- Be careful never to overload a freezer. Overloading prevents it from maintaining a sufficiently low temperature, so items will thaw and spoil.
- While you are packing the freezer work quickly to prevent the freezer temperature from rising and always wear protective clothing to protect yourself from the cold.
- Meat, poultry, fish and dairy products must all be stored in separate parts of the freezer, and different types of items must not be stored one above the other. Store meat items on one set of shelves, dairy items on another, etc.
- Observe the "First In, First Out" (FIFO) principle of stock rotation. That is, always store new deliveries behind or under previously delivered items, so that the older items are used before the newer items.

Procedures for handling non-perishable goods

Non-perishable items include:
- canned items
- bottled items
- dry foodstuffs.

The Executive Chef or Store Keeper must supervise the storage of all non-perishable food items.
- All outer packaging must be removed before they are transferred to the Kitchen Dry Stores. If items need to be transferred into covered bins or storage containers, for example flour and sugar, this should be done in the Receiving area before they are taken to the Dry Store.
- Items in sacks, such as flour, rice or sugar, must either be transferred into the appropriate covered bins, or stored in their sacks on pallets.
- Observe the "First In, First Out" (FIFO) principle of stock rotation.
- Check the use-by or expiry dates on the new deliveries to make sure that new deliveries are not older than existing stock.

Maintaining storage conditions

There are three main types of storage areas:
- Dry Storage – these are the storage areas in which items are stored at room temperature, and include the Cellar, the F&B Dry Goods Store, the Housekeeping Store, Equipment Stores and so on. These areas must be dry, cool and well ventilated. The Chemicals Store is another example. Chemicals must be stored separately from all other items.
- Refrigerated Storage – these are storage areas that are kept at temperatures between 1°C and 5°C. In the case of walk-in fridges or freezers, a temperature gauge should be displayed outside on the door so that the temperature can be continually monitored.
- Freezer Storage – these are storage areas that are kept at temperatures below –18°C.

Dry goods storage conditions

You must follow the guidelines for storing dry goods in order to meet health and safety requirements.

- There must be no items on the floors.
- The floor must be kept clean and free of spills.
- The shelves must be clean.
- Practise the FIFO principle.
- The shelving must be away from the wall to allow for cleaning.
- The area must be dry and free from damp.
- Chemicals and non-food products must be stored separately.
- It must have metal or plastic shelving.
- Crates and sacks may be stored on pallets, which can be moved for cleaning.

Refrigeration storage conditions

Fridges must be clean and managed properly to avoid the food that is stored within them from spoiling.
- Thermometers must be accurate.
- The temperature must be between 1°C and 5°C.
- Door seals, hinges and handles must be clean.
- Light covers must be clean and rust-free.
- Fans, grids and shelves must be clean.

Did you know?

The Health Act Regulation states that every chilling and freezer facility used for the storage, display or transportation of perishable food must be equipped with a thermometer. This thermometer must show the temperature within the storage areas at all times. It must be placed outside the fridge or freezer in a place where it can be seen and where accurate readings can easily be taken.

- Nothing must be stored on the floor, and metal or plastic shelves must be 20 to 30 cm above the floor to allow for cleaning.
- Practise the FIFO principle in stock rotation – first in, first out.
- Do not overload fridges.
- Store raw foods separate from cooked foods.
- Crates may be stored on pallets, which can be moved for cleaning.

Freezer storage conditions

Freezers must be clean and managed properly to meet health and safety requirements.
- Light covers must be free from dirt or rust.
- The temperature must be –18° C.
- All doors and seals must be clean.
- Shelves, handles and hinges must be clean.
- Practice the FIFO principle.
- Do not overload freezers.
- Defrost freezers when necessary to make sure they are clean and working properly.
- Shelves must be 20 to 30 cm above the floor to allow for cleaning.
- Freezers must have metal or plastic shelving.

Stock rotation

Stock is rotated according to the "First In, First Out" (FIFO) principle in order to ensure that product quality is maintained by using older stocks before new stock.
- The FIFO principle applies to all foodstuffs, beverages, some chemicals and some housekeeping consumables, such as guest supplies.
- The FIFO process helps to manage large and increasing stock volumes.
- New deliveries are always stored behind or under older items, to ensure that the older items are used first.
- Pull the older items to the front of shelves so that new deliveries can be packed behind them and, if necessary, remove older items from the shelves so that the newer items can be placed behind or underneath them. This is a good opportunity to clean the shelves.
- Issue older stock items before newer deliveries. If you have stored your deliveries according to the FIFO principle, the older stock will be in front or on top. Issue these items first.
- Check expiry dates again while you are preparing the requisitions. If an item has expired, do not issue it. Rather return it to the supplier or dispose of it.

Quality checks

The quality of deliveries will be checked when the goods are received, but a second check should be done when the goods are transferred to storage as a useful control.
- When you are storing stock, pay attention to various quality indicators such as:
- the condition of the packaging

- the sell-by, use-by or expiry dates
- the look and smell of the products
- any signs of pest infestation.
- If items have deteriorated in storage, such as fresh vegetables or fruit, they must be discarded. The Executive Chef must authorise the disposal of food items.
- If items have expired because they have passed their use-by date, such as expired beers, they should either be returned to the supplier or discarded – with the permission of the Head of Department.
- A requisition form should be raised and authorised for breakages and damaged goods or deteriorated items that are to be written off. This ensures that there is control of items to be discarded.
- If items have deteriorated, you should investigate the following:
  - Were they stored under the correct conditions? If not, take action to ensure that this is not repeated. If it was someone else who stored the items, make sure that you give that person feedback about the problem. Record this feedback in your Report Book.
  - Is there a fault with the climate control (temperature, ventilation, dryness) in the storage area? If so, report this to maintenance immediately so that action can be taken to solve the problem.
  - Were too many of these items ordered which meant that they could not be used quickly enough? If so, give feedback to the person responsible for the original Purchase Order. Make a record of this feedback in your Report Book.
  - Are these items simply not moving or not being used? If so, give feedback to the person responsible for the original Purchase Order. Make a record of this feedback in the Report Book.

Learning activity 7.3

Work alone
You have a lot of experience on how a checklist is drawn up and how it is used.
1. Draw up a checklist for maintaining quality of stock in storage areas.
2. Swap your checklist with a partner.
3. Assess the checklist you received.
4. Discuss both checklists with the person you swapped with.

Unit 5:

Issue goods in accordance with organisational requirements

Procedures for issuing goods

In the same way that all goods received must be received according to organisational procedures and requirements, so too must goods that are issued be processed and managed following specific procedures.

- In order for any items to be released from the stores to any of the departments, it is necessary to fill out a Requisition Form which must be presented to the store manager or keeper. Goods should be issued only against a signed requisition form.
- The requisition forms are completed in triplicate in a requisition book and must contain the following information:
  - the name of the required item as it appears on the Stock Sheet
  - how many or how much of the item is required
  - the name of the department requisitioning the item
  - the name of the person compiling the requisition
  - the date of the requisition.
- The Head of Department from the department requiring the goods must sign the requisition form.
- All issues must be written up on a requisition. Do not allow any items to leave the storage areas unless they have been written up on a requisition form.
- There should be specific times at which Stores will be open for issues. These times should be made known to all departments and must be kept to. Exceptions should only be made in emergencies. This enables Stores to work in an efficient manner, and makes it easier to control deliveries and issues.
- Another way to help processing issue to be easier is to ask that all requisitions be submitted by a certain time. This gives the storekeeper and his or her team time to prepare the requisitions in advance. This speeds up the process of moving the requisitions to the relevant departments.
- Only one requisition should be handled at a time in order to prevent any confusion or the mixing up of requisitions.
- Check that the requisition has been completed correctly before collecting the items required. If there are any problems with the requisition form, get these corrected before preparing it. This is also easier if you get the forms in advance since any problems can be identified before the items are needed.
- Work through the requisition in an orderly fashion, placing all the items on one requisition in one place or in one container, such as a trolley, handcart or box.
- If any of the items requisitioned are not available, cross them out on the form, and note down when they are expected to be available. Do not leave them on the form and undertake to deliver them later. If

these later deliveries are never received, the department records will be wrong and this will affect their financial results. If the items are no longer on the stock list, make sure that the relevant department is informed and then sign any changes you make on the requisition form.

- If you are unable to meet the exact specifications required on the requisition form, such as the correct size of the product, but you do have the same product in a different size, then, before you change the order or make a substitution, check with the department concerned. If you are given permission to make a substitution, change the specifications written on the requisition form, and sign the change.
- Once all the items have been collected from the stores, check them and sign the requisition form.
- When the representative from the relevant department comes to collect the requisition, make sure that he or she checks the items against the requisition and signs the form in your presence.
- Always keep two copies of the requisition form and return the requisition book to the relevant department with the items.

The process for issuing items such as bottles of spirits, beer and soft drinks is slightly different. When you issue these kinds of items proceed as follows:

- Bottles of spirits should be stamped and dated to identify to which outlet the bottle was issued. This is important because for any outlet or department to get replacement stock they must hand in the empty bottle with the correct stamp.
- The storekeeper then discards the empty bottle after the stamp has been cancelled. This is done to try to prevent the unmonitored transfer of bottles between bars and also to prevent the hotel bars from selling non-hotel goods. It is also a useful process to monitor items that are not selling in the bars.
- If beers and soft drinks are stored separately from the cellar in cold storage, first prepare the cellar stocks, and then go with the bar attendant to collect the items in cold storage.

An example of a stock requisition form

Stock requisition			
No:		Date requested:	
Quantity	Item	Ref No	Department
Date issued:		Requested by:	
Authorised by:		Signature of stock controller	

Learning activity 7.4

Work alone
1. Research what a blank requisition form looks like.
2. Create your own form
3. Complete your form according to Organisational Standards.

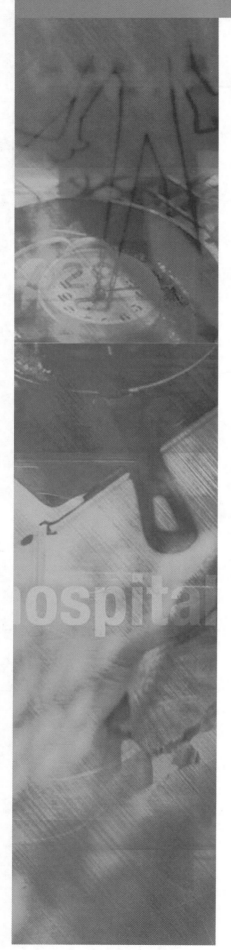

Module 10

Quality checks and documentation

Complete all relevant quality checks and documentation

In this module you will ...

- describe the control procedures and documentation required in the receipt, storage and issue of goods
- describe a typical product specification and why they are important
- describe the impact of supplier lead times on the price of goods

Unit 6:

Control procedures and documentation

This unit will describe the control procedures and documentation required in the receipt, storage and issue of goods

How to handle stock discrepancies

Stock discrepancies can be a big problem in a storage area and you need to know how to handle them properly.

- For partially delivered orders, mark the delivered items on the Purchase Order and note the date of the part delivery. Retain the copy of the Purchase Order until the supplier has delivered the outstanding portion or has advised the hotel that they are unable to satisfy the order in full.
- For each partial delivery, mark the delivery documentation "Part Order".
- On delivery of the final part of the order, mark the Receiving copy of the Purchase Order as "Complete" and send it to the Creditors Clerk for payment.
- If ever you receive an incomplete delivery with no indication that items are to follow and when to expect them, complete a Credit Note, then sign it as well as having the delivery person do so, then attach one copy to the documentation that will be sent to the Creditors Clerk, and give one copy to the delivery person.
- The Invoice must be signed only if all the goods charged were delivered in good condition.

Returning goods

In some cases you will receive goods that you need to reject.

- This happens when goods do not meet your requirements. For example, the goods do not meet your quality standards or the specifications, or they are damaged or have contaminated packaging.
- You must also reject items if labels cannot be read properly – particularly chemicals and food items with illegible sell-by and use-by dates.
- Any problems with goods delivered must be noted on the Invoice, and a Credit Note must be made out so that the goods can be returned to the supplier with the details of damaged or missing stock.

Learning activity 7.5

Work with a partner
1. Write a dialogue which may take place between a supplier and a customer when the customer does not receive all of the goods they ordered.
2. Discuss what you think the customer would have the right to say and what the supplier may say in response.
3. Willing pairs may wish to present their dialogue to the rest of the class.

Minimum and maximum stock holdings

One of the methods of calculating stock levels is to establish the minimum and maximum supply levels for the optimal storage of products. The ideal is to keep only the most essential supplies without running the risk of a shortage. By planning well, the manager should know what he or she will need for one week.

- These minimum and maximum stock levels are known as a "Par Stock". They indicate the maximum stock that should be held, and the minimum stock level that should be reached. Stock is ordered when the minimum stock level is reached.
- Maximum and minimum stock levels will either be set in terms of quantities of items, for example a maximum 4 cases of J&B whisky and a minimum of 1 case of J&B whisky, or in terms of days, for example a maximum 3 days' frozen produce and a minimum of 1 day's frozen produce.
- The purpose of working out these levels is to ensure that there is always enough stock to meet guest requirements and that there is not too much money tied up in excess stock. (You'd do better to keep your excess money in the bank.)
- Prepare department requisitions according to the predetermined par stock levels for each department.
- When stock levels reach the minimum, prepare requisitions in order to bring stock levels back up to the maximum par level.
- The central stores stock levels are managed on the same basis and these stock levels are worked out in order to enable each department to maintain its predetermined stock levels.

Out of stock items

There will be times when the minimum stock levels fall too low and you end up having no stock available. This can happen if there is a sudden increase in business or if deliveries are late.

- If a requisitioned item is out of stock, make a note of this in the Report Book, and follow up with the hotel purchasing department or the supplier. Try to get the supplier to commit to a delivery date.
- Keep departments informed on the progress to get hold of out-of-stock items.
- If you have continuous trouble obtaining a specific stock item make enquiries with the hotel purchasing department or suppliers about substitute items and inform the relevant Heads of Departments.

Overstocked items

Be aware of items that are moving slowly. Make a note of these items in your Record Book and inform the relevant Heads of Department that this stock is moving too slowly. This gives them the opportunity to consider special promotions as a way of moving these items.

Remember that at some time during your shift you must send one copy of all of the requisition forms processed to the Food and Beverage Controller. File the other copy.

Unit 7:

Typical product specification

This unit will describe a typical product specification and why it is important.

Working with specifications

A specification is a document listing the product name, the intended use for the product, its grade, size, and other product characteristics. It also includes general instructions regarding delivery, payment procedures, and other important information. In short, it tells the supplier exactly what the buyer wants. For example, if a buyer were to order a case of apples from a produce company, the company could possibly send any type of apple. Without a specification, the supplier would not know the variety, degree of ripeness, pack, size, and preferred growing region of the apples the buyer needs.

- Specifications are important because there are such a wide variety of products available on the market. The specifications are a control device. Through specifications, management can set policy about which brands, grades, and variety of products will be ordered for the operation.
- Before a buyer can purchase any perishable or non-perishable products, management, with input from the chef, production manager or housekeeper, must write the specifications for these. For example specifications must be made for the foods needed to produce the standardised recipes for the menu items. Large operations typically write formal specifications and smaller operations might use verbal specifications.
- Specifications control the purchasing and receiving procedures. They are used as part of the quality control process and are fundamental to its success. This is because the specifications for each product will vary depending on the potential risks the food may present.
- Food laws all over the world demand that food manufactured for sale must be done so under strict hygiene regulations. There is a possibility of high fines and even imprisonment for those breaking this law and selling food that is unsafe to eat.
- When a retailer makes contact with a supplier they have to be sure that the goods they will get will be of the quality they demand. The first part of this process is to choose a trusted supplier from the very start. The product specifications then form a contract between the supplier and the retailer.
- When deliveries arrive, the delivery note or invoice should be checked to see if this matches the copy of the order: the brands, items, sizes, quantities and other specifications must all match.

Think about it

Even simple things like candy bars have specifications. When you buy one, do you want chocolate, caramel, nuts, cherries, all of these, some of these, or none of these? Do you want 100g or 200g? These are all part of the specifications.

Information on a purchase specification

A lengthy formal specification includes the following information, while a short informal specification includes only a limited amount of this information:

- the product name
- the intended use for the product
- the brand name
- the grade – this is the choice or standard
- the product size – this could include portion size; weight ranges for food items such as roasts, ribs, whole chickens, or whole fish; size of produce
- the packaging – the size of pack, type of packaging material, etc.
- the product characteristics – the colour, amount of trim, type of preservation, degree of ripeness, point of origin
- any acceptable substitutions "or equals"
- any general instructions to bidders – the payment procedures, delivery requirements, and so on.

Unit 8:

The impact of supplier lead times

This unit will describe the impact of supplier lead times on the price of goods.

Managing lead times

Think about it

Lead time is the time that it should take a supplier to deliver goods after receiving the order.

Lead times are the actual times agreed upon and specified on the Purchase Order form, for the arrival and delivery of goods. It is very important to manage lead times to maintain optimum stock levels.

- It is important for suppliers to keep to agreed-upon lead times so that the company can plan for all deliveries according to Organisational Standards and the Occupational Health and Safety Act.
- Changes or inconsistencies in lead times can lead to either too little stock or too much stock in the stores. This can cause cash flow problems for the business if too much money is locked up in excess stock, or it can cause losses if there are no items to sell. The biggest problem for most retailers is that they have very little control over supplier lead times, so this is always a difficult process to manage and control.
- If financial losses occur, then the company may have to add additional costs onto stock or products to recover the extra expense incurred in acquiring the stock. This generally happens when:
  - stock is delivered over a long distance, in which case, petrol costs are high
  - stock has to be couriered in a hurry to reach the company when given short notice periods
  - stock is flown in from another region, which incurs high delivery costs.
- If suppliers cannot meet delivery lead times, or fail to meet the agreed delivery times address the matter immediately with the supplier. Repeated late deliveries are an indicator that you might need to find another supplier.

Reducing supplier lead times

There are two stock holding benefits if you can reduce supplier lead times:
- You won't need to keep as much safety stock to cover for uncertainties in demand during the lead time.
- You won't need to forecast what stock you need so far in advance. This will enable you to do more accurate forecasts and be able to hold less stock in your stores.

You must always be aware of your supplier lead times so that:
- you have enough time to prepare your goods-receiving area for the delivery of the new stock.
- you do not receive more than one delivery at the same time.

- you can avoid delays in dealing with the arrival of stock. The longer you take to deal with deliveries the greater the chance is that the stock could spoil or that stock could go missing.
- you know when you need to add additional costs onto stock or products because of the extra expense incurred in acquiring the stock.

Causes of variability in lead times

There are many different things that can cause lead times to vary such as:
- changes in transportation schedules
- capacity limitations
- equipment shortages, for example too few available rail cars, especially for shipments into ports in the west that are moved via rail to the east
- inspections and customs
- misrouting
- data errors that delay processing
- weather
- labour issues
- security issues.

Module 11

Stock usage

Analyse the physical versus actual stock usage and the practices involved in this process

In this module you will:

- understand why it is important to reconcile physical stock with that recorded on stock sheets
- record stock on a regular basis
- make suggestions on increasing/decreasing the volume of stock held in storage areas
- complete all work activities efficiently including delegation where appropriate.

Unit 9:

Reconcile physical stock

This unit will ensure that you understand why it is important to reconcile physical stock with that recorded on stock sheets.

In the workplace

The Stores Department is responsible for controlling a large and varied number of items. The Chief Store keeper must keep strict controls of all items in use and storage to ensure that adequate stock is on hand for the routine operation of the organisation. This will ensure that that supplies do not run out, that there are minimal losses, that costs do not exceed budget, and that the products and services are consistent and to the satisfaction of the guest.

Reconciling stock

Reconciling is done to check that the actual number of items in stock (physical stock) corresponds with the recorded items on your stock sheets.

The frequency of stock takes will depend on organisational procedures.

Stock takes

Stock takes should be completed on the same day that they are started.

Only authorised staff should be responsible for the counting and recording of stock. In most establishments, two or more people are required to count stock in any one area.
- Items in all departments should be accounted for.
- Damaged items must be recorded.
- Items sent for repair must be recorded.
- Stock must be recorded on the correct documentation.

Stock recorded on stock sheets

Procedures involving the requisitioning and re-issuing of goods are to be recorded, documented and filed appropriately. It is also necessary for the accounts department to have accurate record and verification of transactions within the department in order to reconcile the finances to the costs incurred and thereby discern the profit / loss of the department and the investment value in the stock on hand.

It is important that you have copies of all transactions that take place and involve the movement of stock within the department. Movement is recorded manually on documentation as the transaction takes place.

The Head of the Department should audit all requisitions, stock sheets, delivery notes, invoices, credit notes and any other paperwork related to the storage and movement of stock on a daily and weekly basis to ensure that it is controlled and correct.

Words & terms

To **reconcile** two things, such as, for example, the physical stock with the stock recorded on stock sheets, is to get them to correspond.

Reconciliation is the process of identifying any differences between two related records in which the figures should agree so as to resolve discrepancies and demonstrate proof of accuracy.

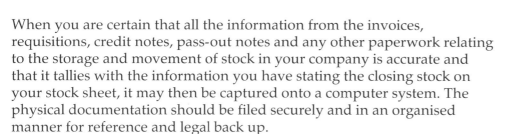

When you are certain that all the information from the invoices, requisitions, credit notes, pass-out notes and any other paperwork relating to the storage and movement of stock in your company is accurate and that it tallies with the information you have stating the closing stock on your stock sheet, it may then be captured onto a computer system. The physical documentation should be filed securely and in an organised manner for reference and legal back up.

The documentation should accurately reflect the status of your stock up to date as well as match up to the relative financial records for the department.

In the workplace

Do not use any white-out fluid on the stock sheet because if you do, you will not be able to prove what the original amount was.

Physical stock taking

Physical stocktaking is the true measure of how well a store has performed in term of gross profit. It allows any differences between the physical stock take figure and book stock to be adjusted to the physical figure in the cost of sales of the organisation. If the physical figure is less than the book figure you have shrinkage; if it is more, you have excess. Both must be investigated to try to identify the reasons for the variation.

Stock losses need to be accurately identified, recorded and assessed against a potential loss forecast on a regular basis.

In most cases the front-line manager will assist in the stock take preparation requirements and the physical count and will also have the responsibility of ensuring that these functions take place and are correctly conducted.

There are a number of staff requirements the manager must address for the stock take to run smoothly and achieve an accurate result.

Interpreting and explaining to team members the policies and procedures of stocktaking

The better informed each person participating in the stock take is, the less the likelihood of mistakes occurring. There are a number of issues that will be covered by procedures such as:
- the method of counting (top left to bottom right of shelves and counting from the order of stock, not the order of stock on the stock sheet
- the methods of recording and making corrections
- what to do with completed counts.

Rostering staff according to allocated budget and time constraints

Stock takes take place at a variety of times depending on store policy. Some stores will close the store or restaurant during normal trading hours in order to stock take. Some will stock take outside normal trading hours and some will remain open and stock take.

Extra staff is generally required to do the stock take effectively and in the shortest possible time and this aspect must be budgeted for. This means allocating specific tasks and using those who have completed their task to assist in other areas where required. One of the main considerations is to ensure that customers are not inconvenienced.

Remember that the fewer staff members available for a stock take, the longer it takes and the more likely it is that errors will occur, since staff may become fatigued or may be interrupted because there is no one else to serve customers throughout the process. Adequate staffing is a necessity.

Method for taking stock

- Clean the entire stock-take area. Make sure it is free of rubbish, dirt and foreign items.
- All stock is to be counted and recorded by item and tallied to a stock sheet.
- All information from the stock tallies must be recorded and completed on the stock sheet to produce a stock report.
- Details should be recorded on stock sheet as follows:
  - Stock type
  - Number of stock items
  - Reference number or code (if any)
  - Position of storage within the stock room or other storage area, for example, fridge, freezer or storeroom etc.
- The items are to be counted by two suitably qualified people to be sure that the procedure is correct the first time around.
- Lose items are to be weighed on a scale, and the weight recorded.
- Measure or weigh each item down to the nearest 10th, if the item in stock is not full.
- Stock sheets must be signed by both parties who assisted with the stock take.
- The Food and Beverage Department must deliver the information on the stock sheet to the Finance Department for data capture and analysis.
- If the stock take proves incorrect against the values in the Finance department, a retake is done immediately.
- Do not start packing out new stock during stock takes.
- Do not be disturbed during a stock take. Do the procedure after hours if necessary.
- Stock takes should take place at least three times each month.

Advantages of stock reconciliation

- This gives assurance that the stock on hand matches the amount of stock that you paid for.
- It provides proof of the department's movements in terms of stock on hand, stock bought and stock used or re-issued.
- It gives you an historic overview of the department's overall performance.
- It provides first-hand legal evidence of a transaction when discrepancies, such as, for example, price irregularities arise.

In the workplace

Stocktaking is an ordered procedure that reflects the following results:
- a stock break down account of current stock as opposed to income and expenditure in the department
- open stock or partly used stock
- sales and purchases
- opening and closing stock on hand in storage.

Inventories or stock sheets

Maintain stock sheets or inventories for all areas and items so that you know exactly what you have in stock.

Record all deliveries, requisitions and issues, as well as breakages, variances and so on to ensure that all items are recorded and all movement tracked.

Keep stock sheets up to date. Some stock is counted daily, weekly or monthly, depending on the area and frequency of use.

Inventory lists or stock sheets should also contain details of the each item, the supplier, the number of items per case or container, the price of each case or item, opening stock, purchases, total stock, total value, items used, value of items used, closing stock and value of closing stock.

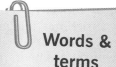

Words & terms

Inventory: A detailed list of all articles, especially articles of property. Also may be the list of items a shop or company has on hand.

Unit 10:

Record stock on a regular basis

In order for an establishment to operate efficiently, there must be an adequate supply of all required items at all times. Required levels of stocks must be planned according to occupancy and average consumption, and minimum levels must be established to ensure that supplies do not run out. Guests expect the establishment to run smoothly, and expect to be supplied with all the items they may require. Stock items must be strictly controlled to prevent losses, theft and damage.

Recording stock

Record stock regularly so as to maintain the required number of items on hand to meet the needs of the establishment. In this way all tasks can be carried out on time.

Only staff members who have been properly instructed should have inventory functions delegated to them.

After a delivery has been received and verified as correct the order need to be entered into the stocktaking recording system to update the stock records. If this does not occur, stock take results will be affected and overstocks can result if the system re-orders the same stock.

Stock control records (whether manual or computerised) will provide you with vital information on what is selling well and what is not. Inaccurate records could result in extra stock being bought in which could be a waste. It could tie up a large amount of money in stock or it could add to stock controls, thus creating a greater risk of losses.

Accurate records assist in stocktaking. Records need to be kept so that when the stock levels are low new stock can be bought in. This will assist with determining when levels are going down.

Accurate records will help prevent loss and theft of items. It is important to record all issued items, so that the correct levels are known and purchases can be made when levels are going down.

Records must also be kept of the items that are damaged or being thrown out because this will assist management in deciding whether the quality of items supplied is acceptable and whether there are solutions for the problems caused by damaged items.

Any signs of missing items should be reported to your supervisor immediately so that this can be dealt with according to your establishment's organisational requirements.

Manual method of recording

This can include a **perpetual inventory** in which written records are maintained for all stock.

It can also be a stock card or book system containing all the necessary information, such as description, stock number, sizes, and cost and selling prices.

The description details and the reference number of the item are noted on the stock card. The maximum stock level (the level that should not be exceeded) and the minimum stock level (stock should be ordered before this level is reached), is also entered on the stock card.

All incoming stock is added to the total on hand and reduced as the stock gets sold or issued.

The stock card method allows the storekeeper to see the balance of the stock level at a glance and he or he can order stock before it runs out.

Manual methods require great attention to detail and a lot of time to complete.

An example of a stock control card

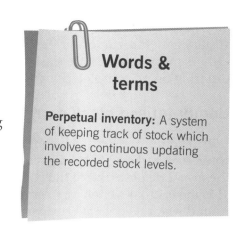

Stock control card					
Department:			Section:		
Item			Reference no.		
Max allowed		Min allowed		Re-order	
Date	Reference	In		Out	Balance

Electronic method of recording

Electronic systems are many and varied, with the most advanced being linked to the point-of-sale terminal and able to provide information on all aspects of the stock.

Some electronic systems often have ordering functions built in, so the system generates an order based on a minimum stock level and lead-time. Others may only provide the sales and stock levels information, with ordering being completed manually.

Computerised stock control method

With a computerised stock control method, the main unit costs are converted and calculated automatically and instantly and are shown on the visual display unit of the computer. This may be printed out if required. This means that a chef, for example, may request a long list of ingredients from the storekeeper, who records the list on the computer by typing in the request items. The total cost of this list of goods is instantly recorded and deducted from the stock list.

Another example of instant computerised figures is the updating of stock when purchases are delivered. The storekeeper types in the purchases from the delivery notes and the computer adjusts the stock level accordingly and adjusts the price if this has been altered.

From this it can be seen how advantageous a computerised system is to the storekeeper. It is possible to have a permanent, up-to-the-minute cost record of all stock on the premises. The stores control system will be a small part of an entire business control system used by all departments of the establishment.

Did you know?

The purpose of record keeping is to track the details of stock, such as, for example, where the goods came from, where the goods were transferred to, how the goods were disposed of, who had access to the goods and even whether those individuals were checked by security.

Documentation used for the requisition of goods

Different kinds of documentation are required.

Requisition form

Complete a requisition form each time items are required from another department. Ensure that the name and signature of the person collecting the goods is clearly written on the form and that the goods required are clearly itemised according to organisational procedure.

Purchase order form

The purchase order form lists the products to be purchased, their price, delivery date, and other important information.

The Head Chef or Duty Manager can complete this form when she or he is ordering stock to be delivered from suppliers outside of the company. The items must be specified correctly and an authorised signature must appear on the form. Also, the desired lead time must be clearly stipulated.

The purchase order form includes the following features:
- a unique number to identify the purchase order
- the name of the ordering restaurant or foodservice operation, its address, and its phone number

- the date of the order
- the signature of the person placing the order
- the supplier's name, address, phone number, and a contact name
- the date of delivery, terms of payment, and any special instructions
- each item to be purchased, the quantity and unit of the item, the item's unit cost, and the extended cost of the item
- the total cost of the order.

After creating a purchase order for the needed items, the buyer sends the purchase order to the supplier and a copy to the receiving clerk.

The receiving clerk receives the items, notes on the purchase order what the supplier has sent, and forwards the purchase order to accounting.

Accounting then compares the purchase order with the supplier's invoice – a bill that accompanies the delivery of goods – to determine the correct amount to pay the supplier.

A purchase order shows everyone concerned what has been purchased, at what price, when to expect it to be delivered, and when payment is due.

An example of a purchase order form

Name of company				
Purchase order form				
Name of supplier:				
Description		Quantity	Unit Price	Amount
Requested by		Authorised by		
Signature		Signature		
Department		Date		

Documents used for re-issuing goods

These documents include credit notes and pass-out notes or books.

Credit notes

These are issued by the supplier's accounts department when goods have been returned to them.

Pass-Out notes or books

These are also called Transfers. They are issued when goods leave the department or company to be given to someone else in another department or company. Transfers or pass out notes/books are used when you are transferring stock items from one department (or an affiliated company in the area) to another. The following regulations regarding Transfers apply:

- No stock item (even left over food) may leave the company to be given to someone without the correct issuing of a pass-out note or transfer.
- The Head of Department or General Manager must authorise and sign the pass-out form when the item leaves his or her department.
- The H.O.D or General Manager of the company receiving the item has to sign acknowledgement of receipt of it, in the pass out book or on the pass out form.
- An invoice is issued accordingly from your accounts department and is consistent with the details in the pass out note or book.

Ensure that the items being transferred are clearly itemised and that the Head of Department or Duty Manager has authorised the transfer and added his or her signature to the form.

Learning activity 7.6

Work on your own
1. Locate an example of both an invoice and a Purchase Order form.
2. Write a paragraph on each one explaining what you understand by the information given.
Place your paragraphs and the documents in your portfolio of evidence.

Damaged Stock

- Ensure that the supervisor completes a goods returned form and that the delivery driver signs it.
- Note the item returned on the invoice and attach a copy of the goods returned note to the invoice.
- The delivery driver must take the damaged stock away immediately.
- Await the credit note from the accounts department.

Unit 11:

Increasing/decreasing the volume of stock

Think about it

This unit will enable you to make suggestions on increasing/decreasing the volume of stock held in storage areas.

Increasing/decreasing the volume of stock

If too many goods are purchased, not only is the restaurant's capital tied up in inventory, but if the goods are perishable, they might spoil. If too few goods are purchased, there is the danger of running out. The right balance between too much and too little stock will depend on the costs of carrying stock, placing orders, and being out of stock, as well as on management policy concerning appropriate customer service levels.

Controlling purchases

One of the controls in purchasing is to know when, or how often, to purchase. Consider that the very act of purchasing costs money, not only in product cost, but in organisational cost as well. It takes time to receive bids, complete purchase orders, phone in or electronically transmit orders, receive the goods, store the goods, and pay the invoices.

The more often a supplier's truck stops, the more the costs to the supplier (and consequently to the restaurant or foodservice organisation) go up as well. It would stand to reason, then, that less frequent orders would be best for the organisation. However, this is not always true for two reasons:

First, with fewer orders being placed, the inventory level must be higher. High levels of inventory tie up the organisation's cash flow. Cash is not only tied up in the cost of the products but also in the cost of the storage space. Storage space, while necessary, does not generate sales but is a cost to the operation. Storage space costs money to build and may take space away from other functional areas such as dining space. In addition to the cost of building storage space, there is a cost to maintaining it. Pest control and regular cleaning are two of the costs of maintenance. In addition, some storage, such as cold storage, requires cooling and ventilation equipment that runs on electricity, thereby increasing utility costs. All of these costs associated with storage space must be covered by the sales brought in by the operation.

Second, not all of the goods purchased lend themselves to being stored for any length of time.

The goal is to keep stock levels as low as possible to minimise all the costs mentioned as well as the insurance costs.

Possessing a high amount of inventory for long periods of time is not usually good for a business because of inventory storage and spoilage costs. However, possessing too little inventory isn't good either, because the business runs the risk of losing out on potential sales and potential market share as well.

Source: http://www. investopedia.com/terms/i/ inventory.asp

In the workplace

The ideal solution is to find the most economical ordering quantities from the best source of supply, at the lowest price!

Complete all work activities efficiently including delegation where appropriate

Completing tasks

It is best to complete one task before moving on to the next one. For example, do not attempt to handle the storage of more than one delivery at a time. In this way you can be sure of completing the task efficiently because you will be concentrating on only this task.

If you have accidents which result in spills or breakages, clean the mess up immediately. Any breakages must be documented in your Record Book so that the stock losses can be accounted for in the stock take.

Keeping the storage area tidy is part of this task.

Keeping work areas tidy

Keep the storage areas tidy at all times so that items can be easily found. In the same way, keeping your desk and other work areas tidy will result in greater efficiency since you will not have to spend time looking for things.

Keeping up to date

Keep paperwork up to date, and record any feedback given on stock storage problems immediately, so that you do not forget. This level of efficiency will ensure the smooth running of this department.

Requisitioning procedures

Make sure that requisition forms that have been completed are filed correctly.

Handle only one requisition at a time. If you try to handle several you run the risk of making mistakes.

Do not allow more than one person at a time into stores to collect requisitions. While one person is collecting the requisitions for his or her department, other people should wait outside. This procedure should be followed in the interests of security.

Delegating responsibility

One of the marks of a good manager is her or his ability to delegate tasks responsibly to other appropriate persons. Make sure that your stores assistant, if you have one, is well trained so that he or she can assist you with the preparation of requisitions. This makes his or her job more interesting and it increases the efficiency of the department.

Assessment Activity 7.1

Assignment

Develop a procedure and checklist for the receipt of goods in a 5 Star hotel.

Guidelines for this assignment

A checklist is

- a reminder of what you're looking for and a record of what you have found.
- a list of action items, steps, or elements needed for a task. Each item is checked off as it is completed.

When you are employed in a 5 star hotel, there will be some procedures involved in receiving and handling items. These include the following:

- Generally, there will be a security guard who will ensure that the delivery area is secure from unauthorised access, so that you will not have to see to this.
- A store person or controller might be responsible for accepting and checking deliveries.
- There would probably be a separate department that would be involved in any transportation of these goods.
- There might be a greater number of store rooms in the establishment.
- In some hotels, there are specific times for issues and requisitions for various departments.
- The range of supplies would be greater than other operations, and control systems might be more extensive.

Assessment Activity 7.2

Case study

You are to complete a stock taking case study including a manual stock take.

Question 1

Write down 5 important procedures that you will have to follow during the stock take. (5)

Question 2

1. Do a stock take in the deep freeze of the following types of meat:
   a) whole rump steaks
   b) whole spare ribs
   c) pre-portioned beef fillet. (3)

2. Do a stock take in the dry store of:
   a) sugar in the storage bin
   b) tins of mushrooms
   c) all the cake flour (in bins and full packets on shelves) (4)

3. Do a stock take in the dispense bar of:
   a) bottles brandy (full as well as open bottles)
   b) tins coca cola
   c) Amarula liqueur (3)

Work experience

1. You are to spend a day working in a stores environment.
2. Write a report on your day focusing on the following:
   - Organisational practices regarding hygiene and the quality and security of good
   - The receiving processes and procedures of the organisation
   - How goods are handled and stored
   - How goods are issued
   - The organisational control and documentation procedures
   - Sock taking procedures

Topic Summary

This topic focussed on maintaining the receipt, storage and issue of goods. It consisted of three Modules.

Module 9 looked specifically at maintaining the security and hygiene procedures in the receipt, storage and issue of goods. In this Module, Unit 1 described the relevant legislation and practices and Unit 2 described how to prepare the receiving area. Unit 3 then looked at how to go about receiving various types of goods, and explained the quality checks required. Unit 4 looked at how to handle and store all goods and the Module ended with Unit 5 which explained how to issue goods in accordance with organisational requirements.

Module 10 explained how to complete all the relevant quality checks and documentation. It consisted of three Units; Unit 6 looked at control procedures and documentation; Unit 7 at typical product specifications and Unit 8 described the impact of supplier lead time on the price of goods.

Module 11 had as its focus stock usage. Unit 9 ensured that you understood why it is important to reconcile physical stock with that recorded on stock sheets. Unit 10 explained how and why to record stock on a regular basis. Unit 11 equipped you with enough knowledge to be able to make suggestions regarding increasing and decreasing the volume of stock held. Unit 12 finished the Topic and the year off by explaining how best to complete all work activities efficiently including delegation where appropriate.

The following are important things to remember:
- Ensure that all goods supplied comply with health, hygiene and security regulations as stipulated in the Occupational Health and Safety Act.
- Follow set procedures for the control of supplies.
- The manager is accountable for the monitoring and control of the receipting process and it is the responsibility of the staff to implement

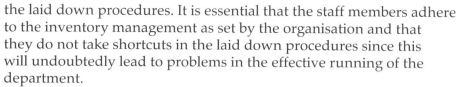

the laid down procedures. It is essential that the staff members adhere to the inventory management as set by the organisation and that they do not take shortcuts in the laid down procedures since this will undoubtedly lead to problems in the effective running of the department.

- It is important to be aware of the lead times of your suppliers for the following reasons: extra costs are generated during lead time when stock is delivered over a long distance, in which case petrol costs will be high. Stock that has to be couriered in a hurry to reach the company when given short notice periods or stock that is flown in from another region generate high delivery costs.
- If suppliers deliver items that do not meet quality specifications, return them immediately.
- Keep accurate records so that you have sufficient stocks and supplies for the operation.
- Follow safety procedures for the lifting, transporting and storing of goods.
- Keep storage areas well organised and clean so that stock can be located easily.
- Rotate stock to ensure consistent quality. Stock that went into storage first must be issued first to ensure that there is a continuous rotation of stock. This procedure will minimise the problem of stock getting old or spoiling. (FIFO system)
- Stock should be issued only against an official requisition form. Ensure that the requisition has been authorised by a supervisor or a person who has the authority to do so.
- Monitor stock levels to ensure that orders can be placed in good time.
- Do not overstock items – this may lead to financial loss, damage etc.
- Check and count all stock regularly, according to procedures.
- Reconciliation is the difference between the physical stock take figure and stock according to the book (records). Stock losses need to be accurately identified, recorded and assessed against a potential loss forecast on a regular basis.

Assess yourself

Assess your understanding of the information covered in these Modules by completing the following table:

	Yes	Partly	No
I am able to describe the relevant legislation and practises regarding, hygiene, quality and security of goods and the possible consequences of non-compliance			
I can prepare the receiving area in terms of hygiene, equipment and staff			
I know how to receive various types of goods and explain the quality checks required			
I am able to handle and store all goods in accordance with organisational requirements			
I can issue goods in accordance with organisational requirements			
I am able to describe the control procedures and documentation required in the receipt, storage and issue of goods			

I am able to describe a typical product specification and why they are important			
I am able to describe the impact of supplier lead times on the price of goods			
I understand why it is important to reconcile physical stock with that recorded on stock sheets			
I can record stock on a regular basis			
I know enough to make suggestions on increasing/decreasing the volume of stock held in storage areas			
I am able to complete all work activities efficiently including delegation where appropriate			

Portfolio of Evidence Guideline

Topic 1: Serve bottled wine	
Assessment Activity 1.1: Assignment *Student's Book* page 44 Answer questions on various customer service issues.	Assessment Activity 1.2: Simulation *Student's Book* page 46 Complete a simulation activity on the service of wine.
Assessment Activity 1.3: Assessed practical *Student's Book* page 46 Provide a wine service in a live situation	Self assessment *Student's Book* page 48 Complete a self assessment grid to assess understanding of the information covered in Topic 1.

Topic 2: Prepare and serve cocktails	
Assessment Activity 2.1: Assignment *Student's Book* page 62 Write a description of the preparation and presentation of 6 six cocktails and six mocktails.	Assessment Activity 2.2: Assignment *Student's Book* page 62 Complete an assignment on the preparation and presentation of cocktails following field research.
Assessment Activity 2.3: Simulation *Student's Book* page 87 Complete a simulated exercise on the service of cocktails and mocktails.	Assessment Activity 2.4: Assessed practical *Student's Book* page 89 Provide a cocktail service in a live situation.
Self assessment *Student's Book* page 90 Complete a self assessment grid to assess understanding of the information covered in Topic 2.	

Topic 3: Provide a silver service	
Assessment Activity 3.1: Assignment *Student's Book* page 126 Complete a short question assignment.	Assessment Activity 3.2: Simulation *Student's Book* page 127 Complete a simulation of silver service.
Self assessment *Student's Book* page 128 Complete a self assessment grid to assess understanding of the information covered in Topic 3.	

Topic 4: Maintain a drinks service	
Assessment Activity 4.1: Assignment *Student's Book* page 165 Complete an assignment on the application of licensing regulations and the management of customers	Assessment Activity 4.2: Simulation *Student's Book* page 165 Complete a simulation in the role of a member of a drinks service team and a food service team.
Assessment Activity 4.3: Assessed practical *Student's Book* page 168 Complete an assessed practical in the role of a member of a drinks service team and a food service team.	Self assessment *Student's Book* page 170 Complete a self assessment grid to assess understanding of the information covered in Topic 4.

Topic 5: Maintain the cleaning programme in a specified area	
Assessment Activity 5.1: Training exercise *Student's Book* page 194 Develop a training programme. Enact the programme with Level 2 students.	Assessment Activity 5.2: Assignment *Student's Book* page 194 Develop an inspection schedule and checklist.
Assessment Activity 5.3: Class test *Student's Book* page 195 Answer short answer questions.	Self assessment *Student's Book* page 196 Complete a self assessment grid to assess understanding of the information covered in Topic 5.

Topic 6: Plan and conduct meetings	
Assessment Activity 6.1: Case study assignment *Student's Book* page 235 Complete all the preparations and documentation for a meeting as per the case study.	Assessment Activity 6.2: Simulation *Student's Book* page 236 Convene a meeting. Run the meeting and complete all necessary correspondence and documentation.
Self assessment *Student's Book* page 238 Complete a self assessment grid to assess understanding of the information covered in Topic 6.	
Topic 7: Maintain the receipt, storage and issue of goods	
Assessment Activity 7.1: Assignment *Student's Book* page 279 Develop a procedure and checklist for the receipt of goods.	Assessment Activity 7.2: Case study *Student's Book* page 279 Complete a stock taking case study.
Assessment Activity 7.3: Work experience *Student's Book* page 280 Spend a day in stores environment. Write a report.	Self assessment *Student's Book* page 281 Complete a self assessment grid to assess understanding of the information covered in Topic 7.